# Playing to the End

publication supported by a grant from
*The Community Foundation for Greater New Haven*
as part of the Urban Haven Project

Anthropology of Contemporary North America

SERIES EDITORS

James Bielo, Miami University

Carrie Lane, California State University, Fullerton

ADVISORY BOARD

Peter Benson, Washington University in St. Louis

John L. Caughey, University of Maryland

Alyshia Gálvez, Lehman College

Carol Greenhouse, Princeton University

John Hartigan, University of Texas

John Jackson Jr., University of Pennsylvania

Ellen Lewin, University of Iowa

Bonnie McElhinny, University of Toronto

Shalini Shankar, Northwestern University

Carol Stack, University of California, Berkeley

# Playing to the End

Elder Black Men, Placemaking,
and Dominoes in Denver

*Steve Bialostok*

University of Nebraska Press | Lincoln

© 2026 by the Board of Regents of the University of Nebraska

A Case of You. Words and Music by Joni Mitchell. Copyright © 1971 Crazy Crow Music. Copyright Renewed. All Rights Administered Worldwide by Reservoir Media Management, Inc. All Rights Reserved. Used by Permission. *Reprinted by Permission of Hal Leonard LLC.*

Portions of chapter 8 were previously published as Steve Bialostok and Marcus D. Watson, "Older Black Men Playing Dominoes: Talking Shit and Creating Black Place," *Transforming Anthropology* 30, no. 1 (2022): 34–47. © 2022 American Anthropological Association. https://anthrosource.onlinelibrary.wiley.com/doi/full/10.1111/traa.12227.

All rights reserved

The University of Nebraska Press is part of a land-grant institution with campuses and programs on the past, present, and future homelands of the Pawnee, Ponca, Otoe-Missouria, Omaha, Dakota, Lakota, Kaw, Cheyenne, and Arapaho Peoples, as well as those of the relocated Ho-Chunk, Sac and Fox, and Iowa Peoples.

For customers in the EU with safety/GPSR concerns, contact:
gpsr@mare-nostrum.co.uk
Mare Nostrum Group BV
Mauritskade 21D
1091 GC Amsterdam
The Netherlands

Library of Congress Control Number: 2025015474

Designed and set in Charter ITC by L. Welch.

In memory of Jane H. Hill and Luis C. Moll

I remember that time you told me
You said, "Love is touching souls"
Surely you touched mine
'Cause part of you pours out of me
In these lines from time to time
—Joni Mitchell, "A Case of You"

## Contents

|     |                                                            |       |
| --- | ---------------------------------------------------------- | ----- |
|     | List of Illustrations                                      | xi    |
|     | Acknowledgments                                            | xiii  |
|     | Notes on Transcription                                     | xvii  |
| 1.  | Beginnings                                                 | 1     |
| 2.  | Denver's History of Racism and Segregation                 | 23    |
| 3.  | Charles Hall                                               | 41    |
| 4.  | Northeast Park Hill and the Struggle to Maintain Black Place | 51  |
| 5.  | Robert Taylor                                              | 73    |
| 6.  | Birth and Evolution of a Black Social and Cultural Nexus   | 83    |
| 7.  | Herman Carr                                                | 105   |
| 8.  | Talking Shit inside the Card Room                          | 117   |
| 9.  | Buford Yarborough                                          | 137   |
| 10. | The Business of Intimacy                                   | 149   |
| 11. | D-Ray Edwards                                              | 169   |
| 12. | Endings                                                    | 179   |
|     | Notes                                                      | 191   |
|     | Bibliography                                               | 207   |
|     | Index                                                      | 217   |

## Illustrations

1. Card room placard — 5
2. Park Hill and Five Points map — 31
3. Holly Square shopping center sign — 54
4. East view of shops on 33rd Avenue — 56
5. West view of shops on 33rd Avenue — 57
6. Mr. Taylor — 74
7. Hiawatha Davis Recreation Center — 84
8. Perseverance mural — 85
9. Barbershop — 94
10. Mr. Carr — 106
11. Author and Mr. Taylor, pallbearers — 114
12. Mr. Carr, Mr. Taylor, Mr. Buford, Grover, and D-Ray — 118
13. Mr. Taylor, George, and Mr. Carr — 126
14. Mr. Buford — 138
15. Mr. Buford's funeral — 165
16. D-Ray — 170
17. Trapper — 185
18. Card room sign removed — 188

# Acknowledgments

Writing a book is never a solitary endeavor. Though it involved long hours of solitary work, this book has been shaped by the contributions of others—through shared ideas, encouragement, and thoughtful feedback. Each interaction, whether large or small, broadened my perspective and helped bring this book to life in ways I could never have imagined on my own.

First and foremost, my greatest debt goes to all the men in the card room. Their openness, generosity of spirit, and willingness to share their lives not only made this work possible but also touched me profoundly. I miss them.

This book has been enriched by countless formal and informal conversations with individuals who live in, have lived in, or are professionally connected to the greater Park Hill neighborhood: friends Frank and Sylvia Sullivan; ceramics instructor Linda Reed; urban planner and activist James Roy II; social and financial leader Haroun Cowans; Urban Land Conservancy president and CEO Aaron Miripol; Mayor Mike Johnston; my barber, Brad Washington; Pauline Robinson Library Senior Librarian Leslie Williams; House of Hair entrepreneurs and community organizers Marcus Pope and Samantha Guillmeno; community advocate Jonathan McMillan; Corey Benjamin, who generously shared stories about his father; card room regular Paul Howard; Denver Parks and Recreation coordinator Charles Black; vocational program coordinator for the Hope Center Otis Preston; and Frank Merriex, who taught me everything by telling me nothing.

Many have provided advice and insights. External reviewers provided invaluable recommendations that sharpened my work. The University of Wyoming has been my academic home from the start and, despite facing numerous financial cuts, provided me with a sabbatical to begin writing this book. Colleagues Allen Trent, Pete Moran, Vicki Gillis, Jenna Shim, Cynthia Brock, Joe Russo, and Mark Perkins encouraged along the way; Nik Sweet's feedback was especially helpful. My former colleague Marcus Watson shared his knowledge of the tradition of playing dominoes, and his insider perspective and cultural insights were instrumental to this book's development. Local Denver historian Phil Goodstein generously shared his expertise and responded to my many questions. Shirley Brice Heath and I first discussed this project in its early stages; later, her deep knowledge and critical eye along with insightful critiques of early chapter drafts pushed me to engage rigorously with the data. Carole Edelsky offered important comments on an early chapter. Kate Wiegele, a wonderful reader, offered both encouragement and indispensable feedback. Jennifer Roth-Gordon understood precisely what this book needed and never hesitated to tell me so in no uncertain terms.

I am fortunate to have had enthusiastic editors at the University of Nebraska Press. Anthropology of North America series editors Carrie Lane and James Bielo saw the potential of this book and were essential in shaping my vision with critical feedback. Editor in chief Bridget Barry believed in this project from the start, granting ample time for revisions. Associate editor Emily Casillas patiently shepherded the latter stages of the process, offering both invaluable editorial insight and reassurance that eased my anxieties. Kayla Moslander ensured that the manuscript moved smoothly through each stage to final publication. I am also grateful to the production, marketing, and administrative staff—Terry Boldan, Tayler Lord, Tish Fobben, Leif Milliken, and Erika Rippeteau—as well as the talented design team.

I am lucky to have friendships that provide me with a deep sense of belonging: Frank Serafini, Andy Brenan, Scott Reuss, Susan Iwamoto, Gloria and Jim Fitzpatrick, Marcee Samberg, Hillel and Judy Salomon, Jace Rogat, David Betty, Brian Odom, Michael Dell'Osso, and Toni Szilagi. Matt Aronson has been my best man—not only at a wedding but also, time and again, through the moments that mattered most. Rudi Gaudio has been a guiding force in both my professional and personal life, offering honesty, attentive listening, and consistently wise council.

I am also grateful to my son, Ethan, as he navigates his own journey and seeks his unique place in the world.

Finally, my deepest gratitude goes to my husband, Joe Lozoya. If I were the type to hang a Christmas stocking, I'd have earned at least one lump of coal for each year spent writing this book. While coal might be fitting, I'd rather honor the priceless support Joe provided at every step. Between training for and running marathons, he proofread each chapter, guided me on formatting, kept me organized, patiently overlooked the mood swings, and offered steady reassurance during moments of despair. I truly could not have completed this book without him.

## Notes on Transcription

Transcribing talk is never a neutral or unproblematic practice. All transcripts enable certain interpretations and advance particular interests. Linguistic anthropologist Elinor Ochs first addressed how transcript layout and the use of symbols reflect the researcher's agenda.[1] Sociocultural linguist Mary Bucholtz writes that because transcribing is always an act of interpretation and representation, it is also an act of power.[2] As this book is meant for a broader audience that includes both general readers and scholars, I have reduced the number of transcription markings to minimize distraction. To show my decisions regarding which parts of conversations to include, anything omitted is preceded with or followed by an ellipsis. In terms of representing how the men sounded, I occasionally include information on stress-prosody by capitalizing words, though I rarely did so at the level of syllables. I tried to capture how they actually sounded in these transcriptions, which included their use of African American Language (AAL).

As sociolinguists have frequently documented and discussed, many African American Language speakers most often vary between what are commonly considered "less standard" (or so-called vernacular) features and what are considered more "standard" (closer to standard English) features.[3] A speaker's distribution of features associated with AAL vs. features associated with standard English will differ according to social factors ranging from age to gender to socioeconomic status, in addition to the nature and context of the interaction, including the level of formality.[4] These linguistic features are equally grammatical and conversationally appropriate; it is wider (and whiter) American society that stigmatizes the linguistic features of AAL and associates them with a lack of education or intelligence, as "bad English."[5]

Finally, laughter, actions, and other paralinguistic communication are denoted by brackets ([ ]).

# Playing to the End

# 1   Beginnings

"Give us fifteen!" Mr. Buford calls out his score loudly, having added the numbers of white domino pips on the exposed end of a line. Mr. Buford, a feisty and loveably cantankerous octogenarian, rarely misses a domino game.

"Partner, you play so pretty," Mr. Hall says. Domino plays, as in other sports, can be praised for their beauty.

"You know what?" D-Ray's throaty tone always sounds agitated. "There's a whole lot of fives and shit out here."

"Huh? . . . I don't see no five." Mr. Taylor feigns confusion. His constant quips keep the others amused.

"Quit talkin' the game!" says Mr. Hall, normally of gravelly voice and laconic manner, playfully admonishing the men's loud, showy, and "out-of-control" talk. His comment is intentionally ironic since boisterous talk is the point.

"You ain't shit!" says D-Ray, who is filled with willful bravado but intimidates no one. It's only a matter of time before his momentary scowl is replaced by a thick smoker's laugh. As Mr. Taylor once described it, the "shit talk" that accompanies the game of dominoes is "a whole lot of nothing"—but they wouldn't have it any other way.

I learned to play dominoes with Mr. Buford, Mr. Hall, Mr. Taylor, Mr. Carr, and D-Ray—who, unlike most of the elderly men in the group, declined the honorific. These retired Black men, ranging from their mid-seventies to ninety, taught me the game with patience and care, even if I never fully caught on.[1]

*How I Discovered Dominoes*

In 2015 I was introduced to the Hiawatha Davis Jr. Recreation Center, where I began participating twice a week in a Silver Sneakers exercise program and took a ceramics class every Wednesday. Like me, most of the participants were seniors, many of whom lived in Denver's Northeast Park Hill neighborhood. Each time I attended, I passed the card room and sometimes stopped to listen in. The energetic banter among the men inside gradually captivated my attention and caused me to slow my pace. Eventually, I mustered the courage to enter, offering a nod and a smile each time I settled at an empty table to watch the spirited card game and merciless teasing that accompanied it. One day, after many visits, Samuel, one of the four Black octogenarians playing that day, approached me after his game ended. He stood up, pivoted with his walker, and—after I naively failed to introduce myself, asked, "Are you undercover?" "No," I responded with a slightly awkward laugh, "I'm just interested in your game. What are you playing?" "Pinochle," he answered.

This brief exchange helped break the ice. Samuel silently pushed his walker back to the card table and introduced me to the men sitting there. From that day forward, whenever I entered the card room, Samuel and I exchanged nods. The regular pinochle players followed his lead.

Then one afternoon, I met Grover. Before entering, he momentarily stood just inside the doorway, with a grin on his face and an Oakland Raiders baseball cap worn backward. A youngster by comparison—he was only in his fifties—Grover drew attention by flicking the room lights and boisterously announcing, "The champ is here!" I would later learn that this performance was typical for Grover. He came over and asked what I was doing. I told him I was interested in the game, but especially in how the men spoke to each other. Grover gave me a puzzled but curious look. After I provided a couple of examples of the banter I'd overheard, he grinned and said, "Yeah, that *is* interesting. I never thought about it that way." Grover then helpfully volunteered one of the most important rules of card room banter: "You don't talk about your wife or your family." He led me to the pinochle table and began explaining the game as the men played. "It's easy," Grover reassured me, perhaps noticing my eyes widen with fear as he talked. I sat at the table for several weeks, usually with Grover by my side, socializing with the men and trying to figure out the game.

Serendipity brought me to dominoes. One afternoon, I happened to stay later than usual and witnessed a changing of the guards around 4:00 p.m. The pinochle players stood up, gathered their belongings, and put the cards away in the closet. Gradually, a new group of elderly men walked in and settled at several tables. I watched my first domino game, which featured even more spirited banter than cards. Later that week, during a Silver Sneakers luncheon, I mentioned my brief observation to my exercise "neighbor." As luck would have it, she lived next door to Bobby Cummings, who had organized the first dominoes game in the mid-1960s and attended every night. She offered to contact him on my behalf.

The following week in the card room, I heard a lean and spry octogenarian say in a ringing voice to the group of men he sat with, "Some guy is supposed to come here and talk to me about the tournament. I don't know what happened to him." I raised my hand like a shy elementary school student, hesitantly vying for a turn. "I think that's me," I said. We moved to a tiny and cluttered office next to the card room. A former medical technician, Mr. Cummings had worked at a local hospital in the 1960s where he started as the only Black employee. He recalled the days at the center when "we used to play in front," referring to the early years when the recreation center was known as Skyland.[2]

Mr. Cummings shared a wealth of information about the domino tournament and its previous management, the origin of the domino sets in the room, and his purchase of new plastic tables to withstand the domino slamming. He also mentioned that the National Basketball Association star Chauncey Billups had grown up at the center and still came around. Mr. Cummings detailed the lobbying and planning that went into the center's massive renovation in 2000, including his efforts to ensure they set aside a room for cards, chess, and dominoes. When I expressed my admiration for the men's unwavering commitment to playing five times a week, he told me that the men drove over every afternoon to play, with most staying for about four hours. "Do their wives care?" I asked. "I don't know," he responded with a wry smile. "But they play!"

Back in the card room, he set up the dominoes for my first lesson. Drawing the required seven tiles for himself, he instructed me to do the same, and then demonstrated how to score. "*This* is gonna be mine now," he explained. "All I can play is the deuce, trey, or blank," he said, offering a primer on domino vocabulary. "What do you match the blank one with?" I asked, hoping that my rookie questions didn't get me kicked out. "Another blank," he said, with a supportive tone. I was learning, though I normally spend my days teaching. With an academic background in anthropology, I teach courses in sociolinguistics, race and racism, and cultural and linguistic anthropology at the University of Wyoming. Thinking initially about my students, I shared with Mr. Cummings my hope that I could audio-record some games but mentioned that I would need the men's permission. "You don't need their permission," he declared loudly for the entire room to hear. After a quick look around the tables, he added, "You got *my* permission."

Technically, his authorization would never have passed an Institutional Review Board overseeing university research, though I did follow up with each of the men individually much later. They gave their permission to use their real names and share their life stories in this book.[3] But I quickly learned that Mr. Cummings was a mischievous and rascally character, greatly admired and highly respected by the other men. He paved the way for me to sit with a group and observe. Eventually, three of those men became participants in my research. At the end of that first evening, Mr. Cummings invited me to come back. I started attending several times a week, and Mr. Cummings always welcomed me, as did the other men I habitually sat next to: Mr. Buford, Mr. Taylor, and Mr. Hall. These four struck me as the room's core—perhaps because they were among the oldest, but also because of the respectful deference they received from everyone else.

Then one day, Grover walked in, still buoyant and obviously popular with the others. "You coming *here* now?" he grinned, noticing me. "Ain't you playing pinochle?"

"I was never actually playing pinochle," I responded. Grover (re)introduced me to the men at the table. "These guys talk shit too," he said, remembering my interest in the topic.

FIG. 1. Card room placard. Steve Bialostok, photographer.

Rather than joining the elders at their dominoes table, Grover opted to sit with the younger crowd—mostly men around his age. Watching them slam dominoes so hard that the table shook and the tiles bounced, I understood why Mr. Cummings had purchased the nearly indestructible tables. I never knew a table game could require that much physical and emotional energy, and I came to admire both their passion and their stamina.

One evening, many months later, and entirely thanks to my domino partner, I was enjoying a winning streak with Mr. Taylor. But after more than an hour of steady play, my mental exhaustion turned into physical weariness. And yet the men I had come to know as "the elders" played on. I spent five years in the card room with these men at the Hiawatha Davis Recreation Center. *Playing to the End* is a tribute to them and all they generously shared with me as I watched them navigate their elder years amid dramatic racial shifts in Denver, Colorado. This is my attempt to honor their lives and the joy and connection they so clearly gained from playing dominoes and "talking shit."[4]

*Playing Dominoes in the Card Room*

The card room at the Hiawatha Davis Recreation Center is the only such officially designated room among Denver Parks and Recreation's thirty recreation centers, but the name is somewhat of a misnomer. Card games only attracted a handful of players in the early afternoon, and not even every day. Many of the men who once played pitty-pat, bid whist, and especially pinochle no longer show up. Some have passed away. But later in the afternoon, like clockwork, a dozen or so elderly Black men begin to arrive. They walk around, greeting each other. First, their eyes meet, and they smile, simultaneously giving each other dap—a handshake of solidarity. This symbolic but physical gesture has long represented Black consciousness, identity, and unity.[5] Soon, a few self-appointed players remove rectangular boxes, paper, and pencils from the small storage closet in the corner. An evening of play unofficially begins when the men settle at two or three tables with the usual suspects. Most of these men have been regulars for decades—both in the card room and before it opened. They begin a social practice so ingrained in their daily lives that it has become a taken-for-granted ritual.

The card room quickly fills with explosive talk and raucous laughter as the rubber bands securing the old snaps on the boxes are removed, and twenty-eight small, black wooden domino tiles are turned face down on an empty table. Dominoes have long been a part of Black culture, both within the United States and throughout the Caribbean and its diaspora.[6] Each player draws seven dominoes from the set. The player who draws the double six or highest double goes first and places one of their tiles on the table. As tradition dictates, the turn rotates to the left, clockwise. In this version of the game, the men place dominoes in a linear fashion, with the number of dots on each tile matching the adjacent domino. The key objective isn't just to run out of tiles but to score points by making the open ends total a multiple of five. If successful, the player earns that number of points. In keeping with the elders' practice, the score (five, ten, fifteen, twenty, twenty-five) must be announced aloud so that everyone, including the scorekeeper, can hear it. A player will broadcast, "Ten!" or sometimes direct the scorekeeper, "That's ten, Mr. Marker!" The goal for a player or team is to "domino"—to accumulate enough points to reach the designated target of 150.[7]

The simplicity of the domino rules and the ability to play with only the briefest instructions belies the game's complexity and intellectual demands. The men play in teams of two, with each move requiring focused problem-solving to score points and block the opposing team. Players are constantly faced with a variety of in-game decisions, from choosing an opening play to countering an opponent's move. I was amazed by the men's ability to infer, from what had been played and who made the play, which tiles the others were still holding. This was true of every elder, including ninety-year-old George, who, after leaving at the end of the evening, often couldn't remember where the bus stop was. Successful players must predict which dominoes each player holds (including his partner's) and anticipate which tile a competitor or partner might play. Being able to silently communicate your hand to your partner, and vice versa, is critical. But I could never figure any of this out.

The final design of the tile layout is not intentional, but rather the result of strategy and a little luck. Some configurations grow elaborately in all directions, resembling an angular skeleton or a Rorschach inkblot. The figure in the game I recount in the chapter's opening looked like three parallel train tracks merging into a primary track at a ninety-degree angle.

Throughout the game, the men's self-amusement is so infectious that I often find myself laughing without entirely understanding what's so funny. The room is filled with enthusiasm. They slam dominoes with such force that the tiles already on the table are displaced; they exuberantly call out scores ("I'll take five!" "Gimme ten!"), toss insults like prizes, and declare "domino" extra loudly, as if the other players couldn't possibly hear.

Players are corporeally immersed, most notably when slamming down a domino. In some instances, such as with Mr. Taylor, his movement resembles the mechanics of a baseball pitcher's windup: his entire right arm rotates forward several times while his hand grips the domino until he finally slams it down on the fourth or fifth rotation. Sheldon's slam, on the other hand, contrasts with the graceful rise of his forearm, his elbow turned upward. Mr. Hall only slams occasionally, with an emphasis on his forearm and wrist. Trapper, however, *always* delivers a full body slam, accompanied by an accentuated monosyllabic sound that can be represented by HUH! Slamming dominoes conveys confidence. A particularly loud slam usually indicates that the player has scored. But the intensity of the slam doesn't always correlate with the quantity of the score. Scoring five, for example, can scatter a line of dominoes just as easily as scoring twenty-five. When he matches a domino but doesn't score a multiple of five, Mr. Hall might simply toss his tile toward his match, expecting someone to position it for him.

As part of their cherished tradition, the men don't just play dominoes; they are practically required to indulge in what they affectionately refer to as "talking shit"—the predominant form of discourse within the card room. For these elders, talking shit, though occasionally provocative or insulting, is primarily a form of playful, uninhibited speech deliberately disconnected from outside concerns. They emphasize that it is meant to be good-natured and harmless, carefully avoiding negativity or hurt feelings.[8] Despite how it might sound, it is viewed as lighthearted banter, almost always sparking group laughter and never intended to create animosity. Engaging in talking shit is seen as essential. As Grover emphasizes, its centrality to their social interactions and domino play cannot be overstated: "You *gotta* talk shit. . . . They know how I get at the table. They know how Walter gets at the table. They know how Big Joe gets at the table. I know how Mook gets at the table. It's no fun if you don't talk shit."[9]

In the card room, the goal is not to play a straightforward game of dominoes; there is a symbiotic relationship between talking shit and physical action. Talking shit is an integral part of the domino experience and of the room's energy. After the banter and dominoes described in the chapter's opening, Ronnie, seated with three others at the adjacent table, delivered a brief monologue that epitomized shit talk. He burst into a high-pitched, celebratory whoop, enthusiastically announcing his score—and the competitive flair with which he achieved it—to no one in particular. "Fifteen with a double, I ain't changin' my bones! I ain't changin' my bones! That's fifteen with a double! Gimme fifteen. You asked for me. You got me! I'm tired of winning! [He cackles.] He *was* ahead. He *was* ahead. He *was* ahead! [He cackles again.]"

Fueled by a shared spirit of passion, enthusiasm, and joy, the elders spend a significant portion of their days at home, eagerly anticipating their nightly gatherings in the card room. The card room provides them with familiarity, racial solidarity, and a sense of respect. Most of the elders here go by the honorific "Mr.," a title they never heard applied to their fathers or grandfathers when they were growing up. Though many have moved to Denver's suburbs, they commute to the center Monday through Friday to play dominoes and talk trash. The card room nurtures their social bonds and keeps them connected. However, they, along with many other Northeast Park Hill residents I spoke with, express a sense of melancholy about the gradual disappearance of what was once a predominantly Black neighborhood. This community had been a cornerstone of the recreation center, and conversely, the center had played a significant role in the life of the neighborhood. The elders in the card room are keenly aware of their neighborhood's demographic shifts, which have also affected the center's transition from a majority-Black to a majority-white institution. The elders, who had always been a steady but unmarked presence, now see themselves as conspicuous survivors in a transformed environment. The evolution of Denver and the Northeast Park Hill neighborhood looms in the background of the card room, an inescapable contextual backdrop that I explore further in chapters 2, 4, and 6.

*Conducting Research in the Card Room*

While I can't pinpoint the precise moment when my experiences in the card room shifted into an ethnographic project, I am deeply appreciative of the generosity of spirit that led the men to welcome me warmly night after night. Mr. Taylor and Mr. Hall put aside their competitiveness to team up with a timid novice who could do little more than tally dots and occasionally keep score. Mr. Buford informed me that Grover had told the others that he approved of my presence: "We were wondering what this goddamn white guy was doing here. Grover said that you was okay." Slowly, I transitioned from a mere observer to an occasional player, embracing the participation needed for the "participant observation" research methodology that anthropologists value. But it wasn't until a series of related incidents following the annual domino tournament that I began to think of my time there as "research."

Mr. Cummings had repeatedly expressed frustration about the lack of publicity for their beloved domino tournament from Parks and Recreation. Knowing that I "wrote articles," he asked if I would write one about them. I explained that although I didn't write that type of article, I would be happy to reach out to someone who might be interested in covering their story. I emailed a local white television news reporter.[10] Considering what might pique his interest, I framed the story around the nightly domino games, blending details I had observed with insights I had inferred. In particular, I highlighted how the men staunchly rejected narratives that associate aging with decline, dependence, and incompetence. I also portrayed them as "survivors"—Black men who had aged in a society where Black men disproportionately die young. Despite the challenges of living in a society that often marginalizes and isolates Black men, these men had forged meaningful social connections in the card room.

The correspondent responded politely and forwarded my email to a nationally known white broadcast reporter who traveled across the country highlighting "heartwarming" stories about ordinary people. The local correspondent sent me his reply. It read in part, "I'm not sure it quite hits the bar for us. . . . Right now I just have a hard time seeing it as a network feature. For example, I don't see these men as 'survivors' just because they're Black and they lived into their 80s. That seems overstated. And I'm having a hard time picturing a domino tournament that could carry for 3 minutes."

Despite this quick and disrespectful dismissal, I agreed with Mr. Cummings that their activities warranted some form of public recognition. I had come to deeply appreciate the significance of the card room, especially during periods when my own personal life felt chaotic. I found myself increasingly drawn to its nightly rhythms, the adherence to the unwritten rule to "not talk about your wife or family." I could feel the sense of community in that small room, and I felt fortunate to be, if only temporarily, a part of it. Occasionally, someone would affix a photograph to the wall of a departed elder who had once been a member of the card room. These men never sought nor cared about notoriety, but I knew that the card room and its members had a story to tell—one that went beyond mere pictures on the wall. I wanted to help tell their story, but I also wanted to tread carefully and respect their space.

After visiting the card room three to five days a week for months, I approached the elders I felt most comfortable with, asking each privately if I could visit them at home for a conversation about dominoes and what I had been observing and learning. When I visited those who agreed, I shared some of my personal and professional background. I explained the journey that had led me to the card room, starting with my pinochle observations and responding to Samuel's question about what I was doing in a Black social space. My attempts to clarify my research intentions sparked some confusion, as none of the men could understand why their daily routines were noteworthy or of any interest to others. I explained that, with their permission, I hoped to eventually record them and take notes as they played. I also expressed my hope to ask them questions about what I had observed and heard during the games.

During our initial meetings, I didn't immediately introduce a consent form for their signatures. Instead, I shared my hopes for a potential shift in my role in the card room, from novice player to researcher, and asked for their feedback. I visited their homes two or three more times—sometimes just to watch television together or have casual chats—before five men agreed to join my research project.

*Participant Observation beyond the Card Room*

I eventually moved into a house a mile from Hiawatha Davis, within what I fortuitously discovered was reasonable walking distance to the homes of half a dozen men from the card room. This new location allowed me to explore the businesses, nonprofit organizations, and churches within a six-block radius of the center. As I began to participate in neighborhood meetings and activities as a resident, I grew increasingly troubled by the neighborhood's challenges. For example, living in a food desert was a minor inconvenience for me, but my aging neighbors lacked transportation to the nearest grocery store, two miles away. Before I became a resident, I had generally remained quiet during community meetings about the changing landscape, particularly the gentrification of a block just a mile south of the center. But I soon found it difficult to separate my roles as researcher and resident.

My identity as a neighbor began to shape my research questions and deepen my involvement. I became angry when new white residents openly expressed concerns about their own public safety and voiced anti-Black fears. In one memorable exchange, a white man condemned the "blight" at one end of a gentrifying street, where Black men "loitered" in front of a liquor store. At the opposite end of the same block, just five hundred feet away, a new microbrewery had opened. "When Black men stand in front of a liquor store, you call it a blight," I said. "When white men stand in front of a microbrewery, you put out tables and invite them in." But my own presence in the neighborhood was equally complicated: in just three years, I saw my block shift from about 60 percent Black to 75 percent white. And I sometimes chose to frequent "gentrified" spaces, like the local Denver pizza chain that opened next to a new multimillion-dollar micro-unit apartment complex.

Being present in the neighborhood deepened my understanding of local issues and also led to connections—sometimes in unexpected ways. I'd walk my dog past that "blighted" liquor store and end up striking up conversations with a few regulars. They shared stories of being forced out of their homes to make way for new development. To better understand the shifting racial dynamics and people's experiences of these changes, I spoke with two of the remaining shop owners as well as several new business owners. I discovered House of Hair, a barbershop with a thirty-year history of providing haircuts and engaging in social activism, just an eight-minute walk from my house. Brad, who became my barber, grew up down the street from Skyland (the name he still used for the recreation center), played basketball there, and had purchased his home a block away, near where his family still lived. Brad knew the center's history, its supervisors, and the "old guys" who played dominoes. Several elders, including Trapper, were regular customers at House of Hair. I'm certain that Trapper, who rarely spoke to me inside the card room, became friendlier once we happened to get our hair cut at the same time.

Marcus, the barbershop's owner, decided that I needed to "have some fun in my life" and invited me out for cigars and bourbon—a challenge, since I neither smoke nor drink. After learning that the one female barber, Sam (Samantha), liked chocolate chip cookies, I'd periodically bake some and bring them in for her. "People in the shop notice this," Marcus told me, smiling as I struggled to finish even half my glass of bourbon. Each time I entered or exited the barbershop, Marcus and I exchanged handshakes. Over time, he took the lead in teaching me the art of the dap, breaking it down into slow motions that often elicited laughter from onlookers. Though I initially felt awkward, I gradually improved, until my movements became more fluid. "There you go," Marcus remarked the first time I did it reasonably well. However, I never put my newly acquired skill into practice in the card room.

*My Insider-Outsider Position*

Despite the overall friendliness of most of the men in the card room, it was generally clear to all that I remained "out of place." Pierre Bourdieu's sports metaphor of having "a feel for the game" aptly describes the essence of an insider, emphasizing an intuitive understanding of what is expected and "a sense of one's place."[11] The elders' ritualized interactions—their bodily comportment and talk—marked the card room as a distinctively Black space. On a few occasions, I was able to successfully and playfully mimic their reactions to scoring points ("*That's how you make fifteen!*"), which elicited laughter from the group. Other times, my outsider status was confirmed through common and required ritual social interactions like greetings. On a typical evening, as elders entered the card room, they would circulate, extending either a fist bump or dap to everyone present. Some men took quite a while to navigate the route from door to chair, even though they had greeted each other the day before. My presence would surprise all but the regular elders. The occasional players greeted me with a polite conventional handshake and addressed me formally with a "Hello, sir."

The initiation of a domino game through tile shuffling provided another context for the negotiation of my insider-outsider position. The meticulous and seemingly mundane act of shuffling, crucial for maintaining the integrity of the game, involved a series of coordinated movements. The shuffler adroitly arranges his fingers and both palms upon the face down tiles. He begins to rotate his hands to mix the tiles, the alternating synchronization resembling the act of washing the table. Normally rotated rapidly, the tiles remain under the shuffler's control—they rarely turn upward or split off from the whole. Once they are scrupulously mixed, the shuffler releases all the tiles by shoving them slightly toward the center of the table. When I took my turn shuffling, my awkward and unrefined gestures contrasted sharply with the smooth and controlled actions of experienced players. This drew attention to my lack of dexterity and eventually became a subject of playful jokes among the elders.

My insider-outsider position took on more depth with the five elders central to my research. They teased me and shared laughter over my faux pas and awkward moments. They also provided guidance on appropriate social norms. On one occasion, as I observed the younger individuals playing, talking shit, and the youngest using a variant of the n-word, Mr. Taylor advised, "You can't ever say that word. I don't like it. *They* can say it. *You* can't." Sometimes they joked about me with others. While introducing me to his relative visiting from out of town, Mr. Carr announced, "This is Steve. He's a *white* guy," prompting group laughter. In one domino game in which I participated, Mr. Hall referred to me as "Mr. Steve" before catching himself and reverting to simply "Steve." D-Ray pointed out Mr. Buford's frequent vulgarity to me: "Steve, can you believe an old man talks like that?" My presence, in this case, helped him indirectly insult Mr. Buford.

Despite all that we shared, over the course of the five years of my research, I consistently grappled with the idea that my presence brought about the very thing these men sought to avoid and presented an incursion into the safe Black space that they were cultivating. Yet, upon raising this concern with each participating elder (and several others), they encouraged me to continue frequenting the card room. "We know you now," Mr. Hall told me. Mr. Taylor also sought to reassure me: "Anyone can come in here." Mr. Cummings repeatedly extended invitations for me to return. Mr. Buford was the only elder who openly questioned my presence. He and I started having breakfast together at his favorite restaurant every few weeks. Always straightforward, he initially peppered me with questions about my background—where I was from, if I had ever been around Black people, and why I would be interested in their space. After several breakfast conversations, visits to his home, and meeting his family, a mutual understanding seemed to blossom, mitigating his suspicion and fostering a genuine connection. As time passed, my presence in the card room became more expected and less of an anomaly.

Through this journey, I gained an understanding of the significance of a homeplace—the way a group of a few dozen men could turn a sparsely filled room of tables and chairs into a place infused with profound social, cultural, and personal meanings.[12] This book traces how the elders engage in Black placemaking through their everyday participation and play in the card room.

*Black Placemaking*

Given the long U.S. history of racial separation of Black and white bodies, encompassing slavery, Jim Crow segregation, redlining, racial terror lynchings, and gentrification, the theme of displacement is central in the lives of many Black people.[13] The esteemed scholar bell hooks describes how Black people have continuously created alternative "homeplaces," havens imbued with a sense of belonging within a nation that continuously devalues, dehumanizes, and demonizes Black people.[14] Katherine McKittrick has analyzed how white Americans have historically obstructed the development and existence of Black spaces, aiming to erase not only these spaces but also the relationships, cultural practices, and people associated with them.[15] Saidiya Hartman characterizes Black space as *stealing away* and seeks to honor "unlicensed movement, collective assembly, and an abrogation of the terms of subjugation in acts as simple as sneaking off to laugh and talk with friends."[16] Black placemaking thus includes individual and collective acts to build alternate spaces that are sites of respect and dignity and points to a "future of alternative conditions—spatial freedom and freedom in place."[17] Amid the continued indignities of the color line, Black placemaking emerges as a powerful expression of spatial resistance, challenging white entitlement and offering refuge.

Through placemaking, Black people resist being cast as victims of history and create "sustaining, affirming and pleasurable" communities.[18] Black placemaking entails fun, witty, soulful, smart, biting, and rejuvenating acts and culturally significant rituals.[19] The creation of Black place enacts a rejection of the status quo and of the white gaze that diminishes, degrades, dehumanizes, and erases Black life.[20] Resisting the gaze of white people through Black placemaking allows for spaces "where we can simply be—where we can get off the treadmill of making white people comfortable and finally realize just how tired we are."[21] Black placemaking cultivates an abiding, celebratory, and almost nation-building sense of Black belonging. It suggests what Tina Campt refers to as a "practice of refusal." A practice of refusal recognizes a social order "that renders you fundamentally illegible and unintelligible. It is a refusal to embrace the terms of diminished subjecthood with which one is presented and to use negation as a generative and creative source of disorderly power to embrace the possibility of living otherwise. The practice of refusal is a striving to create possibility in the face of negation."[22]

Through this study of the card room, I examine the resourceful and artful ways Black people escape objectification in an anti-Black world.[23] According to the elders, the card room stands as the last public venue in Denver for playing dominoes, outside bars or lounges where betting occurs. Black places often persist as precarious, contingent, and delicate entities—and the story of the card room, in the renamed Hiawatha Davis Recreation Center in Northeast Park Hill, is no exception. Its significance as a Black space—due to the men's continued efforts—underscores the ongoing struggle for autonomy and self-determination in a society marked by anti-Blackness, structural inequalities, and racial injustices.

*Play-Frames, Ritual and Performance*

In the card room, the game of dominoes and its accompanying talk can be understood as an example of resilience and escape that takes place through play. While scholars continue to debate a precise definition of play, there is broad agreement that play involves temporarily stepping away from ordinary life into a distinct "sphere of activity with a disposition of its own."[24] The "play" in this context does not just refer to the game of dominoes; it also centers around the verbal play of talking shit. The goals and outcomes of talking shit can best be explained through three interconnected concepts: play-frames, ritual, and performance, as I discuss further in chapter 8. Play entails characteristics such as intrinsic drive, voluntary engagement, and a lack of purpose other than its own enjoyment.[25] It also encompasses rituals. As anthropologist Mary Douglas observed, rituals are predictable behaviors that provide a frame for action: "A ritual provides a frame. The marked-off time or place creates a special kind of expectancy, just as the oft-repeated 'Once upon a time' sets the stage for fantastic tales."[26] Similarly, shit-talking is a ritual that accompanies the game of dominoes.

Rituals center around tradition, fostering a sense of history and cultural continuity, as well as feelings of belonging and identity. They establish the beliefs and practices of a community, in which participants demonstrate one's faith in others. Even the repetition of certain ritualized actions, such as slamming down dominoes, serves to draw people together. Just as collective prayers and meditations act as powerful symbols of shared identity and "bridge differences within group settings marked by diversity," the card room rituals bind the elders to the space and to each other.[27]

Victor Turner explains that rituals are also cultural performances, and Richard Bauman points out that verbal performances make a speaker accountable to an audience and hold their speech up as "subject to evaluation for the way it is done, for the relative skill and effectiveness of the performer's display of competence."[28] The elders' ritualized cultural performances signal to the audience to interpret what is said in a special sense: "Do not take it to mean what the words alone, taken literally, would convey."[29] Domino play and talk can be understood as performances meant for the elders' own amusement and for the evaluative eyes and ears of others in the room. As a form of cultural performance, their "play" allows participants to "embody their place in the scheme of things."[30]

While the elders would all undoubtedly agree with the claim, as Mr. Taylor said, that talking shit is about "a whole lot of nothing," I argue that talking shit is far more than "nothing"—through domino play and talk, the elders construct a sense of self and communal belonging and turn the card room into a safe and comfortable Black place. Together, they create and find refuge from the "lived sedimentation of white power and privilege that perpetuates violence upon Black bodies."[31] In doing so, they channel resilience and care into a space that they fiercely defend from the threats of encroaching gentrification, cultural erasure, and displacement.

*An Ethos of Care*

Black caregiving and placemaking are both critical in a world that refuses to recognize Black humanity—a world that renders Black bodies "inhuman, disposable, and inherently problematic."[32] Fred Moten underscores the diverse ways in which Black people establish alternative spaces to practice "seeing one another, loving one another, and granting one another breathing room in a world where anti-Black racial violence is normalized and asphyxiating."[33] Christina Sharpe insightfully explores the notion of care within the context of Black life and experience. She delves into the complexities of care amid a past and present filled with violence and oppression, highlighting the ways in which care operates as both a source of and a site of resilience for Black individuals and communities in an anti-Black world.[34]

Just as the elders' domino playing defies stereotypes of aging that include mental and physical decline, their joyful and energetic camaraderie also contradicts ideas of cantankerous or lonely old men. Mr. Hall, though not the oldest, serves as the caretaker for the room. During my first year, he occasionally moved my tiles (violating unspoken rules) to a more advantageous position. When others objected, Mr. Hall would respond, "He's just learning." In later years, he would sometimes show me how I could have strategized better or scored more points. But the men did not see themselves as caregivers. When I pointed out to Mr. Taylor that "no one in the card room offers to be my domino partner more than you, even though you know that there's a good chance we'll end up losing because of me," he quickly brushed aside my observation. Yet there are many ways to engage in an ethos of care, as Christina Sharpe points out, including—and going beyond—"the provision of what is necessary for the health, welfare, maintenance and protection of someone or something."[35]

When I could, I tried to do things for the elders. Mr. Hall let me help him into his jacket at the end of the night. I often helped Mr. Buford into his car, especially as he got progressively weaker. I once spent an evening driving George around on errands, shopping, and carrying bags of groceries into his home. I called and texted to check in on the elders, and I treated them to meals whenever they could join me for an outing.

I stopped by their homes and visited, and I once shoveled snow off Mr. Taylor's sidewalk. But these were not acts of "care."

Hiʻilei Hobart and Tamara Kneese define "radical care" as collective care or "a set of vital but underappreciated strategies for enduring precarious worlds."[36] They explain how care can "push back against structural disadvantage" and consist of "*a feeling with*, rather than a feeling for, others."[37] The elders would not have described their own relationships with each other as relations of care—nor would "caregiving" be readily obvious to anyone observing their interactions in the room. They trickled into the card room around 4:00 p.m., staying four hours, often playing past the "fifteen-minute warning" they got from Eli every evening. Sometimes someone brought buckets of chicken to share. They rarely shared personal details about their outside lives, and the elders didn't frequently talk on the phone or socialize outside of this space. But as they slammed dominoes and talked shit together in this room for up to twenty hours a week, they were *with* each other, and this helped them survive—and thrive. Their relationships are a kind of "radical care," and this book is filled with stories of how they benefit from what they share with each other.[38]

*Telling Other People's Stories*

Insiders have long engaged in the observation, preservation, and celebration of their own history and traditions, bolstered by their strong cultural competence and a deep awareness of the sensitive nature of sharing their stories with outsiders. One of anthropologist Zora Neale Hurston's most significant contributions was writing as a "native" anthropologist before it became fashionable.[39] Dana Ain-Davis and Krista Craven Del Hierro's work in feminist methodologies also highlights the transformative power of ethnography in amplifying the voices of marginalized communities.[40] By engaging deeply with the lived experiences of individuals, we can foreground their narratives, challenge dominant discourses, and foster greater inclusivity in academic and public dialogues. The power dynamics of who is "trained" and vested with the authority to conduct research and publish continue to be skewed toward "educated" white men like me, and Amy Shuman points out that telling other people's stories is fraught with representational and ethical complexities.[41] One important corrective is to be clear about the limitations of my study.

This book is about a specific group of older Black men as written by a white outsider who came to know them over a period of five years. For some of the men in this book, their stories will be shared after they have passed away. I have discussed this book with the elders many times, and when possible, I also spoke with some members of their families. Any story shared with others is partial and told from a particular viewpoint. In my case, I spent time with elderly men in their later years, visiting them from time to time in their homes (and sometimes with their wives) and socializing with them for a few meals a month in their preferred restaurants, generally for breakfast or lunch. But mostly I got to know them and the community they forged in the card room through their nightly games of dominoes and their willingness to include me in my various roles: sometimes as an observer taking notes and recording their conversations and sometimes as a novice participant in their nightly games.

I feel privileged to have learned more about their individual journeys and the people and experiences that mattered to them. I didn't conduct formal life story interviews; instead, personal narratives often emerged organically, sometimes sparked by casual questions. Some elders seamlessly wove life history details in and out of other conversational topics. When I realized I wanted to write up their individual stories, I worked closely with each elder to confirm their interest and to double-check details. Included in this book are some of the stories that they chose to share with me and chose to allow me to share with a wider audience. Just as I edited the stories as they appear here, the men undoubtedly edited the details they revealed to me. The brief biographies that I intersperse throughout the book hint at the richness of their experiences and the profound insights they have gleaned from decades of watching the world change around them. I wish I could have shared even more of their stories, and I wish they had all lived to see their stories in print.

*Outline of the Book*

The book unfolds in a dual rhythm, alternating between chapters that explore the racial, cultural, and spatial context surrounding the Hiawatha

Davis Recreation Center and those that foreground the lives and reflections of the elders whose nightly domino games anchor this story.

Chapter 2, "Denver's History of Racism and Segregation," situates the recreation center within a longer urban history of racialized displacement and segregation. From the transformation of Five Points into a thriving Black neighborhood under conditions of exclusion to the gradual encroachment of gentrification into Park Hill, this chapter establishes the broader structural forces that shaped—and continue to unsettle—the lives of Black residents in Northeast Denver.

Chapters 3, 5, 7, 9, and 11 offer intimate portraits of the five elders who generously shared their life stories. Charles Hall reflects on his journey from Roswell, New Mexico, to a career in education and a sense of belonging in the card room. Robert Taylor, a former military man and Xcel Energy foreman, speaks to the perseverance required to overcome addiction and racial barriers. Herman Carr's tales of basketball, military life, and deep community ties reveal a man of integrity and warmth. Buford Yarborough brings the power of oral storytelling to the fore, his life marked by hardship, service, and resilience. And Donald "D-Ray" Edwards emerges as both a keeper of memory and a vocal critic of changes that have eroded communal care and rootedness. Through these narratives, readers glimpse a Black masculine intimacy rarely represented in public discourse.

Chapters 4, 6, 8, and 10 interweave themes of spatial politics, cultural transformation, and resistance. Chapter 4 investigates ongoing racial shifts in Northeast Park Hill, capturing the tensions between integrationist rhetoric and the lived experience of displacement. Chapter 6 explores the transformation of the Skyland Recreation Center into Hiawatha Davis, charting the ways Black communal spaces are renamed, restructured, and ultimately repurposed under gentrification. Chapter 8 turns inward to the card room itself, where nightly games of dominoes become acts of cultural endurance and mutual recognition—where "talking shit" operates as a mode of bonding, teaching, and making place. Chapter 10, "The Business of Intimacy," considers how emotional closeness and platonic love circulate between men who rarely speak of such things directly, particularly in the relationship between D-Ray and Mr. Buford.

The final chapter, "Endings," reflects on loss—of people, of space, of continuity. The deaths of several elders, disruptions wrought by the COVID-19 pandemic, and the quiet erasures accompanying institutional changes all signal a precarious future for the card room. And yet, what endures is the story: of a community shaped by struggle, held together by ritual, and animated by the ordinary grace of presence.

# 2  Denver's History of Racism and Segregation

At one point, Mr. Hall, Mr. Buford, Mr. Taylor, Mr. Carr, and D-Ray all resided within a one-mile radius of each other in Denver's north and northeast Park Hill neighborhood. Most had been there since the neighborhood's early 1960s transition from a predominantly white community to a predominantly Black one. At the time of my study, only Mr. Hall, Mr. Taylor, and Mr. Carr continued to live in the same homes they had occupied for decades. They were now surrounded by white neighbors. In this chapter, I explore Park Hill's historical, sociocultural, and political dynamics that gave rise to the pronounced racial shifts in the area. These racial dynamics are essential for understanding the origins and evolution of Black spaces within Northeast Park Hill and, more specifically, in the card room at the Hiawatha Davis Recreation Center.

*Denver's Shifting Black Spaces*

Denver today bears little resemblance to the city once half-jokingly referred to as "a big Cowtown." The Mile High City, once considered a poor second cousin to booming cities on the coasts, now boasts a vibrant downtown skyline filled with construction cranes—so numerous the *Denver Post* dubbed them Colorado's "new state bird." A national "crane index" ranks Denver higher than San Francisco, New York, and Washington DC for its number of tower cranes. Developers continue to raise the bar with skyscrapers featuring premium office spaces, luxury apartments, sky terraces, and multimillion-dollar penthouse condos. For example, Union Station, the city's train and light rail hub since 1881, underwent a $54 million transformation, completed in 2015. It now also houses a high-end hotel, neighborhood shops, restaurants, and bars.

In the mid-nineteenth century, Colorado experienced a gold rush, attracting a diverse range of people. As Denver grew, Black people began settling in the city, initially working as miners, laborers, and domestic workers. Many settled in an area near downtown Denver, later known as Five Points due to the intersection of Welton Street, 26th Ave, Washington Street, and 27th Street.[1] Gentrification has transformed Five Points, once the historic center of Denver's Black community and known as the "Harlem of the West" for its vibrant music scene, into the city's latest trendy district: RiNo (the River North Arts District).[2] With its numerous art galleries, shops, microbreweries, an event center, a large high-tech music venue, and "essential restaurants," the city magazine *5280* declared in 2016 that "the vibe in this 'hood is more relaxed than LoDo [Lower Downtown Denver]."[3] The white appropriation of "hood" described a place where 99 percent of Denver's Black population once lived.

Black migration to Denver's Five Points neighborhood was followed by a shift to specific areas in Park Hill. Founded in 1887, the much broader Park Hill neighborhood boasts a rich heritage. Starting from two miles south of what is currently Hiawatha Davis, developers transformed predominantly agricultural land, brickyards, and dairies into a charming neighborhood adorned with tree-lined streets and houses showcasing Victorian and Queen Anne architectural styles.[4] Park Hill, and especially its southern sections, was an almost entirely white enclave for its first seventy years until the enactment of the Colorado Fair Housing Act of 1959. Black city residents had previously lived several miles to the east. Eventually, the northeastern section of Park Hill became home to Denver's largest concentration of Black residents. But long before northeast Park Hill became the city's "historically Black neighborhood," Black people had lived in Five Points. While much of Denver's history of racism and segregation mirrored broader patterns of racial discrimination and inequality prevalent throughout the United States in the late nineteenth and twentieth centuries, Black life in Denver specifically is deeply rooted in Five Points' history of segregation.

*Five Points, 1864–1950s: Birth of a Black Community*

Five Points was not always a Black community. It first emerged between the 1870s and 1880s as an elite, white streetcar suburb that included a mix of residential structures—some grand and stylish, others more modest—where many middle-class residents lived alongside their wealthier neighbors. Goodstein describes how the city's first streetcar system promoted rapid growth and development, enhancing real estate values along the route.[5] A major high school, churches, hotels, and restaurants emerged. Temple Emanuel, the first major synagogue in Denver, was erected in 1882 in the Curtis Park vicinity of Five Points. But by the early 1890s, Capitol Hill, about two miles south of Five Points, had become the new prime location. It was there that Denver's wealthiest families built some of the most elaborate mansions in the American West. Five Points' population shifted from white to Black over the next three decades, as whites moved farther from downtown.

Between 1880 and 1890, Denver's Black population nearly tripled, bolstered by the railroads' arrival in 1870. The increased economic activity attracted many Black workers, and Black residents constituted almost 4 percent of Denver's population in 1890 (3,254 in a city of 106,713). By 1893 both Denver's segregation and a growing number of industrial jobs brought even more Black people into Five Points than any other area of the city.[6] Despite the 1895 state law that guaranteed all Coloradans access to the state's public places regardless of race or color, racial segregation and discrimination were more the rule than the exception. When large numbers of Black workers, many formerly enslaved people from Georgia, were imported by the railroads in the 1870s to lay track, most white people would not rent to them. The railroad companies created a segregated district within Denver at 22nd Street for Black laborers, known then as the "Deep South." With a growing Black population, and homeowners excluding Black families from moving into all-white neighborhoods, Black settlement shifted entirely to Five Points.

In the early twentieth century, Five Points emerged as a vibrant hub, home to approximately six thousand Black residents. Despite its industrial nature, characterized by printing presses, factories, and lumber yards, it also housed numerous Black families.[7] A vibrant community of professionals such as physicians, attorneys, and dentists thrived alongside members of the working class including porters, cooks, janitors, domestics, and various service workers. Public facilities were constructed to accommodate the growth, such as Denver's first Black fire company.

Local residents had access to amenities that included three newspapers, a YMCA and YWCA, baseball clubs, and more. By 1920 Black-owned businesses prospered, with the Welton Street business district, in the heart of Five Points, emerging as the largest Black business community in the West. This business district and the property continue to be owned by local Black investors.[8] Five Points' nine churches also played a pivotal role by offering newcomers and residents a sense of place, community, unity, and pride. Throughout the 1930s, 1940s, and 1950s, Five Points functioned as Black Denver's center of social, residential, professional, and industrial development.[9]

During these same decades, Five Points also garnered national attention as an entertainment destination for prominent jazz performers. Establishments there featured such major national figures as Count Basie, Billie Holiday, Lionel Hampton, Louis Armstrong, Ella Fitzgerald, Duke Ellington, and others contributing to its legacy. The Rossonian Hotel and Nightclub—which still stands at the five-point intersection that gave Five Points its name—was *the* destination for artists and a social space for Black gathering. It was also the most prominent signifier that Five Points had shifted from white to Black space.[10] Other popular establishments ran along Welton Street, as Enbrown writes, "The Points was the bee's knees and the cat's meow, a place to settle in and sip some (at times) legal hooch and listen as a canary on stage sang to the hypnotic beat of a skin tickler. The musical mash, the 'sweet brutality of hopes and dreams, both achieved and dashed, and the freedom to let loose with heart and soul,' everything got played in the Points."[11]

When Black World War I veteran Benny Hooper returned to Denver after the war, he opened the Ex-Serviceman's Club in downtown Denver as a place for Black servicemen and others to eat, play billiards, and stay overnight. The police raided it, claiming the establishment was the center of illicit drinking and crime.[12] After Mayor Benjamin Stapleton insisted that he find a new location, Hooper moved his club to the heart of Five Points and called it the Deluxe Recreation Parlor and Ex-Serviceman's Club. He eventually opened a dance hall next door, with a balcony that seated more than one thousand patrons—far more than could fit in the Rossonian's small lobby. Hooper often donated his dance hall space and many of its proceeds to churches, civic groups, and charities. He became a beloved member of the Five Points Black community and was known as the "Mayor of Five Points."

*The Klan in Denver, 1920–1926: The City Draws the Color Line*

Although Denver did not experience the same pervasive state-sanctioned violence and discrimination that roiled the post–Civil War South, the Ku Klux Klan gained significant popularity in Colorado during the 1920s. After World War I, the population of Five Points grew with an influx of Black migrants from the South. This period also saw Black residents moving into previously all-white neighborhoods, while the city's immigrant population expanded. Alongside these ethnic and racial shifts, social issues such as crime, corruption, and alcohol abuse seemed to spiral out of control, particularly for local white Protestants in positions of power.[13] This sense of social anxiety created an opening for the Klan to gain influence.[14] Inspired by the film *The Birth of a Nation*, the Klan of the 1920s included white supremacists who, while still fervently anti-Black, broadened their hatred to include Catholics, Jews, and immigrants of all nationalities—groups they believed represented a conspiracy against the "Puritan civilization" that had made the United States great.[15] This version of the Klan was also far more organized, widespread, and effective than its earlier counterpart. Klan members infiltrated Denver communities, identifying perceived problems and then promoting their "solutions" to white residents. Klan membership in Colorado peaked in 1925 at fifty thousand members, making it the second-largest Klan presence in the United States at the time, after Indiana.[16]

Denver's Klan remained a hate group, but it was a hate group enmeshed in all matters of city government. In 1920 there was no Klan present in Colorado. But in 1921 the Klan's first recruiter, Georgia's highest-ranking Klansman, arrived in Denver. Benjamin Stapleton, who would be elected mayor in 1923, privately welcomed the Grand Dragon's support. Four months after the Klan founded its small and secretive Denver Doers Club in the elite Brown Palace Hotel in 1921, Klansmen announced their existence publicly in a letter to the *Denver Times*: "We are a law and order organization assisting at all times the authority in every community in upholding law and order. Therefore we proclaim to the lawless element of the city and county of Denver and the state of Colorado that we are not only active now, but we were here yesterday, we are here today and we shall be here forever."[17]

In 1923 the *Denver Post* condemned Benjamin Stapleton's election, noting the landslide victory and referring to the Klan as "the largest and the most efficiently organized political force in the state of Colorado today."[18] Indeed, the Klan's power and influence were so overwhelming that Denver (and Colorado generally) became known as "Klan central" in the United States. In response, Denver's small Black community, with the support of the NAACP and two Black newspapers—the *Denver Star* and the *Denver Statesman*—mounted a counteroffensive against the Klan. The Klan also targeted companies that hired Black employees, organizing boycotts to intimidate businesses. Despite these threats, the Black community remained resilient and took care of itself.[19]

Stapleton was open about his support for the Klan, and through his efforts, the organization took control of Denver politics. In 1924 he declared, "I will work with the Klan and for the Klan in the coming election, heart and soul. And if I am re-elected, I will give the Klan the kind of administration it wants."[20] Stapleton hired Klan member William Candlish as chief of police, appointed Klan members to important cabinet offices, and allowed the Klan to use city resources.[21] In fact, one could not be elected to office in Denver without the Klan's endorsement. That same year, Klan members in Colorado were also elected to the governorship, the U.S. Senate, and much of the state legislature. Hooded men marched through town while opponents were kidnapped and pistol-whipped.[22]

The Klan prioritized the prohibition of racial mixing in public accommodations, with Five Points as their prime target. But residents of Five Points fought back. Klan members burned a cross in front of the house of Black dentist Clarence Holmes, an early civil rights advocate who founded the Denver Interracial Committee in 1916 to expose the Klan. Holmes headquartered the committee's office in the heart of Five Points' Black business district.[23] In response to the Klan's activities, the interracial committee, along with the local NAACP chapter (established in 1917), actively resisted. In retaliation, the Klan threatened the local NAACP president, warning him to curb his efforts. In 1922 a letter on Klan stationery was delivered to Ward Gish, the custodian of an apartment house, demanding that he leave Denver because of his "intimate relations with a white woman." The letter went on to say, "N——, do not look lightly upon this. Your hide is worth less to us than it is to you."[24] Gish turned the letter over to the police and temporarily left Denver.

Black thinkers and activists such as Marcus Garvey, W. E. B. Du Bois, and James Weldon Johnson visited the Five Points area frequently, offering hope and inspiration to the community. Nevertheless, racism and segregation remained entrenched in Denver. Attempts to live outside the Five Points boundary were dangerous, as those who did so faced threats and acts of violence. For example, the *Rocky Mountain News* reported that on the evening of July 7, 1921, someone hurled a bomb from a moving car while mail carrier Walter R. Chapman and his wife sat in their front room, leaving a six-foot crater in the front yard.[25] Mr. Chapman told the police that after he bought the home on Gilpin Street—east of the city's "color line"—a white man approached him and threatened to blow up the house if they stayed in the neighborhood. A note left at the scene warned, "N—— tenant . . . you have come into a district where you are not wanted. You have ruined property. Get out and stay out or take the consequences. They will be severe and merciless." This was part of a series of bombings targeting middle-class Black families who attempted to move eastward, closer to the exclusive City Park neighborhood.

The Klan's influence in Denver had effects. White communities formed "neighborhood improvement associations" to create and enforce racially restrictive covenants.[26] Even after the Supreme Court held that such covenants were unenforceable in 1948, they continued to be observed privately. These associations played a significant role in resistance to integration during the 1950s. It wasn't until 1957 that the Colorado legislature repealed the nearly one-hundred-year-old law prohibiting interracial marriage.[27]

*Moving East: Five Points to Park Hill, 1950–1970s*

Denver's lengthy history of redlining excluded Black, Indigenous, and other people of color from homeownership for most of the twentieth century. By 1950 more than 250,000 Black people lived in Five Points. Redlining maps assessed the suitability of neighborhoods for development or investment, and Five Points was labeled as "an old area now occupied by a combination of Negroes, Mexicans, and a transient class of workers . . . [and] Denver's closest approach to a slum district."[28] Like in other urban areas across the United States, redlining prevented Black residents from building wealth.[29] George Brown, a Black *Denver Post* reporter, began uncovering Jim Crow–like practices in the city.[30] Brown uncovered segregation in public spaces such as movie theaters, restaurants, swimming pools, and other outdoor recreation and amusement centers. He wrote, "Jim Crow has the Negro going or coming. He will not let the Negro buy outside the restricted zone, and he creates barriers to prevent many from buying within. I tried to buy a house inside the boundaries and I couldn't get adequate financing from any bank because they said the house was in an area which is deteriorating and becoming blighted."[31]

Beyond these discriminatory banking practices, the City of Denver deliberately neglected the Five Points neighborhood. In the 1940s and early 1950s, for example, the Denver Water Board extended new water lines only to white neighborhoods, leaving Five Points residents with inadequate indoor plumbing—or, in some cases, none at all.

Following World War II, fueled by "massive federal spending" in Denver, "an influx of newcomers and pent-up demands for new cars and new housing unavailable during the war led to a boom that changed a drowsy provincial city into a sprawling metropolis."[32] The city's population grew by 29 percent in the 1940s, from 322,412 to 415,786. The Black population doubled, rising from 7,836 in 1940 to 15,059 in 1950. As a result, Five Points became overcrowded by 1949, with many of its 13,500 residents living in cramped nineteenth-century homes built below safety standards. White property owners often subdivided these old homes into small rental apartments.[33]

Elsewhere in Denver, construction met demands. Park Hill "came back" in the sense that, north of East 32nd (later renamed Martin Luther King Boulevard), thousands of inexpensive ranch houses were built, most under one thousand square feet. These brick-and-cinderblock homes lacked the architectural detail of the Victorian homes in the older, southern section of Park Hill and were much smaller. However, they provided relatively affordable starter homes for recently married veterans or employees of nearby Stapleton Airport and the Rocky Mountain Arse-

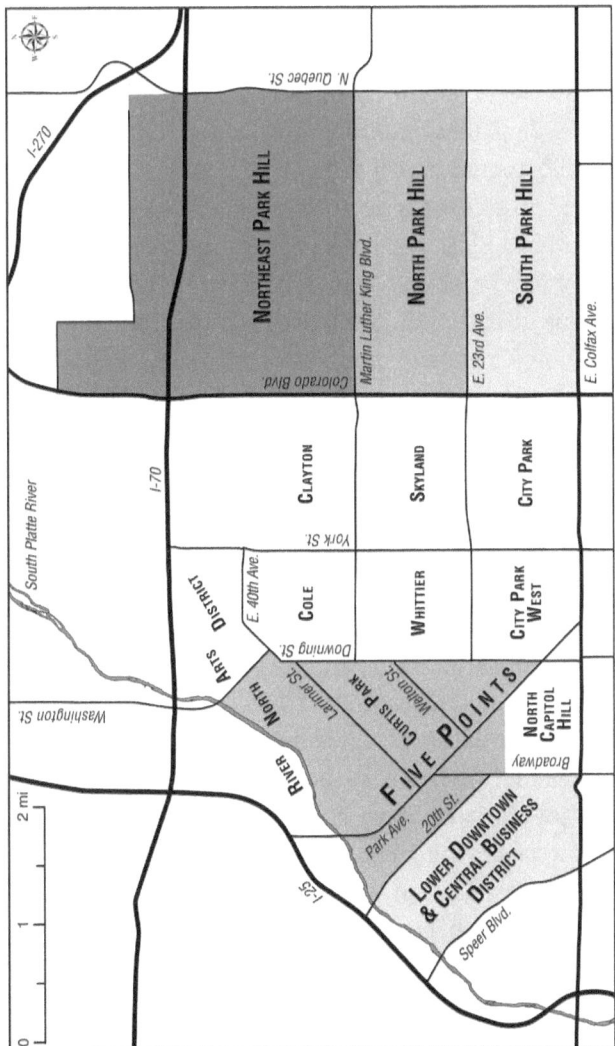

FIG. 2. Park Hill and Five Points. Map by Gabriel Moss.

nal. While the new homes didn't resemble the traditional Park Hill style, living in Park Hill still carried a sense of prestige.[34] Zoning ordinances in Northeast Park Hill allowed for duplexes and triplexes, whereas the older section of Park Hill consisted exclusively of single-family homes.[35]

In 1947, two years after J. Q. Newton was elected mayor of Denver—following nearly twenty years of racist and status quo policies under

Benjamin Stapleton—he acknowledged that "Negros are holed up in a small area which is getting worse and worse. . . . They are victims of an unwritten law. Sooner or later there must be a breaking through."[36] Despite the overcrowding, tensions arose among Five Points residents regarding what to do about it, with some urging middle-class Black residents to stay and protect the historic Five Points district. Even the *Denver Blade* encouraged Black residents to preserve the unique character and identity of Five Points. As John Wallace wrote, "The original Negro settlers of this district and their heirs created an environment and atmosphere of refinement and intelligence."[37]

As the Black population in Denver expanded, especially the middle class, many began moving out of the Five Points neighborhood. They gravitated eastward toward homes near Colorado Boulevard, the two-lane highway that separated Five Points and surrounding Black neighborhoods from the more stylish, white-dominated Park Hill. With the passage of the Colorado Fair Housing Act in 1959, more Black Denverites in the 1960s began crossing Colorado Boulevard into Park Hill's northern neighborhoods.[38] Homes in North Park Hill, though smaller and less grand than those in the southern part of Park Hill, still carried the appeal of the Park Hill name. Fair housing laws, along with efforts by the city's Commission on Community Relations to monitor real-estate discrimination, made it easier for Black families to move into the area.[39] But living in Park Hill proved to be anything but straightforward. As *Denver Post* reporter Charles Roos noted, "Negroes are permitted to buy houses in Park Hill, at least north of 26th, but they encounter great difficulty elsewhere in the Denver area." The policy of allowing Black people to buy homes in North Park Hill reflected an earlier approach that permitted "Negroes to extend their ghetto when it becomes physically necessary but not to allow them to disperse."[40]

While mortgages were available for middle-class Black families—typically railroad porters, physicians, attorneys, and other professionals—who could afford homes in the more affordable northern sections of Park Hill, those who crossed the color line found themselves the subject of intense curiosity.[41] I met Owetta, in her eighties, at a large community meeting and at nearly every community gathering thereafter. A well-respected organizer and beloved figure in Park Hill, she has lived in her home since the 1960s. However, when she first moved in, her white neighbors were not pleased "to see a Black face coming to a white neighborhood." She eventually put up a fence around her property to signal to her neighbors, "I'm not here to bother you." Owetta's experience mirrored that of many older Black residents who moved into Park Hill in the early 1960s. "I didn't bother nobody," said Rosco, an octogenarian who was the first Black person to move his family onto his block. His daughter, too, didn't "bother" the white children playing in the area, because, as she put it, "We knew their names, but they didn't want anything to do with us. They didn't want to play with us."

White residents, concerned about the changing racial makeup of the neighborhood, sold their homes in a panic and fled to the suburbs, reflecting the national trend of "white flight" in the mid-twentieth century.[42] Black people described watching "For Sale" signs sprout like dandelions next door and across the street from the homes they had purchased.[43] White residents, accusing Black people of "re-segregating" the neighborhood, were often aided by unscrupulous realtors who spread rumors that Park Hill was on the verge of becoming "Dark Hill," Denver's next "ghetto."[44] Some realtors even refused to show houses to white buyers who were interested in moving into North Park Hill. When future resident Art Branscome and his wife, Bea, tried to purchase a home there, they "had trouble getting a loan for this place. The first two or three mortgage brokers we approached said, 'No way. If you were Black, we'd give you a loan, but we're not giving loans to whites in that neighborhood anymore.' Finally, we got a loan from a banker who lived in Park Hill."[45]

*The Tipping Point: Integration on White Terms*

In 1960 a group of white self-identified progressives in Park Hill gathered at Montview Presbyterian Church, located in the heart of the neighborhood. The meeting, titled "The Changing Character of the Park Hill Neighborhood," was convened to address the ongoing desegregation of Park Hill, as middle-class Black families continued to purchase homes in the area. At the time, many white residents of Denver feared "ghettoization" and the decline of historic central urban neighborhoods due to white flight.[46] This initial meeting led to the formation of the Park Hill Action Committee (PHAC), which was established by thirty-five prominent white residents representing eight Protestant and Catholic churches in the neighborhood. The mission of PHAC, as stated in 1960, was

> civic action and education for all the residents of Park Hill. We will seek to maintain Park Hill as a desirable and stable community predominantly composed of single family residents, without discrimination as to race, creed, or color. . . . We will encourage white families both to avoid panic selling, if members of a racial minority group move into their neighborhood, and to welcome them as neighbors, as they would any other family. It is not the purpose of our organization to keep Negroes or other minority families out of Park Hill; nor are we promoting their movement into the area. We are merely seeking to apply the laws of God and man to the human relations problem that exists in the community. We will actively support laws and practices intended to make any housing in the city and state available for purchase by any buyer who is able to pay for and maintain his property. We will welcome any such buyer into the Park Hill community.[47]

At its most idealistic, PHAC sought racial harmony, advocated for an open city, and welcomed Black people into the neighborhood. It also lobbied—and in some cases, boycotted—real-estate interests in an effort to end racial discrimination in local property markets. PHAC demanded that realtors stop circulating rumors that Park Hill would become an "all Black ghetto in ten years."[48] Additionally, PHAC campaigned for tougher statewide fair housing laws. Its members welcomed Black families moving into the neighborhoods, organized a yearlong moratorium on home sales, and worked to persuade white homeowners not to move. These efforts were successful to the extent that many whites remained, while others, attracted by large homes at significantly reduced prices, also moved in.[49] PHAC's work brought Park Hill national attention, including a visit from President Lyndon Johnson and his motorcade. Martin Luther King Jr. spoke at Park Hill Methodist Church in 1962 and again at Montview Boulevard Presbyterian Church in 1964.

On the other hand, PHAC clearly wanted to maintain a sense of social stability, which meant keeping Park Hill a largely white enclave. Its members quite explicitly sought to prevent panic selling with the underlying goal of avoiding encroachment of blight into the neighborhood and to preserve property values. Black families moving into the area were seen as a problem to be managed rather than a fully welcomed change. To that end, PHAC actively and selectively recruited only "desirable" Black buyers to live in Park Hill. Members crafted a survey for prospective Black homeowners, asking for biographical details, the racial demographics of their real estate agents, and their intended length of stay in the community.[50] PHAC also distributed a questionnaire for white residents that included questions such as "Would you contemplate moving out . . . if this neighborhood . . . was entered by another Negro family?" Additionally, PHAC sought to strictly enforce zoning regulations that allowed only single-family homes to be built.

Over time, PHAC emphasized the R-O zoning classification, which permitted only individuals from the same family to occupy a residence.[51] This zoning not only aligned with churches' preoccupation that immoral (unmarried) couples not cohabitate—including relatives, gay couples, or roommates—but also effectively prevented homeowners from renting out rooms. The R-O zoning designation prevented Park Hill residents from subdividing homes into apartments, rendering the neighborhood economically, if not racially, exclusive. PHAC's rhetoric of inclusion, therefore, was accompanied by ideologies of normativity.

R-O zoning gave the impression that race didn't factor into inclusion, so long as residents adhere to community standards. However, white values were embedded in PHAC members' belief system, reinforcing middle-class heterosexual normativity and emphasizing prosperity, safety, and respectability. In reality, PHAC's leadership was concerned that Park Hill's quiet, pleasant residential character was being threatened by what they described as an "appalling" influx of nontraditional housing—both multifamily units and single-family homes falling into disrepair.[52]

By 1962 white residents began to worry that too many Black people had moved into northern Park Hill—far more Black families than white ones—and once again expressed concerns about resegregation.[53] By the mid-1960s, 90 percent of the children enrolled in schools in North and Northeast Park Hill were Black, as were 50 percent of the residents north of 32nd Ave, making the concern about resegregation a valid observation.[54] South (white) Park Hill tolerated Black neighbors so long as there weren't too many concentrated in one area.

To mitigate the so-called Black invasion, PHAC, in collaboration with the Northeast Park Hill Civic Association, published a two-page flyer in 1965 titled "The Facts of Negro Housing," with the subtitle "Why Move Where It Can Hurt Integration . . . When We Can Move Where It Can Help."[55] The flyer urged Black people seeking homes in Park Hill to look elsewhere.[56] Volunteers distributed twenty thousand copies door to door in neighborhoods north of Colorado where many Black people lived. The flyer argued that Black people moving into Park Hill had been deceived, that the neighborhood was becoming "resegregated," and that they should seek homes elsewhere to prevent segregated schools. It also outlined some of the provisions of the Fair-Housing Act and information on where to report violations. Ultimately, the flyer placed the responsibility for preventing segregation on Black people themselves, urging them to move to any part of Denver that was not Park Hill: "NEGROES, for the first time, will be responsible—not whites. Negroes cannot blame whites for new ghettoes, now that a strong Fair Housing Act has made NEGROES FREE TO LIVE WHERE THEY LIKE. . . . Do Negroes want to undercut their hard-won Fair-Housing Act? Do they want to give ammunition to bigots who say Negroes REALLY prefer segregation?"[57]

The original Park Hill—South Park Hill, going north up to 26th Ave—remained white, while Black people continued moving into the northern and northeastern sections.[58] Concerned about this Black infusion, PHAC recognized that white families now needed to relocate to Park Hill, especially when other desirable (white) neighborhoods were not facing similar integration pressures. PHAC actively recruited middle-class white professionals from—as its newsletter put it—the sterile, "unappealing life," and "long commutes" in the suburbs. White residents who chose homes in Park Hill, rather than in the suburbs, were prominently featured in the PHAC literature, while Black homeowners moving into Park Hill were never given the same attention. PHAC's advertising and public relations campaign caught the eye of white homebuyers. One such campaign included an ad that ran for six months in the Sunday *Denver Post* in 1961, listing homes for sale and emphasizing the benefits of life in the neighborhood. Members of the real estate industry reported that the ads "resulted in the greatest demand for Park Hill homes that cooperating realtors had seen here in years."[59] In response to reports that more Black people than white people were moving into Park Hill, PHAC intensified its efforts to attract white homebuyers. The organization sent promotional brochures to local media and real estate agents, highlighting the neighborhood's exceptional qualities and the elitist benefits of living there. "In Park Hill," one brochure read, "you can be pardoned for feeling quietly pleased about yourself . . . just a bit smug."[60]

To be fair, from today's standpoint Park Hill has long had a well-deserved reputation as a politically connected Denver neighborhood, one that has addressed major social and legal issues. Denver's first racially integrated churches were in Park Hill, and local desegregation efforts included plans to integrate public schools. However, based on my observations at multiple community meetings, much of the political "action" today is limited to progressive platitudes. White residents south of MLK often portray today's Park Hill as a beacon of racial harmony, a diverse and accepting neighborhood—what some might call the proverbial "City upon the Hill."[61] Residents (and various websites) proudly claim that Park Hill is an integrated community, but they tend to overlook the fact that most of the Black population is concentrated in Northeast Park Hill. This narrative of integration is still promoted by the Greater Park Hill Community (GPHC). Formed in 1970 from the merger of the Park Hill Action Committee and the Northeast Park Hill Coalition, GPHC is a politically progressive, well-connected organization. Like its predecessor, PHAC, it has promoted racial tolerance, desegregation, and stronger fair housing laws and lobbied the city to improve Park Hill's streets, parks, and schools.

GPHC has a proud history of community service, advocating for community health and healthy living, and running an emergency weekend food pantry. It is probably best known for its free monthly newspaper, *Greater Park Hill News*, annual summer home show, garden walks, Fourth of July parade, and arts festival. GPHC boasts on its website that Park Hill is "an ethnically diverse and integrated neighborhood that prompted a visit from the Rev. Martin Luther King."[62] As a result, Park Hill has been consistently promoted, on a national scale, as a prime example of inclusive and integrated community living. However, despite its census-driven diversity statistics, Park Hill continues to exhibit patterns of segregation similar to many other major U.S. cities.

*Woke but Not in My Backyard*

Racial segregation within Park Hill means that white people continue to make up the majority of the neighborhood and constitute the primary participants of GPHC meetings and events.

Significant community events, such as the annual Park Hill Garden Walk, are complemented by the popular summer Arts Festival hosted by the GPHC in exclusive South Park Hill—a neighborhood most Park Hill residents would readily describe as clean, comfortable, and safe. While a 2021 Fourth of July parade featured a Black Lives Matter sign, it was carried by an all-white marching band. These public displays of racial tolerance, however, do not seem to encourage white residents to engage with or mingle in Northeast Park Hill. I met some white parents who expressed interest in enrolling their children at a local Boys and Girls Club but were unwilling to consider the one just a short distance away in Northeast Park Hill.[63]

The stated intentions of racial inclusivity are also undermined by the food served at these "community celebrations." When I showed the menu for one of the food trucks to my ceramics instructor at the recreation center, she was unimpressed. As a Black woman who had grown up nearby and whose father still lived in her childhood home, Linda was candid about who the menu was likely intended for. "Black people don't eat that," she said without hesitation. "We eat what we call soul food. We're used to food from our culture. That's our food. The food on the truck—unless it's a Black-owned food truck—we don't eat avocado sandwiches. We eat black-eyed peas or pinto beans. We don't eat hummus. What's hummus? We still eat beans, but it ain't no hummus."

For all that, the neighborhood's progressive veneer isn't all show. Notably, Park Hill was the focus of a 1973 case challenging de facto school segregation, which went all the way to the U.S. Supreme Court. Petitioners sought the desegregation of Park Hill schools, and the Supreme Court ruled in their favor. Today, social and racial justice signs are prominently displayed in the front yards of many homes. During the 2024 presidential election, Kamala Harris signs far outnumbered the few Donald Trump signs in this largely liberal neighborhood.[64] The organization Park Hill Neighbors for Equity in Education holds regular meetings where important dialogues take place. On their website, they state, "In August of 2017, a group of Park Hill neighbors gathered for a dialogue about diversity, equity and inclusion, particularly as they relate to the four neighborhood elementary schools in Park Hill. . . . That conversation highlighted the need to raise awareness across the community of the inequities among our schools and to work collaboratively to address them."[65]

Still, while white Park Hill's stated commitment to diversity and inclusion may mark an improvement over generations of legal and de facto segregation, it has not led to meaningful change in support of Black inclusion. As we move forward, the voices of community members will guide us through the layered experiences of Black placemaking in Park Hill. We begin with Charles Hall—his story of belonging and connection grounds broader themes of community, resilience, and hope in the rhythms of everyday life. From his journey between Roswell and the card tables of Denver, we glimpse the intimate ways Black space is made and remade. Later, three more voices will offer collective reflections on shifting racial dynamics, the pull of nostalgia, and the ongoing struggle to preserve cultural identity amid gentrification. But first, we turn to Charles, whose life story anchors these broader currents in the lived experience of place.

# 3  Charles Hall

The affable Mr. Hall typically wrapped up an evening of dominoes with the phrase, "We really had fun." He'd carefully place each tile pip-side-up in the box, then close the box and secure it with two rubber bands before setting it back in the cupboard. It always struck me as a tender action, as if tucking the dominoes in, saying, *You take a rest. We'll see you tomorrow.*

Mr. Hall, now in his late seventies, has a slim build, a kind face, and tired eyes. He was usually the first to greet me when I sat down next to his table, offering me a friendly handshake and a big smile. "Steve, always good to see you." He would teach me strategy during the game, and then as we were packing up, he'd repeatedly gesture to remind me of my wallet, which I'd habitually stow under my chair. At the end of an evening when the weather was bad, Mr. Hall would advise me, "Steve, drive carefully. Slick roads out there." He addressed everyone with the honorific "Mr." He even referred to the scorekeeper as "Mr. Scorer." He called each domino collaborator his "partner" when he delivered compliments—"Good job, partner;" "Get him, partner;" or "Partner, you play so pretty." And he occasionally called upon his self-possessed sturdiness to rally the troops, such as the time an unknown woman walked into the card room and sat down in front of the television for thirty minutes. Her presence quashed the elders' talk entirely, and soon the table became a pressure cooker of forced whispers and subvocalizations. Mr. Hall's peaceful gestures reminded everyone to remain cool and quiet.

"Most of the time I have fun," Mr. Hall once told me. "I laugh and listen to jokes. That's part of my personality," he said. "Who do you know that's unhappy and laughs at the same time? Mine is truly my feeling, and sometimes it's not every day. But sometimes something happens at home. Then I come down here, and I get to feeling good, and those things that happen at home or one of my friends, God just kind of takes that away, and I'm in that happy-go-lucky laughing mood. I think if you can laugh and feel relaxed and feel good about yourself—no one's going to feel good about themselves and not be able to laugh at the same time."

*Roswell, New Mexico*

Charlie Hall was born in 1945 in the northern Texas town of Henderson, thirty miles from the Louisiana border. He was third in a family of four. Eventually his mother would have seven more children with a different husband.

"Why are we leaving Daddy?" the precocious four-year-old asked his mother. "Your dad and I don't see the same things," his mother answered. Two years later, Charlie's mother remarried. Their stepfather's construction job took them all to Roswell. Charlie's only visit to see his father again took place when he was ten. "He looked at us and never quit playing dominoes. . . . He never got up to embrace, say hi, where you been and nothin'. So my mom said, 'Let's go.'" The next time they saw their father was at his funeral.

Mr. Hall's mother, now in her nineties, has remained an ever-present and beloved figure in his life. "I never miss goin' home," he says. From Denver he would drive to Pueblo, Colorado, to pick up his three brothers, and the four of them would make the six-hour drive home every Thanksgiving, Christmas, and summer. Charlie's mother protected him and the others from their unpredictable and moody stepfather. "Living with him was chaos. A very mean person. He kept a roof over my head. He kept food in the house. But working all the time. . . . He never took time." It was his mother who kept the family together. "We all came together, played together. I look at that, and God give it through my mom." She worked hard and still managed to stay involved in her children's lives. "She would never miss a game. No matter where we were playing. You could hear her from the stands out on the field. She was special."

*Sneaky Prejudice*

In the early 1900s, there were few Black residents living in Roswell. Over the years the Black population increased, but they were forced to use separate restaurants and public facilities. By 1960 the Black population in Roswell was 1,644 out of a total population of 39,593. During that decade, when the world-famous all-Black Harlem Globetrotters performed in the Roswell High School gym, local restaurants and public facilities refused them service.[1]

"South part of town for us. Northern parts for the whites. . . . We had our own rec center, but we heard about this new rec center over on the north part of town. Me and some of the guys walked over on Friday afternoon, and they ran us out. Told us to go back to our side." Mr. Hall recalls stories of "prejudice" that still get "stuck in my mind" and vividly describes an incident in which white men severely beat up a "migrant Black man who stole bologna at the old Horn's Food Store." Newspaper accounts support Mr. Hall's memory of Roswell's racism in the 1960s, when the NAACP finally opened an office there.

When Charlie was ten years old—back when cotton was big in the plains surrounding Roswell—he, his brothers, and his stepfather worked in the fields, doing the very job that his mother had hoped her children would never have to endure. Charlie hated the work. The heat was already oppressive when they began at 6:00 a.m., and his fingertips ached from the sharp ends of the cotton bolls. "When you put your hands in, if you don't have gloves on, you cut your hands and stuff. I'm ten or eleven years old. . . . You got up at five in the morning, and then we pick out there. In New Mexico, the heat is tremendous. . . . The shoulder strap filled with cotton was heavy."

Charlie would put in several hours of hard labor before the school day began. He picked cotton through high school, until "my mom stopped our father and said, 'Now they want to play sports, and there's a chance for them to win scholarships.'" The kids were talented athletes, which Charlie attributed to his mother's own athletic prowess. Sports and education were important to her. "My mom always preached two things. You're going to go to church, and you're going to go to school."

Charlie knew only segregated schools before attending Roswell's only high school. There, racial tension took the form of what he called "sneaky prejudice."

> When I got to high school, you know, white here, Black over here. Blacks had a certain place on the campus they hung around, and whites

went to all the drive-ins for lunch because they had the money. . . . As far as classrooms, they couldn't separate you. . . . But you knew whether that teacher was prejudiced or not. Just through his or her actions. . . . We'd get our tests back and . . . compare. I got the same answers he's got [a white student], but I got a C or a D and he got an A or a B.

In college, Charlie was two years older than his peers. He attributed this to the discriminatory retention practices in Roswell, where white teachers routinely held back Black students. "I didn't graduate until I was almost nineteen. [T]hat's why I was real bitter when I got to [college]. I'm in the same grade, but I'm older than freshman." Such policies reflect structural racism that continues to affect students of color today.

Despite these challenges, Charlie became a star football player. But during his junior year in high school, he and other Black athletes discovered that their white coach hadn't shared college recruiting letters with them. Eventually, an athletic director "made ten, twelve calls to recruiters who came a runnin'," Mr. Hall said. One recruiter brought him to Western State College in Gunnison, Colorado, where he played halfback and defensive end while majoring in physical education and minoring in sociology. "It was a dream of mine to go to college. I always wanted to go to college, because that was my driving influence to get out of Roswell. When I was younger, I didn't want to go into the military. The Vietnam War was going on. But I always wanted to go to college."

*Discovering Park Hill and the American Dream*

Western State College was five hundred miles from Roswell, two hundred miles south of Denver, and in a rural area with a small population. It was a small, rural campus—ideal for a young man who had never been away from home. "I met more friends, and I accomplished more things. The football aspect of it kept me going," he said. He enjoyed campus life, but the "overall town" proved less than welcoming. "Backwards," as Mr. Hall described it. "They didn't understand me, and I didn't understand them. Like they close the curtain and say, 'The store is closed.' You know, stuff like that. Bigotry and prejudice. It was everywhere." But overall, "I had a great time in college—the sports atmosphere, the educational atmosphere, socializing—college life that I never would have experienced if I don't get up and go." A transformative friendship shaped Charlie's vision of what was possible for him as a Black man:

> We had a football dorm for football players. Here come this big, tall—Fred. "You don't play football," I said. "This is a football dorm." "I know. I'm your roommate." I said, "What?" "I'm your roommate." He come watch me play football. And at basketball I go watch him. We party and get to know one another. So we started liking one another, you know. Befriend one another. . . . So I was waiting on my bus ticket to come up for spring break. Mom said, "Son, I'm really short [of money]. You should stay up at school." I said, "Mom, don't worry about it." . . . Fred heard me talking. He said, "Man, you ain't going on the bus?" I said, "Man, I'm just going to stay up here. I'll find a job and make a little money up here." He said, "No, come on. You'll go to Denver with me." And I said, "Oh man, I don't want to be a crowd." He said, "There ain't no crowd." . . . I had never been to Denver. . . . So two weeks, everybody was getting out, going home. . . . So we packed our clothes and stuff.

They arrived in Denver and drove toward Park Hill. "I'm looking at these great big, beautiful homes and I say, 'God damn, look at all these Black people . . . cutting and trimming and stuff. . . . These Black folks here got all these jobs . . . cutting these people's grass and stuff. I could probably get me a summer job here.' . . . Fred looked at me and he said, 'What you mean?' I said, 'Them Black folks, working for the white folks, cutting their lawns.'" It hadn't dawned on Charlie that "these Black folks" were cutting their *own* lawns.

> We pulled up, and I said, "Fred, big old beautiful home. Fred, do you live here?" He said, "Yeah man, get out." I'm sitting there in awe. Honest to God, I'm almost in shock to see. So . . . he pushes a button and the gate opens. Automatic gate opens, and we come on in and his mom comes to the door. . . . We walk in and she showin' me around. . . . Fred say, "Come into my room." I go into his bedroom. I said, "Well, I can sleep on the floor." I said, "I don't want to sleep on that beautiful couch in the living room. I just get me a pillow and a pad." He said, "This is the guest bedroom." I said, "What?" He said, "When I bring friends, this is their guest room." I'm used to first come,

first served with eight boys. Two beds, three, three—two slept on the floor. I was in shock.

The whole week he took me around Denver. . . . His mother had a brand-new Oldsmobile. She let us ride around. Brand new and I'm sitting right here. The only thing I ever rode in is the back of a pickup truck, a cotton truck. And he looked at me said, "Man, you don't have this in Roswell?" I said, "No, man." Then we go to church, big old beautiful church. And same thing, parents, big, beautiful cars, dresses, oh wow! And here I am in an old pair of jeans, and it registered, it registered, it *registered* the way these people live here. And the way I used to live. I said, "This can happen. *This* could happen." Last year of college, I came home for spring break. I said, "Mom, I ain't comin' back here to live." She said, "What you mean, Son? You all be out of school." I said, "What can I do?" I said, "Ain't no Black teachers here. I'm in education. They got Black teachers in Denver. They got Black coaches." She said, "You kidding?" I said, "No ma'am." I said, "That's where I want to live."

I said, "Black folks live completely different there." She said, "What do you mean?" I said, "They got kids in high school got brand new cars. You ought to see these homes in Park Hill. They call it Park Hill. You oughta see these brick homes." That's the way I identify them, as brick homes. Because back there all they have is wooden shacks. . . . "Out there—they come a dime a dozen in Denver, and Black folks are living in them." I love Park Hill. When I came, and what I saw—Black folks own this? Owning a brick home?

After graduation, Charlie landed a job teaching middle school social studies and physical education in North Park Hill, in the school where he had been a student teacher. "Black principal, Black nurse, Black supervisor in PE." He initially lived with Fred's family, then moved into an apartment. "I wanted to be like that. I wanted be part of that," Mr. Hall said, describing his excitement about joining the Black middle-class community of Park Hill.

Ten years later, after being offered a job as a high school coach with a salary increase, he saw his dream become a reality. Still, he acknowledged, "it wasn't easy, not by a long shot." During his twenties, he moved between various apartments and rented homes. But with the help of a friend's father—a realtor who "pulled a few strings" in the mid-1970s—he was able to purchase the home where he still lives today. Over time, his Black neighbors have been replaced by white residents. While he would have preferred the neighborhood "stay Black," he reflected, "It was white at one time. Everything goes in 360 degrees."

He met his former wife at a nightclub on the east side of town. Angela brought her son into the marriage, and during their twenty-three years together, they had a son of their own. Before that, Charlie had led an active social life as a single man. "Back then, it was going to nightclubs and going to house parties . . . friends everywhere. I've always had a knack for meeting people. . . . It just seemed like God attracted them to me. I attracted myself to them. I never had any problem making friends or being lonesome."

Mr. Hall lived a half mile from Holly Square, where he enjoyed playing dominoes at the barbershop. But after several years, "They closed down . . . and I found myself for about a year and a half or two doing nothing. I can only do so much work around the house. . . . I wasn't doing anything. So a couple of people said, 'Man, they got dominoes down at the rec center in Skyland. . . . They have a special room there for dominoes, playing cards.'" Off he went.

*Mr. Hall in the Card Room*

Mr. Hall enters the card room with an infectious glow of happiness. He moves around greeting everyone with a handshake, a smile, and a kind word. Without exception, each handshake expresses an equal amount of warmth. Mr. Hall eventually makes his way to the table with the other elders. Occasionally, he will hear a former student calling out, "Coach Hall!" Warm handshakes, grins, and conversations follow; these are the only things that ever draw Mr. Hall away from a game. He remembers every name, and seeing their faces brightens his day. "I got a lot of great moments, but when an ex-student, now an adult with family, they'll address me as Coach Hall or Mr. Hall, it's very, very personally rewarding." Similarly rewarding are his relationships in the card room.

> Here's what I see, Mr. Taylor got a family. Mr. Buford had a family. Mr. Cummings had a family. I *had* a family, but I don't have it anymore, and

I look forward to this every day, just to say hello. Being around those fellows, and learning things, you know. Just to hear them talking, you learn a little bit from them. It's given me something to wake up for in the morning and look forward to. I come down here, and I meet some wonderful, wonderful people.

Indeed, Mr. Hall may occasionally learn "a little bit from them," or about "where they're from and how they were raised," even though the men rarely reference their personal lives. Politics don't interest him, nor does he care "who's got more money in the room"—a nod to how Trapper often boasts about his possessions. But just hearing someone say hello "has given me longevity."

Mr. Hall is simultaneously a player and audience in the card room—he offers an occasional laugh, a grin, sometimes a poker face, but he always stays focused on the game, and he almost always wins. He doesn't come up with his own quips or engage much in the banter. In response to an off-color remark from Mr. Taylor, he often calls out, "Quit, Mr. T!" in his raspy voice, smiling. But he never truly wants Mr. Taylor to stop sharing his bawdy jokes.

The retired coach Mr. Hall is still a coach in the card room. When he shows me a more strategic domino move, he's patient and kind: "Just wanted to show you." Then I hear his reassuring refrain: "You're still learning." He is guided by deeply religious and spiritual principles. He rarely swears, always striving to "be an example" to the youngsters. But they never play as good-naturedly as he'd like, so he sticks with the elders.

*Post-COVID: Summer 2021*

After several months in isolation and the suspension of card room activities due to the COVID pandemic, Mr. Hall and I—both vaccinated—finally got together in his backyard, more than a year after the center had first shut down. His full head of hair was longer than I'd ever seen it, and he was as thin as a rail. He was a month shy of his seventy-eighth birthday, and his face looked frail. He walked with a forward gait, less assured, as though dragging the weight of his legs and feet. "I'm workin' hard trying to keep myself out of depression," he told me. "I get down, down, down. I worry about things I can't do nothin' about." He expressed this despair each time we spoke. The man who "never had any problem making friends or being lonesome" had become quite lonely. Each time we spoke, he'd say, "I miss the guys." Normally, his day was about "getting my adrenaline going, waiting for 4:00 to come." During the pandemic, it was just more television.

Coach Hall had always tended to his flock. He believed that everyone was "one of us" and worthy of care—no one was ignored, no one rejected. His leadership was not aggressive or domineering, but inclusive, with respect for "all kinds." The fact that he saw his former students as part of his big family reflected this. But now, it broke my heart that no one was caring for him.

After an hour of catching up, "Gotta go get my oil changed" was my cue to leave. "You go to that Grease Monkey nearby?" I asked. "No," he said. He went somewhere farther away that he'd been going for a long time. "I know the guys there," he said. "We talk. They take care of me." Before we parted, Mr. Hall nodded and said, "God bless you"—a phrase he often shared, familiar and quietly heartfelt.

I drove home thinking about the power and meaning tucked inside a simple oil change.

## 4   Northeast Park Hill and the Struggle to Maintain Black Place

One day, I arrived at the recreation center to find a sign outside the exercise room, announcing its temporary closure for several days due to equipment replacement. Later that week, I joined Mr. Hall, Mr. Buford, Mr. Taylor, and Paul as they played dominoes. Paul, the only card room regular who also used the exercise room, couldn't help but comment on the long-awaited upgrade, and I asked, "Why do you think they're putting it in *now*?" Paul, Mr. Hall, Mr. Buford, and Mr. Carr responded simultaneously, almost as if choreographed. "More white people." In this chapter, I explore Black residents' responses to racial and cultural displacement. Despite their sense of losing familiar surroundings, they reject the notion of placelessness and adamantly "refuse" to be rendered invisible.[1]

While a few elders occasionally voiced concerns about the shifting racial makeup of the neighborhood, their primary source of discontent centered on the uncertain future of the card room. Unexpected occurrences—such as management's decision to repurpose the room for a single event or temporary closures for maintenance—often triggered fears about the card room's potential demise. "They want to take away the card room" became an increasingly common refrain, fueled by the growing influx of new white members now using the same spaces and equipment that mostly Black patrons had established, nurtured, and used.

Outside the center, my observations confirmed their concerns about both racial shifts and the loss of space. Young white parents strolled past Hiawatha Davis with indifference, seemingly oblivious to the Black men standing outside talking. Northeast Park Hill census data aligned with the elders' observations. From 2000 to 2021, the Black population in Northeast Park Hill decreased from 68.5 percent to 43 percent and in North Park Hill from 56 percent to 30 percent.[2] Residents could not ignore these demographic shifts.

For over a year, I attended the monthly Northeast Park Hill community meetings, where both Black and white attendees expressed concerns. White participants, many of whom had recently moved to the neighborhood, viewed their presence as contributing to neighborhood integration and fostering equality. Black residents, however, perceived these changes more negatively. For example, Rose, a Black resident who lived less than a five-minute walk from the center, observed a significant shift in her once all-Black-owned block. She noted that now, half of the homes on her street were occupied by white residents. Lisa, also Black, said with an undertone of bitterness, "This community is changing. More white people are moving in. They're taking away what was here. They want to do different things." She spoke about how she "gives back to the community. I guess the community really don't matter to them."

In her study of shifting racial dynamics in Washington DC, Sabiyha Prince notes that gentrification "generates mixed feelings," and that both white and Black residents likely hold differing perspectives. However, the Black residents I spoke with were largely pessimistic. They viewed the demographic changes as a "taking of space," akin to invasion and colonization. They worried that the influx of white people contributed to the erosion of norms and values, and the stripping away of Black history and culture.[3]

*The Rise and Decline of Businesses and Cultural Hubs in the Holly*

Spanning one hundred square blocks, Northeast Park Hill features many single-family homes, frequently interspersed with multifamily duplexes and triplexes. Within this community, multigenerational working-class families navigate the challenges of an evolving economy: the neighborhood's unemployment rate is double that of the Denver metro area. In 2000 the typical household income in Northeast Park Hill was $37,468, which was significantly lower compared to North Park Hill ($58,392) and the overall city of Denver ($55,129). It was also less than half of the average income in South Park Hill, which stood at $88,479. Additionally, nearly 24 percent of residents in Northeast Park Hill were living in poverty, a much higher rate than the poverty levels seen in the rest of Denver (14.3 percent), North Park Hill (9.4 percent), or South Park Hill (6.9 percent).[4] The neighborhood includes public housing and other permanently affordable housing options. Northeast Park Hill residents affectionately refer to the heart of their community as "the Holly." This informal designation stretches from Skyland Park, where the recreation center is located, to its immediate vicinity, and extends toward Holly Square, the former site of the Park Hill Shopping Center. From there, 33rd Ave continues west for less than half a mile, passing homes, apartments, a family health clinic, and eventually reaching the site once known as Dahlia Square Shopping Center.

The Holly is a space that vibrantly illustrates Black placemaking through social memory. It served as a vital gathering ground for the elders, each of whom cultivated everyday ties within its landscape. Mr. Carr picked up hardware supplies while his wife had her hair styled nearby. Mr. Taylor walked through the Holly each day on his way to work. Mr. Cummings worshipped at the church just behind Skyland Park. And at the Dahlia Shopping Center, Mr. Buford and his wife regularly enjoyed Chinese food together—a simple pleasure woven into the fabric of their shared routine.

The shopping center, once celebrated as the largest Black-owned mall in the United States, opened in the 1950s on the grounds of the former Ferry Brickyard, at the intersection of Dahlia and Elm Streets. Boasting 8.3 acres, the complex featured diverse amenities, including a lounge, a Chinese restaurant, a roller-skating rink, a bowling alley, and various local stores. However, by the 1990s, the closure of its main anchor grocery store, combined with an occupancy rate below 15 percent, ultimately led to the shopping center's eventual shutdown. Dahlia Shopping Center also fell victim to a broader trend, as regional shopping shifted to larger, modern centers along major thoroughfares in the 1970s and '80s.[5]

The demise of Dahlia Shopping Center had profound implications for Northeast Park Hill. In 2016 the Mental Health Center of Denver transformed the vacant site into the Dahlia Campus for Health and Well-Being, keeping the shopping center's name. The construction of the campus initially faced community resistance due to the stigma sur-

FIG. 3. Holly Square shopping center sign. Steve Bialostok, photographer.

rounding mental health services. Efforts were made to engage the local community through listening sessions, one-on-one interactions, and outreach by community brokers—respected Black residents of Park Hill. Upon completion, the campus hosted community events featuring music, food, and several local vendors. However, many of the campus's clients do not live in the surrounding neighborhood.

The Park Hill Shopping Center (Holly Square), a four-acre outdoor complex, was built in the late 1950s between 33rd and 35th Avenues, from Hudson to Holly Street. This shopping center served as one of Northeast Park Hill's social and economic cores for more than forty years. At its peak, as many as fifty stores occupied the space. A strip mall with other small, locally owned businesses also developed across the street. However, the Safeway supermarket abandoned the neighborhood in the 1970s, and attempts by the shopping center's management to permanently attract another grocer were unsuccessful. As a result, Holly Square began to decline despite several decades of remodeling. Since some businesses still attracted locals, Holly Square remained a community hub. However, turnover was frequent, and many businesses came and went.

The introduction of crack cocaine in the 1980s, along with the arrival of Los Angeles–based street gangs, further affected the area. Park Hill became the Bloods' territory, with Holly Square serving as their base. The neighborhood on the west side of Colorado Boulevard, up to Five Points, was Crip territory. Crack dealing and rampant violence became widespread, and the shopping center, though still open, was marked by graffiti and pockmarked with bullet holes. Ultimately, the destruction of the Park Hill Shopping Center was caused by a gang-related arson that engulfed the entire complex.

This massive fire left both literal and metaphorical holes in the community. With the help of the City of Denver's Office of Economic Development, the Urban Land Conservancy (ULC) purchased Holly Square in 2009 under its community land trust, aiming to preserve the property for community use. The ULC oversaw Holly Square's demolition and facilitated its rebuilding. Twelve remaining concrete pillars were transformed into "peace columns," each bearing the image of a different civil rights activist and the word "Peace" written in that person's native language. However, the overall redesign of the six-block area left many wondering who truly "owned" the neighborhood.

The buildings across from Holly Square, untouched by the fire, have maintained their original 1960s appearance. Once home to a variety of businesses, including a bicycle shop and a financial company, the row of buildings has consistently featured a chicken restaurant. Despite receiving numerous offers for the aging building, the owner—formerly a dry-cleaning business proprietor in one of its spaces—refused to sell. Instead, she remained steadfast in renting exclusively to tenants committed to serving the Northeast Park Hill community.

In 2016 I met Richard, the owner of a popular store that sold a variety of odds and ends. Both customers and passersby frequently stopped by to casually chat with Richard or browse his eclectic selection or do both. Small groups often gathered on the sidewalk in front of the store, enjoying the atmosphere. Inside, Richard sat behind a glass counter while a loud fan circulated air during the summer months and the television blared next to him. Warm, talkative, and open to discussing anything,

FIG. 4. East view of the shops on 33rd Avenue, across from the Park Hill Shopping Center. Steve Bialostok, photographer.

Richard welcomed me with genuine interest the first time I visited. Encouraging me to record our conversations, he shared deeply about his own history and the Northeast neighborhood where he grew up, just a few blocks away. He viewed the neighborhood's changes since the arson fire as generally positive, believing that there was more police protection "now that more white people moved in."

Richard often introduced me to people who came into the store, explaining that I was a "researcher from the university" studying the neighborhood. These introductions gave me the chance to casually ask relevant questions. One customer argued that the entire building should be demolished. "What happens to me then?" Richard smiled. The gentleman joked that Richard's store would just relocate across the street. In contrast, some residents focused on loss. One elderly man, among the first Black residents of Northeast Park Hill, still lived in the same house down the block from the Hiawatha Davis Recreation Center. He said that everything changed after the fire. "It's not a Black neighborhood anymore." Outside Richard's shop, he gestured toward Holly Square. "Look at it," he said with disgust. His arm swept toward the Boys and Girls Club in the Nancy P. Anschutz Center, a twenty-eight-thousand-

FIG. 5. West view of the business strip on 33rd Avenue. Steve Bialostok, photographer.

square-foot multimillion-dollar building that replaced a retail store he recalled shopping at before the arson. He said nothing more, walked to his car, and drove away. While some longtime residents expressed regret that they could no longer shop at Holly Square or gather to talk, many others were indifferent, responding with comments like, "It's change" or "Things change."

In June of 2017, on my way to a community meeting, I saw Richard standing in front of his store. "I have some bad news," he said. "I'm closing the store at the end of the month." Shocked, I asked why. "It used to be that I would take money out of the store and put it in the bank. But lately, I've been taking money out of the bank and putting it in the store. I can't keep doing this. Things were going well for a few months, but not anymore. The neighborhood has changed," he said, carefully avoiding the elephant in the room. "White people moving in?" I offered. Richard hedged at first. He explained that the "new people" moving in weren't interested in the items he had to sell. "I thought you were glad white people were moving into the neighborhood," I clarified. "I am," he responded. "It's helped with the crime and made it safer for kids." He gestured toward two street-mounted video monitors that appeared to connect to the local police station. "Now, when the Bloods come here to make a dance video, the police are here in just minutes. But I wasn't thinking about the other side." Sadly, Richard's plan to open another similar store elsewhere never materialized.

*Stories of Belonging, Cultural Displacement, and Resistance*

To more fully situate the card room within the Hiawatha Davis Recreation Center, as well as the broader context of the neighborhood and U.S. racial dynamics, I share the stories of three Black residents who each, in their own distinctive way, strive to counter the cultural erasure and displacement they perceive unfolding in their community. They experienced the influx of "more white people" as a sign of the erosion of deeply cherished norms and values, a shift that resonated strongly with them.

*Roderick: Three Park Hills*

"This is my hood," Roderick exclaimed proudly as we drove into Denver's South Park Hill neighborhood in the spring of 2015. We had come down here to eat lunch together at Qdoba, a casual Mexican restaurant, and were now driving back to his workplace in Northeast Park Hill. His embrace of South Park Hill took me by surprise. Had Roderick been walking rather than driving down the street here, some white locals might have looked at him as if he were spatially "out of place." True, Roderick had grown up and now worked in Park Hill, but not *this* Park Hill. Over the decades, the original Park Hill neighborhood has expanded northward, and the northeastern section—where Roderick worked—has the highest concentration of Black residents. Roderick, a Black man in his early forties with short-cropped hair and a goatee, was friendly and open when we first met months earlier. A former member of the Bloods, he had and served a long prison sentence. After his release, he and a close friend cofounded a nonprofit youth violence prevention program, based in the building that had once housed former state assemblyman Mike Johnston's office.[6]

The white upper-class surroundings we drove through bore no resemblance to the Northeast Park Hill neighborhood where Roderick had once told me that "plenty of shit goes down." The only thing that "went down" in this exclusive neighborhood was the annual juried Park Hill Arts Festival. South Park Hill was considered one of Denver's (and Colorado's) top neighborhoods.[7] We drove past 17th Avenue, where towering mature trees cast shade on the wide street and where the median was large enough for a neighborhood football or soccer game. The sidewalks bordered gorgeous homes constructed in early twentieth-century architectural styles. They included large historic mansions and smaller Queen Ann Victorians, Craftsmans, turn-of-the-century Tudors, and Colonial Revivals—all elevated and set back on manicured lawns. A white real estate agent, in a statement laden with racialized undertones, remarked, "You can just tell that people care about their houses." We went by homes that would be featured in the annual Park Hill Home Tour, a Denver tradition dating back to 1978 when a local realtor organized it "to showcase the rich history and diverse architecture of the neighborhood."[8] Some of these residences were featured in the annual Park Hill Garden Walk, where owners "open up their hearts and their gardens for all to enjoy."[9]

Roderick and I proceeded north past 23rd Avenue, the route of Park Hill's Fourth of July Parade where an almost entirely white crowd cheers for mostly white Boy Scouts, local politicians, and participants on floats and bicycles and in classic cars, fire trucks, and marching bands. The parade website called it "Denver's historic Park Hill neighborhood, one of the city's largest, oldest, and most diverse areas."[10] We drove by commercial amenities that would appeal to white middle-class residents: a local coffee shop and bakery; a neighborhood wine bar; a pizzeria; a trendy restaurant considered one of Denver's best. The area had none of the suburban aesthetic of architectural sameness, uniform stucco houses, or carpet grass. Residents expressed their individuality through the distinctive landscaping on display in their front yards: colorfully painted objects or even painted plants, raised garden beds of all shapes and sizes, creative uses of space and repurposed materials (broken chairs, old ironwork), and even freshly grown vegetables for passersby to share.

But as we pushed farther north, the landscape began to change. We passed more modest single-family homes with simple lawns. In North Park Hill, the tree-lined streets began to diminish. We headed toward Holly Street, through a single block of Fairfax once known as "Soul Food Row." A strip of businesses on the west side of Fairfax included a liquor store that one recently arrived white homeowner—part of the wave of gentrification in the area—had described as "blighted," along with a couple of barbershops, a convenience store, a bike shop, and the headquarters of the Greater Park Hill Community neighborhood association. Empty Newport cigarette cartons littered the sidewalk. On the opposite side of Fairfax, an A & A Fish Market stood next to two homes slated for demolition. Recently, I had moved to a 1925 bungalow half a mile to the east.

Two miles north of our starting point, Roderick and I took Holly Street across the four-lane Martin Luther King Boulevard, reaching a third section of Park Hill. As Jonathan Tilove writes, "It has become a commonplace of popular culture to identify a Martin Luther King street as a generic marker of Black space and not incidentally, of ruin, as a sad signpost of danger, failure, and decline."[11] This major thoroughfare intersects with several Black neighborhoods in Denver. This particular section of Park Hill marks the final remaining majority Black neighborhood in the city. Online posts reinforce Tilove's claim, characterizing this *other* Park Hill as "rough around the edges" and advising potential residents to "be careful if you do move to that area."[12] On PBS's *News Hour*, it was referred to as a "neighborhood left behind."[13] Denver's infamous 1993 "Summer of Violence" remains in the memories of longtime residents.[14] Underdeveloped commercially but overdeveloped industrially, Northeast Park Hill—now a thriving epicenter for recreational marijuana— was once a hotbed for the drug dealing that sent Roderick and many others to prison. As Roderick and I moved through the neighborhood, the smell of marijuana wafted from the dispensaries and grow houses that are now common in low income and minority areas of Denver.[15]

Roderick directed me to a small local park. We sat on the grass, and he talked about growing up in Park Hill. Our drive from south to north intensified my attention to the surroundings. Around the park, the trees were fewer in number and less mature than those in South Park Hill; the sidewalks were noticeably narrower; the homes, uniformly composed of yellow brick, were small and crowded together; rock gardens filled the flat front yards; chain-link fences were abundant. Roderick abruptly decided to take me to visit his childhood home a short drive away. "It'll probably jog some memories," he said. As we approached, he pointed. "Right over here." I followed his gaze to a sunburned brick duplex with a weathered brown shingled roof sitting back on property shared with identical duplexes. "This is Denver Housing," he said, or as he went on to call it, *the projects*. "We lived here. This was our house." He repeated the address, noting that the back unit with the clothesline still hanging "was ours." I searched for some shade while he sat on the dead grass in the hot summer sun. "Welcome to my universe," he said, then insisted I begin recording our conversation. When his cell phone rang, Roderick answered and spoke to his cousin. "We came over here to my old house. I show this little fool, Steve, where I grew up. [Laughing] Yeah. Do you want to come over here? We ain't doing shit. We just chopping it up. I'm just showing him where I grew up at over here."

As we waited, I pointed out the different Park Hill neighborhoods we had driven through to get here. Roderick responded,

> They [white people] consider this to be like *Northeast* Park Hill. It's like, since when? It's always been Park Hill. We never had it broken down into sections. But you know, you can kinda tell what is considered Northeast Park Hill 'cause the other side, that's all white folks. . . . They've found a way to divide Park Hill, you know, fit the common denominator of the whole process of gentrification, all of that. It's just, you know, reminds us that this is still *our* neighborhood. You know what I'm saying? A lot of these guys still live around here. It's just, you know, like I said, it's just a matter of really feeling like you belong nowadays, and that's hard. You know? A lot of folks that live in this area still feel like all of this stuff being built around them, is not even for them.

"Even Hiawatha Davis?" I asked.

"There's a lot of community organizations that used to be able to operate in there, have meetings, all of that. Now they *charge* people.

You gotta book time and they just make it seem like they don't really cater to anybody around here. You know what I mean?"

Roderick's younger cousin, Jared, arrived quickly. "Ever since I been a baby I been around him," his cousin said. "He always kept me with him." "Yeah, always," Roderick added. Jared continued reminiscing: "I've always hung out with him. Always. He used to come get me and take me to basketball practice. Come pick me up from basketball practice. Take me home from the game when I was playing basketball." Roderick looked up and down the street. "You know what trips me out about this? When I was a kid, all day, right here. My grandma rented in Park Hill and moved from *here* to Montbello [another neighborhood in the northeast of Denver].[16] I remember she always kept saying she wanted [to buy] a house in Park Hill. But she couldn't find none. You know what I'm sayin'?"

"She say she didn't want to leave Park Hill," Jared added.

"She wouldn't know *this* Park Hill," Roderick said, referring to Northeast Park Hill demographic shifts with sarcasm.

"What was the Park Hill that she would know?" I asked.

"This a place where everyone would come. I miss it. The Holly is the heart of Park Hill. People used to come to Park Hill from all over, but now that has changed."

White residents living farther south of MLK Boulevard might not agree that Holly Square represents the "heart of Park Hill." Instead, they often identify it only as Northeast Park Hill, distancing themselves from the Black part of the Park Hill neighborhood north of MLK. A longtime Black resident recounted feeling "confused" the first time he heard the term "Northeast Park Hill," adding, "It's all Park Hill." Another Black resident echoed this sentiment, emphatically stating, "It's just Park Hill." In contrast, many white residents of South Park Hill expressed a different perspective. Eric, a South Park Hill resident, shared, "When I moved here, I made sure I was in South Park Hill, and I didn't want to go north of Martin Luther King Boulevard." Laura, another white resident of South Park Hill who has devoted significant time to advocating for equity in Park Hill schools, expressed her frustration: "I think people in South Park Hill think *that's* Park Hill, and they don't even know there's anything up there." During a walk through the Park Hill Street Fair in South Park Hill one early fall, I encountered a vendor's booth displaying a large map labeled

"Park Hill." Notably, the map excluded the northeast section, making the omission a literal act of rendering the space "ungeographic."[17]

However, Roderick adamantly refused geographic marginalization. Like other Black residents, he staunchly identified with Park Hill rather than acknowledging the label of Northeast Park Hill. Roderick's proclamation of *This is my hood* when we were in the south section of Park Hill carried a distinct lack of irony. His words evoked the spirit of James Brown's anthem affirming Black pride and empowerment: "Say it loud—I'm Black and proud." Roderick's act of refusal transcends overt protest but allows him to navigate and resist oppressive forces in his daily life. Tina Campt has theorized a practice of refusal as an active assertion of the right to exist and thrive in spaces that have historically been hostile or indifferent to Black lives.[18] By rejecting geographic labels imposed by white residents, Roderick and others wield refusal in order to assert their belonging in a context of systemic racism that attempts to diminish or erase Black presence. Through acts of remembrance and reframing, they engage in Black placemaking, reclaiming and redefining their neighborhood on their own terms.

*Cynthia: Describing a Community*

Throughout the summer of 2018, I sat regularly with a group of mothers at Skyland Park across from the Hope Center in Northeast Park Hill as they watched their sons practice football with the Park Hill Pirates. Children of all ages from the neighborhood came to these practices. I observed the team and spoke with the coaches, who, like the players, were rooted in the community. Denver summers are hot, so I would park myself under the same shade tree each afternoon, watching as the coaches prepared the boys for their weekend games. The Pirates have been a part of Northeast Park Hill since 1968. Mayor Hancock frequently referenced in his speeches that he played for the Pirates as a youth. "They just retired my number 32," he told the audience during his 2019 reelection campaign kickoff. Some of the men in the card room had also coached the Pirates over the years; in fact, Mr. Cummings had founded the team.

Nowadays, many families involved with the Pirates live outside the neighborhood. Cynthia, the team's vice president, helped me understand why they braved heavy traffic each weeknight from their suburban homes in Aurora for their sons' football practice. "Don't they have youth football in Aurora?" I asked. Yes, Cynthia explained, and the other mothers enthusiastically agreed: they all felt that the Pirates' coaches were unparalleled. They had higher expectations, more rigorous drills, and a deeper personal commitment to the players. While the football program was the primary draw, their trips were also a form of pilgrimage. All of them had once lived in Northeast Park Hill, and returning each night felt deeply meaningful. "It's like coming home," Cynthia said, a sentiment again echoed by the others. "This is my neighborhood. I grew up here. This is home. This is my hood."

The back side of the Hiawatha Davis Recreation Center, easily visible from where we sat at the park's edge, prompted more memories. After accidentally referring to Hiawatha Davis as Skyland, Cynthia quickly corrected herself. "I only think of it as Skyland." No evidence remains of the outdoor swimming pool built there in 1963, but the mothers reminisced about the fun they had swimming, especially jumping off "the high diving board." They also recalled the "little baby pool," now an empty relic, enclosed behind a wrought-iron fence against the card room's exterior wall. When Cynthia mentioned that swimming there had been free, another mother corrected her: "It cost a quarter to swim."

Cynthia's memories of Skyland shifted our attention to a spot next to the swimming pool, where she pointed out that "basketball in the back" was still being played. A friend chimed in, "There were always two picnic tables, and people would throw a blanket down." Cynthia added with a grin, "That's where the men rolled dice." That memory sparked laughter and prompted others to share their own recollections. They all agreed that everyone was lucky not to have been seriously hurt, given the many police chases that occurred inside Skyland Park while the Pirates practiced. Police navigated through crowds of players, coaches, and parents, chasing down drug dealers and buyers, prompting a hasty dispersal. Offenders, clutching drugs, money, or both, scattered in every direction. Cynthia's stories revealed her deep attachment to the neighborhood, a connection forged at the intersection of individual and collective memories.

It was a stronger community back then [when I was] growing up. Like, I come from a large family. So when we rode our bikes, everyone was around. There was just more community. There was a stronger community back then. When everybody went to school, everybody knew everybody. You know, it's just—you got more and more schools, you got more and more people, you've just got different people. And people are like this no more [pointing toward the kids playing football]. The center—that's where we went. That's where we spent *all* of our time. I mean, Rec cards were fifty cents. [Laughing] You know what I mean? Nowadays a Rec card is three-hundred-something dollars. You know, how are you supposed to tell your kid, "Let's do this?" So, it's just a different time. Kids aren't in the rec center anymore. You know what I'm sayin'? That changes *everything*. You know. People moving in, and they're catering to a different *type* of person.

I did not pursue the topic further, but she brought up "different people" twice, signaling a sense of cultural displacement. Cynthia expressed her concerns with the practice of "buying low, flipping, and selling high." "People are losing their homes, and people get them at low prices and they fix 'em up. Like my aunt and her house. I think when they ended up getting rid of it, it was like $160,000 and the house could have easily been worth over $300,000. The person went in there, redid everything, sold it for almost $400,000."

Cynthia continued to contrast her fond memories of the close-knit Northeast Park Hill neighborhood with the more consumer-oriented atmosphere of her current home in Aurora. She acknowledged that Aurora offered a range of amenities, including shops, restaurants, and modern homes. "But when I look at what we have right here," she said, gesturing toward her friends and then to the coaches helping the boys practice, "this—" she paused, referring to the neighborhood, "is amazing to me. What we have right here. It makes me proud." She reminisced about where she and her friends used to ride their bikes as children. She especially missed "the center—that's where we went. That's where we spent all our time."

One mother, who once lived just south of MLK Boulevard, recalled riding her bike across the street as a child to spend time in the neighborhood where she "belonged." She spoke fondly of "the Safeway, the beauty salon, Skyland Center, the liquor store" (where she'd buy her mother's cigarettes with a note and five dollars), and the "little library in the Dahlia." When I shared how impressed I was with her detailed memory, she responded quickly, "It's easy to remember. It was one of my first experiences of community, because you gonna run into any one of your neighbors who lived somewhere in a ten-block radius. This was my neighborhood." Another mother chimed in, emphasizing that both Park Hill Shopping Center and Skyland were places where "we got to watch out for each other."

I asked about South Park Hill's frequently mentioned distinction between Northeast Park Hill and North Park Hill. "I never heard about it," she said, "until a few years ago when someone asked which part of Park Hill I used to live in."

Cynthia elaborated on behalf of her friend: "When I ask her what she meant, she [the neighbor] asked if I had lived in Northeast Park Hill or South Park Hill. I said, where's that at? Growing up, you never had that thinking. You thought, this is just Park Hill. In my mind and anybody, we just live in Park Hill."

Cynthia also brought up the microbrewery near the hotel on Quebec. A 2013 renovation of the old, vacated firehouse, the microbrewery is perhaps the most stereotypical signifier of neighborhood gentrification. Situated in the far northeast corner of Northeast Park Hill, it is across the street from small single-family homes built in the 1950s, inhabited by longtime residents. Although there are no art galleries, coffee shops, or upscale restaurants nearby, "luxury urban townhomes" were constructed adjacent to the microbrewery. Cynthia expressed her belief that "they should have put it somewhere else. A microbrewery in Park Hill!" she scoffed. "Where are all the Black people?" Cynthia had a distinct understanding of what constituted the "moral geography" in Northeast Park Hill, and a microbrewery hardly aligned with that vision.[19] She (correctly) identified the microbrewery as a business that catered to a white demographic. According to one Yelp review in 2023, "The opening of this place in the old fire station that closed a few years ago has brought vibrancy to a part of town that could really use some."[20]

For Cynthia, the microbrewery symbolized racial exclusion, echoing what Elijah Anderson found in his research in west Philadelphia: "For many local black residents, who are mainly working class or poor, the brewery represents the vanguard of a white invasion. The blacks resent its presence and few would ever think of patronizing this place."[21]

Despite the changes, revisiting the old neighborhood for her sons' weekly football practices provided Cynthia with the opportunity to recreate a sense of Black community and reconnect with Black space. Alison Blunt has argued that nostalgia can be a productive force, fostering agency through a profound connection to home.[22] In describing her former neighborhood as her "hood," Cynthia confirms Geneva Smitherman's definition of a *hood* as "the neighborhood where you live or have grown up; your roots and a place where you feel welcome and at home."[23] Her determination to continue to occupy this space, however partially, constituted a resilient declaration of belonging.

*Geraldine "Geri" Grimes*

I first met Geri Grimes at the monthly Holly Area Redevelopment Project (HARP) meetings, a community-led initiative focused on gathering input about the future of the former Park Hill Shopping Center. Ms. Grimes served as the chairperson of these meetings. At first, I observed quietly, but as my interest grew, I began to approach her afterward with questions and requests for clarifications. She was always open and receptive and eventually invited me to visit her office for further discussions.

When Geri Grimes died on May 11, 2022, the Urban Land Conservancy—with whom she had a close working relationship—offered the following memorial: "Ms. Grimes was a pillar in her community and beyond, providing leadership to organizations such as the Center for African American Health, Denver Early Childhood Council, Colorado Black Women for Political Action, HARP, and many more. She was the president/CEO of the Hope Center for twelve years, and worked there for close to forty years, creating an exemplary program for early childhood education and programs for adults with disabilities."[24]

Numerous articles and posts highlighted her activism and leadership, particularly her efforts to revitalize the Holly neighborhood. During our first interview, she described herself, above all, as a proud "African American woman who represents my community." That community—where she had lived for more than half a century—was where I witnessed her tireless commitment.

> You look at the strengths and you build upon the strengths within your community or within an individual and by doing so it might address some of the concerns that you have, but if you never address the strengths and you only talk about problems, it's like there's no starting point, that there is nothing already there that you build upon. So my approach in the meeting . . . is to say, *This community is rich in many, many things and we also recognize the issues and concerns within our community*. But our community is not built on issues and concerns. The reason for the success and the longevity of Holly Square was because of the strengths.

Like so many who live or have lived in Northeast Park Hill, she recalls

> a place of safety to embrace your culture, embrace the things that were valuable to you. That was still a place on Holly Square to embrace. You have the stores, and you knew your small business owners. You knew them as friends or people in the community. They weren't these distant people. Their kids went to high school with you, so it was always a connection with who was serving you in those places as well, and you knew the places *not* to hang out in. Let's be real, there was places that you could say, "Okay, it's a little rougher in this club than it is in this one." You knew after certain hours it's time to go home because a different group will come into the club. So I kinda knew the neighborhood, and I especially think about the seventies and eighties, because I talk about my kids growing up during that era. The reason everybody is connected . . . is because the neighborhood was a neighborhood where everybody knew each other. Now you're most likely to not even get to know who your neighbor is next door.

I asked about changes, and she responded, "There's so many. You're talking about small businesses having closed down. When gang activity came about in the nineties, that changed the climate of the neighborhood. Neighbors now, it's so much different because you're talking about people who can't live in the neighborhoods that were traditionally neighborhoods of color and they can't live here anymore."

She recalled Skyland—"before it was renamed Hiawatha"—as "the hub of people young and old."

> They grew up within the rec center. The former directors there were so much part of the community. The people that they served and came into their building, first-name basis. It really did feel like you were part of, you know, if Johnny was doing this, then rest assured everybody would know about it. They knew when the kids were having difficult times. They knew when the kids were having wonderful times. They knew about their neighborhood, they knew about the kids that lived in the neighborhood, they knew about the kids growing up.

Ms. Grimes described a community of "caring and mutuality," with "children playing ball in nearby vacant lots, riding bicycles, shopping at the Dahlia, walking to Holly Square to do some more shopping, spending time at the center." Skyland was part of the neighborhood landscape. Like Cynthia, Ms. Grimes expressed frustration with gentrification:

> Why wasn't gentrification important when we were raising *our* young ones? Why wasn't it important before? All of a sudden, it's important. That's real for people. Not that they don't want to move forward. They recognize that it was a race issue. Gentrification is a simple word for saying white people moving into Black neighborhoods. But they want to make it sound so good—"gentrification." So you can put whatever pretty name you want to it but in reality, what are we talking about? We're talking about white folks displacing Black folks. Losing homes whether you owned them or not. If you lived somewhere for thirty years, and all of a sudden your rent goes up sky high, that's still another way of pushing you out. And we talk about the economy and blame it on the economy. We talk about now we need affordable housing. We knew all that stuff beforehand. We're no dummies. This world has not been built on dummies. We know exactly what we're doing. And until somebody hollers about it, then it's like "we need to be sure not to displace people." Let's be real. If they could knock down Mrs. Wil-

son's property tomorrow, it would not be looking like *anything* that's a reflection of this community. Look at what has happened in Curtis Park. You know you walk in and it's not a feeling of *integration*. It is just another form of segregation. Now it's just all white. That's the difference. You know, I grew *up* here. . . .

I walk out in my neighborhood that I have lived in for forty-four years now in Park Hill. I'm gonna tell you, even my grandkids are like, "Why are we getting so many white folks on the block?" Because they're *not* used to that. But what they're *more* not used to is the fact that when they walked out before it felt much friendlier. I got one [white] neighbor, they happened to be there four years now and rarely and barely speaks to us. I almost have to *force* them to speak. My husband is very different. He's a very friendly person, so he'll just keep trying. I would just end it. We leave about the same time every morning around 6:30. She's so busy trying *not* to look at me and jump in her car. Not a simple good morning. I'm not gonna hold on a conversation. Don't worry. But it doesn't make you feel part *of*. And then the neighbor that's diagonally across—she's probably living there thirty years or so—and we talk about it. But it's not so much who's moving in, but the *feeling* coming from that.

Many Black residents in North and Northeast Park Hill, like Ms. Grimes, commonly expressed dissatisfaction with unfriendly interactions with new white neighbors. Ms. Grimes continued:

My grandkids, they're over at our house a lot. So they see a new neighbor that has a child, they're ready to play. And this family's like, no, no way. I want my kids, my grandkids to run outside and—one of my neighbors has a child almost the same age as my grandchild, and I think she would *love* to run over and play. But I gotta restrict her.

We tell our kids not to worry about it. They don't want to play with you, that's fine. You guys still can have fun. I was almost at one point, almost—like, you know how you speak to someone every morning because you see 'em? And you realize they're not saying anything back to you, and you try to ignore it and just say, "You know, I'm gonna be the bigger person." She's not gonna speak. She's trying to jump into her car just to avoid. You know, why are you here? Why are you in the neighborhood? And if you asked me her name and her partner who live there, I couldn't tell you. Before, we knew *all* our neighbors. And of course all our kids knew all the neighbors. Because it's all just part of your neighborhood. Right? And you know who's on your block.

Over two years of interviews, Ms. Grimes painted a vivid portrait of community life, change, and challenges. She mourned the loss of a vibrant community, where familiarity among residents fostered care and mutual support. Ms. Grimes framed the transformation through the lens of racism, pointing to shifts in social dynamics within her own block. She noted a decline in interaction and the rise of anti-Black racial fear, particularly among newcomers. As sociologist Brandi Summers states, "Newcomers often disregard the residents and communities that had been formed and thrived for years before their arrival."[25] Ms. Grimes lamented the disappearance of a close-knit community and experienced a profound sense of loss as familiar bonds weakened under the pressures of gentrification.

*Conclusion*

Roderick, Cynthia, and Geri Grimes offer a nuanced understanding of Denver's Park Hill neighborhood, particularly Northeast Park Hill, where the racial dynamics have undergone significant transformations. Roderick's refusal to conform to imposed geographic labels shows his fight to hang onto Black space. He resists historical marginalization and exclusion, asserting the right of Black individuals to shape and define their own spaces, thus contributing to Black placemaking. Cynthia's stories explore the power of nostalgia and the ongoing creation of community bonds to resist Black displacement. Her reflections evoke a longing for a past marked by communal cohesion while highlighting the disruptions caused by gentrification and displacement. Ms. Grimes emphasized the resilience and agency of the community in navigating the impacts of gentrification. Her focus on recognizing and leveraging community strengths reflected a proactive approach to addressing challenges while preserving the essence of the close-knit neighborhood. She served as a local warrior, leading efforts to safeguard cultural heritage and social bonds amidst the currents of change. As I discuss in later chapters, the card room similarly stands as a bulwark against gentrification's encroachment, symbolizing resilience and defiance in the face of urban upheaval.

# 5    Robert Taylor

"Your mother could pull a twelve-footer, man?" Mr. Taylor said, looking up with a surprised expression. The man sitting across from him at the domino table, not a card room regular, was talking about growing up picking cotton. He had described putting the cotton into twelve-foot-long bags called croker sacks.

Mr. Hall chimed in to affirm the newcomer's claim. "My mother would fill it up, and my daddy would take it out to the field."

Mr. Taylor responded politely, "She couldn't fill a twelve-footer. Think about it. And when you go home, ask her." He knew bullshit when he heard it.

*Boyhood Life*

Though he was born Robert Truman Taylor in a cotton field in Lake Providence, Louisiana, on September 27, 1944, everyone called him Truman. "I was born in a family of nine. I was number eight," Mr. Taylor told me. His mother was filling a nine-foot croker sack when she went into labor. Truman was delivered "right there in the field" with the help of his mother's sister, who'd been working alongside her. The sister took them to their nearby home on a twenty-acre piece of land purchased years prior by Mr. Taylor's white Irish grandfather.

Growing up, said Mr. Taylor, "I picked cotton just like everyone else, and I had to do my chores." The small plot was their primary source of income, and they somehow made it work. "We didn't know we were poor. We just knew that we had each other, and everybody around us was in the same boat, so what could we compare it to, then?" But in retrospect, Mr. Taylor described "poverty beyond description. We just had to make do with what we had and be happy with that."

FIG. 6. Mr. Taylor. Steve Bialostok, photographer.

Weeks after our croker sack conversation, Mr. Taylor and I sat down to eat in the Walmart Subway, and I asked him about having corrected Mr. Hall. He said, "The average cotton sack—you probably never seen the bag they put the cotton in—you put it on your shoulder. It's a long bag behind you." He went on to explain the hot, backbreaking process that began by pulling the fluffy white lint from the boll. He'd try not to cut his hands on the sharp ends. He paused, remembering my original question. "Mr. Hall knows nothing about cotton." Cotton was grown in New Mexico, where Mr. Hall grew up, but not to the same extent as in Louisiana—especially in Lake Providence, the heart of the Mississippi Delta cotton kingdom. But today I wanted to know more about Mr. Taylor's early life. "I'd keep the books for my dad. He couldn't read. Couldn't write. . . . The [cotton] business is to make as much money as you can. That's the only resource you got. I was *raised* in the field. . . . When the cotton was there, *you* were there. If you can't carry a bag, you'd give it to your daddy, or put it on *his* back. It was a way of life."

Cotton wasn't a year-round crop, so different times of the year meant working for others. The daily wage at the time was three dollars, and Mr. Taylor recalled a police officer coming to their home and arresting his father for refusing to work for less than that. His father was 6'6" and 280 pounds, an intimidating man who "didn't take bullshit, even from white people." "They wanted to break him. Beat him down. Let him know that he ain't the boss. He gotta do what he's told. That was the way it was. And you had to live through these things in order to survive. He's just trying to make it to another day. . . . So he stood up that day. He stood up for his family. That, I really appreciate. And maybe that's where I got a little backbone from."

In response to my question, "Were *you* afraid when you were younger?" he said, "Sure. You *had* to be afraid. Policeman came to your house, you knew he was coming for something. Either to beat you up and put you in jail, put your family in jail. Usually when they came to our house, I had business out in the woods." Truman's parents raised him to know his place—"not to question a white man, what he did, or why he did it. That was the way it was."

Watching how the white world chewed up and spit out his father gave Truman the backbone he needed to "take no shit" from anyone. That didn't mean he would "get in your face" or not be compliant for police stops, but he would "not be afraid anymore." At the same time, he didn't want to be "outspoken like Martin Luther [King] and the rest of them." He wouldn't force himself into a whites-only restaurant, for instance. "My thought was that the cook was Black, and you can get the same thing that they're eating out there if you just go in the back door. . . . That was wrong, but what're you gonna do about it?"

He'd been a good student in his all-Black elementary school but had no desire to attend college, "because I wasn't that smart. I didn't want school. I didn't *like* school." Truman didn't know what he wanted to do, but he did know that "I don't want to do *this* [picking cotton] for the rest of my life. There's gotta be something better."

*Getting Out of Lake Providence*

Truman knew that "it was time to go" after he graduated from high school. He told himself, "I gotta make some money, somehow." His older half brother owned a small general store in Niagara Falls, New York, and encouraged Truman to come work with him. He worked from 8:00 a.m. to 9:00 p.m. every day except Sunday, when he worked a half day. He sent much of his earnings back to his parents. And only a few months after Truman left Lake Providence, his mother became sick and died. He was just nineteen, and she was in her early forties. He returned with his brother for the funeral.

After another year in Niagara Falls, there was still "no money" in that little corner store. Frustrated, and with a nineteen-year-old's desire "to see some girls," he joined the military and boarded a plane for the first time for basic training in San Antonio, Texas—where he laid eyes on running water and a shower for the first time. From there he went to Biloxi, Mississippi, and spent nine months training "to intercept Morse code." He went on to serve in Turkey and Japan—and learned how to clean a latrine, play pinochle, and "drink like a fish."

Four years after entering the military, Mr. Taylor made a decision. "I had a lot of experiences that I know I never would see again. I'd never do again. Visited a lot of places. Should've made a career out of it, but . . . I was adventurous. I wanted to do something different. Plus them ol' girls was looking pretty good in civilian life, so I got back out. No job again, no skills."

*Work and (Not) Being an "Uppity Negro"*

He returned to Lake Providence looking for work. Frustrated, he spent most of his time drinking. After "a hot week or two" he left for Phoenix for "six or eight months" before drifting to Denver. Thanks to his military service, he got an entry-level position at a Ford dealership. "I shagged cars. They come in off the transport trucks, I checked them all in. I cleaned them up, and I tagged them. I checked them for every little thing that could possibly be wrong." But Mr. Taylor ran into obstacles. "For a while I worked for the dude who was training me. He was white. I was sticking out. When it came down to making extra money, he hired everybody else in the shop but me to work nights. . . . They let me know I ain't got no future there."

Eventually he landed a job repairing home gas meters at Xcel Energy utility company. After five years, he moved to the warehouse to stock shelves. "A lot of people didn't like to see me be successful in the job I was in," he said. He and another Black employee were physically assaulted. White employees kicked them from behind, pretending to be joking. "That's what they do to you. Try to keep you down. Kick you in the ass. I'd catch his foot right here. Now, where's the other one?" I asked if he thought his efforts convinced his white coworkers of his worth. "White people are kind of strange. . . . [T]hey going to push you as far as they can. And then they going to back up. They know how much you can take. Then they're going to try to get rid of you after that. . . . So you got to play a little game with them. Make them think you're crazy."

When the warehouse foreman position became available, "I didn't quite make the cut. I said 'Bullshit. I'm going to be a foreman, one way or the other!'" He sounded angry, thinking about it. "That makes you, what do they call it, 'uppity.' Uppity Negro. A troublemaker." But persistence eventually paid off, and he was promoted to foreman, a position he kept until he retired.

*A Permanent Home in North Park Hill*

At Xcel Energy, Mr. Taylor met a woman who eventually became his "fourth or fifth" wife, he told me, unsure of the exact number of times he'd been married. His first wife became involved with drugs and left him in less than a year. They were living in a three-bedroom apartment in a Denver suburb. "We doing good. And all of a sudden, 'Hey, I got to go.' I said, 'Where you going?' Well, some dude she met. He introduced her to dope."

Wife number two didn't last much longer, but together they bought his current North Park Hill home on a corner surrounded by a cyclone fence. This gave him stability, a sense of comfort, and control. His home is small and intimate, with yellow brick and white trim, more weathered than other homes on the block. If there had ever been a luscious lawn, it is long gone. But after once losing the home to his ex-wife and eventually buying it back, he feels rooted in this house.

When Mr. Taylor moved into the home in the 1970s, living among Black folks, he felt a sense of community. He recalls a joyful neighborhood where "a whole bunch of families used to play basketball right there on that garage." Customarily we talked inside his home. But with COVID restrictions in place in 2021, we spoke in the fenced-in backyard, next to his two cars. He pointed to a free-standing garage that I'd always thought was a storage shed. "I had a hoop put up there. They played ball every day. My backyard used to be the playground."

Five decades after he bought the house, with just Mr. Taylor and one other Black family left, social life on the street has changed dramatically. One of the first white neighbors even suggested that he couldn't afford to live there. "I mind my own business and just tug along now that I got the little guy [a two-year-old grandson]. And a lot of times we just go down the block, and here I am running behind him, so that must be strange to them as they're looking out the windows."

Hearing Mr. Taylor was easier outside, even with the noise of passing cars and nearby lawnmowers. When we sat in his living room our conversations competed with theme music and gunshots from the Cowboy Channel. Sometimes we'd stop talking to watch his favorites—*Wagon Train*, *The Rifleman*, or *The Big Valley*. Mr. Taylor spent a good part of his day on a gray La-Z-Boy recliner, watching television and/or playing dominoes on his iPhone.

He was always agreeable to talking anywhere, but he seemed most at ease at home, with dinner on the stove. One topic was his years of drinking. His alcoholism contributed to the departure of his second and third wives. Why did they knowingly marry an alcoholic, I wondered. "They knew that I had an income that was a little bit above average. And I didn't have demands. . . . They never tried to find out why I was a drunk." It made me sad to think that Mr. Taylor imagined they only wanted him for his money.

*Dominoes and Community*

The old Xcel Energy warehouse was just east of Skyland Recreation Center. From the 1970s through the 1990s, Mr. Taylor walked to work, passing Skyland but paying it little attention. The liquor store was a frequent stop, but twenty years before we met he'd stopped drinking entirely—with no support group, no help. Just cold turkey. He'd calculated the money spent on liquor over the years. And he "wasn't taking care of my family," he said. "I was pissed off at my dad.... So I just started drinking, and drinking, and drinking. And then it hit me one day. I'm doing all this, and I'm winding up just like him. Only I'm drinking, and he never was a drinker."

Mr. Taylor's memories are conflicted. On one hand, "I was afraid of him.... He said *do* something, you did it. No reason, no explanation required. Just do it. So I can say a lot of time that I raised myself.... If you did what he said, he was okay. If you didn't, you got your track shoes on." On the other hand, "He took care of us as best as he could.... Nine kids is kind of hard to take care of when you ain't got no income."

His father never hit him. "He wasn't a fighter, but nobody messed with him. He was too big." He lived until ninety, dying two years after Mr. Taylor brought him from Louisiana to live with his sister in Denver, where he suffered from Alzheimer's.

*The Pot Calling the Kettle Black*

Members of stigmatized groups can sometimes endorse the same stereotypes about their own groups that members of the majority have. Even though I knew this, it was still hard to hear. Mr. Taylor repeated so many corrosive stereotypes—Black folks can't manage money, don't run businesses well, don't respond respectfully to police officers, and should work harder—that I finally began to accept that he believed what he said. After I told him that "the average Black college graduate earns less than the average white high school no-college graduate," he responded, "Because they don't apply themselves." When I said that Black people in America haven't been able to accumulate wealth, he said, "Because they sell out."

I nearly blew a gasket, though, when he began repeating former President Ronald Reagan's racist tropes about Black women on welfare (the "welfare queen"). Mr. Taylor kept insisting that Black people can't manage money and that they don't know how to run businesses. "Look around you," he said. "Five Points used to be owned by Black people. Where are they now? All you have to do is die and leave what you got to your kid. All your kids got to do is die and leave it for *his* kid. Then you keep it in the family, things can grow."

Like Mr. Taylor, other Black conservatives insist that Black people who fail could have succeeded as much as white people if they had wanted to.[1] Without a doubt, Mr. Taylor frames his life like many Black conservatives: he was hardworking, not lazy; morally upright, not immoral. Mr. Taylor presents his life story as that of a self-made Black man who overcame countless obstacles. As he tells it, he bootstrapped his way out of Lake Providence, out of the cotton fields, out of poverty, and into a successful career. He overcame racism at work, moved into a Park Hill home, and got out of alcoholism without a support group. When I asked what his two greatest achievements were, this was his answer:

> I can figure that out real easy. Number one was being there for my kids. Even though I didn't raise them, I had never spent much time with any of them as I should have as a father, but they still know me and they still respect me, and they appreciate me for what I *did* do. So it's not my greatest, but I'm glad I didn't abandon them. . . . And the second greatest thing was being able to control my habits.

Mr. Taylor's tone grew quite deliberate as he tried to figure out how to describe a third achievement—his current successful marriage. "I wanted to say that was just a stroke of luck, that I got a decent wife out of the whole bunch." He laughed but remained serious. "What? I must've done it, so it's got to be an achievement. Come on, man."

*Mr. Taylor and the Card Room*

Despite our many arguments on the topic, it was obvious to me that Mr. Taylor didn't actually live by this "pull yourself up by your bootstraps" ideology. His oldest daughter, diagnosed at a young age with obsessive-compulsive disorder, lives in the basement and is dependent on his care. He is thrilled when his unmarried daughter brings his young grandson over for him to babysit. Similarly, it is only Mr. Taylor who provides transportation for any man from the card room who needs it. "You're like a carpool," I said. "What you going to do?" Mr. Taylor would respond. "You let him walk home or give him a ride."

He rescues others whenever necessary. Once George got lost downtown and somehow managed to contact Mr. Taylor for help locating his car. Mr. Taylor immediately enlisted Mr. Carr's help, and they walked the streets of downtown Denver until they eventually found the car. George has often needed rescuing. Once I arrived at the center at about 6:30 p.m., just in time to see Mr. Taylor walking out. "George called and needs a ride," he said. We drove nearly four miles to find George standing in front of Trader Joe's. Mr. Taylor took him home, a half-hour drive, and—as always—made sure he got inside his apartment safely.

Mr. Taylor just laughed when I presented the contradictions between his actions and his personal philosophy. I wondered aloud if what he told me about his beliefs "was all bullshit." He strongly denied it. I ended our conversation with a story about my father-in-law, originally from Mexico, a migrant worker for decades until he started a roofing business. "I don't think he really understood what I did for a living," I told Mr. Taylor. "A university professor. A researcher. What little he understood he didn't think was really work. It wasn't working with my hands." Mr. Taylor laughed as I went on. "There are times I think you look at me and think, God he's stupid."

"Yeah." Mr. Taylor's smile was cynical. "I can feel it. I think he's right."

## 6 Birth and Evolution of a Black Social and Cultural Nexus

Catty-corner from the Blazing Chicken Shack stands the cultural touchstone of Holly Square, located five miles from downtown Denver in the Northeast Park Hill neighborhood. Before you see its formal name at the entrance on Holly Street—the Hiawatha Davis Recreation Center—your attention is drawn to the large murals painted on the two-story concrete slab walls. A clenched brown fist resembling a skeleton echoes the adjacent Nelson Mandela quote: "It always seems impossible until it's done." On the side of the building facing 33rd Avenue, look closely and you'll see various colorful geometric shapes that suggest the word "knowledge" within the profile of a head. Adjacent to the painting is the quote "Some say knowledge is power. I say the use of it for good is real power." Hiawatha Davis Jr., its author, once lived in this historically Black neighborhood. The center—named in his honor—memorializes a much-beloved man who spent his adult life advocating for social justice. On a pleasant day, as you walk toward the entrance, you'll pass Black men talking and laughing. Enter the small foyer, and you can pick up a free copy of *5-Point News*, *Denver Urban Spectrum*, *Body of Christ*, and *Denver Weekly News*—local Black newspapers. Against the back wall, a large display case holds decades of sports trophies and framed photos dating back to the 1970s when staff knew all the participating kids' names.

Glass windows across from the front desk allow receptionists to keep an eye on a few teens hanging out in the game room across the hall. The room doesn't compare to the massive Boys and Girls Club directly across the street. Hiawatha Davis's game room has only one pool table, one ping pong table, a couple of couches, and a small television mounted on the wall. Down a short hallway opposite the locker rooms and vend-

FIG. 7. Hiawatha Davis Recreation Center. Steve Bialostok, photographer.

ing machines, the largest room in the center—the weight and cardio room—feels crowded when more than seven people work out at once. It straddles the short hallway, which wraps around the back with the arts and crafts room, the gym entrance, and a small multipurpose room and kitchen. But the real action, and the largest crowd, is in a room across from the weight room. A green placard on the wall reads "Card Room."

The center fosters a vibrant cultural environment, serving as a space for community connection and heritage. It is frequently sought out by Black-focused organizations for community-based and youth-related activities and meetings. By my third year of research in 2018, with its predominantly Black membership, it still embodied the distinctive Black sense of place that people like Cynthia recalled from an earlier era. Mostly Black men lifted weights in the exercise room and played basketball in the gym. Silver Sneakers classes, led by the popular Michael, were tailored to the preferences of a predominantly female audience and featured the sounds of Motown hits. Charles, the recreation coordinator, animated his spin classes with a curated playlist from his phone featuring a variety of Black artists. Linda, the dedicated ceramics instructor who had volunteered for a decade, wore an African apron and played Denver's local hip-hop station while assisting students and crafting her own pieces, which were

FIG. 8. Perseverance mural. Steve Bialostok, photographer

Black- and African-themed. Sam spent a year meticulously painting an entire set of ceramic Black soldier chess pieces. Group prayer occurred in a government building without discussion of its appropriateness, suggesting a spiritual link between faith and the recreation center. One day, following our Silver Sneakers class, about two dozen participants, predominantly Black women, gathered in the moderate-sized multipurpose room to celebrate Miss Elsie's ninetieth birthday. The Black male elders in the card room formed their own unique community, nested within this still predominantly Black center, just as the recreation center itself was nestled within the historically Black section of Park Hill. History, community, and racial familiarity drew the card room players back.

Denver's mayor also kept coming back. The recreation center was once Mayor Michael Hancock's homeplace. On the evening he declared his candidacy for a third term, from Hiawatha Davis's basketball court, the

Denver mayor emphasized to the sizable audience that he had roots in the neighborhood and spent a significant part of his youth at the center. During his speech on January 16, 2019, Hancock introduced his official announcement with a personal anecdote: "Grandma Dolores lived just across the street from here, at 35th and Holly. She died thirty-six years ago in 1983. However, as we grew up and spent weekends with her, we would come to this center known as Skyland back then, and we would swim and play basketball and football in the park."

The mayor concluded with a fervent declaration that "Skyland" provided "a sense of community where we felt safe." Given Denver's racist past, along with the ongoing threat of gentrification and displacement, maintaining the center as a Black space required effort from those who remained. This chapter explores the emergence and evolution of the center, first known as Skyland and later as Hiawatha Davis, a small, local recreation center that offers valuable insights into Black placemaking and the impacts of gentrification.

*Birth of Skyland Recreation Center*

By the 1960s the United States had undergone significant social and economic changes following the post–World War II economic expansion. While the country enjoyed a period of prosperity and growth during the 1950s, the 1960s saw "white flight" and suburbanization, which led to increased levels of social inequality and racial segregation in American cities. President Lyndon Johnson's 1964 "War on Poverty" introduced a range of policy initiatives and programs aimed specifically at urban communities. Recreation spaces were emphasized as one way to provide opportunities for social interaction, physical activity, and community engagement in "disadvantaged neighborhoods."

In 1967 Denver's Commission on Community Relations produced the document *The Summer of 1967: Northeast Park Hill*, in which it raised specific concerns about youth:

> Another factor to consider is that the shopping centers in Northeast Park Hill have been the traditional gathering places for the Negro youth from all areas of the city. These "gatherings" at the shopping centers indicate the need for recreation for these groups. One wonders

what would have been the situation if the gathering places were in the midst of the "poverty" of the Negro ghetto.... The neighborhood contains a large park, Skyland, at 33rd and Holly Street which has tennis courts, a swimming pool, a softball diamond and basketball courts. Outside of a bowling alley at the Dahlia Shopping Center and a bar, there is no indoor recreational center for the Negro neighborhood.[1]

Soon after its construction, the Skyland Recreation Center became accessible to the public for a limited number of hours each day. During this time, additional recreation centers were built in several poor neighborhoods. Due to its modest size, Skyland Recreation Center could accommodate only a few activities in undersized, partially enclosed rooms near the front entrance. These spaces included a half-court basketball area with a rubber floor, a gym equipped with chipped and cracked weights, and a single stationary bike and treadmill. Another area housed a small kitchen where men gathered to play cards, chess, and dominoes. When new athletics director Keith arrived in 1990, he recalled, "In the neighborhood, there were very few Caucasians. If there was a Caucasian on the block, it was rare. It was mostly Black. I was considered the token white boy when I first got here. They called me, 'white boy.'" "Did they know your name?" I asked. "They'd just say, 'Where's the white boy?'" Management didn't expect Keith to "last more than six months. No one really stayed here." By then, gang activity had proliferated throughout Holly Square, and Skyland Park had become a focal point for related issues. "The [empty] pop cans held either drugs or money," Keith recalled.

> They would lay them in the park. So there would be a Mountain Dew there. And then all of a sudden you'd see a Pepsi can there. Don't pick up the pop cans. There used to be a playground, not where it's at right now, right over here by the pool area. Don't clean up the area over there because that's where all the drug deals and all that's going on. They would put the money in the pop cans. So if you picked up the pop can, you're either getting drugs or getting money.

Keith vividly remembered that his first day on the job, April 7, 1990, was also his first introduction to the pervasive crack cocaine trade. Feeling thirsty and noticing there were no vending machines in the recreation center, he crossed 33rd Ave to go to the convenience store. While there, he witnessed a drug bust.

In spite of frequent gunshots that rang out in the park and bullet holes in the walls of shops at Park Hill Shopping Center, a moral force field shielded Skyland Recreation Center from gang violence. Keith remembered that even though "lots of gang members" loitered outside, the membership at Skyland didn't decrease. "They [gang members] respected the building," Keith said. "There was never any graffiti painted on the walls." The center was "a safe haven." "This is the Blood's area. You don't mess around with the center kids. The Bloods recruited, but they kept this place sacred. So we had a Crip come in here. Tried to play basketball. We had to take him back to that office, call the police, and the police had to escort him out. There were other places for him to play in his territory, but he wanted to play here." Keith also learned that the Skyland Recreation Center was inseparable from the community. "I learned a lot my first ten years, just being 'round the community," said Keith. "If you're not doing something for the community, the community will call you on it."

*From Skyland to Hiawatha Davis: The Beginning of Displacement*

On March 8, 2000, Mayor Wellington Webb broke ground for a $6 million renovation of the Skyland Recreation Center, which was renamed Hiawatha Davis in honor of the late Black Denver city councilman who died in 2000 after serving the district for sixteen years. "Hiawatha Davis," said Happy Haynes, Denver Parks and Recreation executive director, "was one of the first of the original centers to get that renovation and facelift. And it was designed to sort of try to create opportunities for transformation in a community [that] was really suffering." Goodstein writes that a year after the renovated center opened, the building had transformed into more than just a facility. It had evolved into a fully equipped "athletic club" with paid memberships.[2] While "athletic club" might be an overstatement, the center had expanded from thirty-one thousand square feet to nearly forty thousand square feet. It now featured a second-floor running track, a large multipurpose room, an indoor pool, expanded locker rooms, more restrooms, and additional windows. The newly renovated facility also included a designated space for the men who had once gathered in the kitchen: a card room, created exclusively for them.

Despite census data indicating that Northeast Park Hill had started to transition from a predominantly Black community to a whiter one in the 1990s, the community center's membership remained largely Black, as I learned from Bob. I met Bob, who is white, in one of Charles's spinning classes. He had served in the Peace Corps for two years starting in 1972, and his connection to Hiawatha Davis began in 2003.

> There were still probably, I'd say, 80 percent or 85 percent of the people here were African American. And they were working out and stuff like that. The pool didn't get very much use because that wasn't their focus. And so for me it was really nice because I could, and still can, go to that Olympic-sized pool and swim there. . . . But when we started coming at that time, there was a lot more, how should I say, trash talking in the weight room, and a lot of people yelling and hollering. . . . But I've noticed since probably the last five years it's really become a more—there's more whites here than African Americans, with the exception of the guys in the card room that play dominoes and all that. That's sort of their abode.

Bob's use of a racialized space framework resonates with what many white members told me. The once-dominant African American population had clearly given way to an increasing number of white patrons. Despite the intention to "create opportunities for transformation in a community," the construction of the new recreation center aligned with the emerging demographic shifts in the neighborhood. At the time of the renovation, Denver city officials aimed to honor a former councilman by renaming the center. However, given the strong neighborhood ties and significant racial changes, it's not surprising that many locals—especially those of a certain age, like Cynthia, Roderick, and Geri Grimes, as well as the mayor—continued to call it Skyland. Place names hold symbolic importance and carry racial connotations. While the decision to rename the center Hiawatha Davis was meant to honor a specific Black figure, the name Skyland represented, to outsiders, a space associated with gangs, drugs, and (Black) unsavoriness. Of course, this was not all that Skyland represented to locals, many of whom resented the shift from a name associated with Black criminality and gang activity to one tied to a carefully chosen Black role model.

As Duncan Light and Craig Young emphasize, a name that holds valuable symbolic capital for one group may inflict symbolic violence on another group, particularly the local community.[3] Jay Winter defines sites of memory as places where groups express a "collective shared knowledge of the past, on which a group's sense of unity and individuality is based."[4] In his study of gentrification in the San Francisco Bay Area, Samy Alim finds that Black teenagers felt deep connections with—and a deep sense of loss over—Black spaces that had disappeared before they were even born.[5] While Skyland may not have attained the iconic status of landmarks like the Statue of Liberty, the Northeast Park Hill community had already imbued Skyland with considerable social and cultural significance. The shift in name carried profound personal meaning for individuals deeply connected to Skyland, who viewed it as actively erasing the local community, culture, and history.

*A Place to Just Be: Nostalgia, Memory, and the Changing Landscape*

A group of elders sat around a card table watching Mr. Buford, Mr. Hall, Mr. Taylor, and Mr. Carr play. The television news report about the possible restoration of an old building in Five Points prompted Mr. Buford's question. "Do you recall Benny Hooper?" Mr. Buford asked no one in particular, his question punctuated by his distinctive laughter. Benny Hooper's, a casino center ballroom, had opened in the 1920s originally for Black servicemen. Mr. Buford continued with an exclamation of "oh man" before launching into a tale he had once told me about the night he approached three women at a Five Points bar. "I'm sitting at the table, didn't know nobody. They made themselves acquainted with me, and they was all lookin' beautiful. Man, they were talking their asses off. I was having fun with these girls, drinking and shit." His story prompted other recollections about Five Points, including nostalgic memories from decades earlier of where people had lived, played, drunk, met women, and danced—stories of how their social lives used to be. Barbara Johnstone writes that "individuals' relationship to groups are mediated through shared memories, shared memories organized around place and the stories that belong to places."[6] Mr. Carr recalled another story, his cousin driving through Five Points telling the then-twenty-seven-year-old, "'Don't go there. Don't go there. Don't go there.' Shit," Mr.

Carr said. "That was one of the first places I went." Mook remembered Benny Hooper's growing larger over time, with more seating and a two-story hall with a balcony. They remembered events and other landmarks including clubs and restaurants. Napoleon recalled "gambling shacks and everything else" in and around Five Points. "We used to walk in the bar. There's my dollar. There's my dice, throw a dollar on the floor, somebody would throw one there." Without memories of place, writes John Zeisel, people lose their sense of self.[7] There were stories about having "all kinds of fights over women," with some proclaiming innocently, "and it wasn't my fault." "It sure has changed," Mr. Hall said, sounding especially wistful. The collective nods and uh-huhs brought more stories about neighborhood loss, their sense of a "longing for what is lacking in a changed present . . . a yearning for what is now unattainable."[8]

Several men recalled their teenage years playing basketball at the Glenarm Recreation Center in the heart of Five Points. Glenarm had once been home to the "Black YMCA," officially known as the Colored Men's Department. The Colored Men's Department was a three-story, 1881 Italianate-style building purchased in 1914 to serve as a recreational and educational site for Five Points' growing Black community. Locating the second branch in Five Points was not entirely benevolent, however. White leaders hoped that placing it there would reduce the number of Black people visiting the YMCA's main building a mile away. The Colored Men's Department featured a reading room with billiards, a boys' club room, a gymnasium, a branch of the Denver Public Library, and a swimming pool in the basement. Two floors included rooms that could accommodate up to sixty men, mostly railroad porters and waiters. The Colored Men's Department was a Black place where men and boys could relax and feel comfortable being themselves.

After listening to the elders' stories, I spoke with Dave, the supervisor of Glenarm Recreation Center and former supervisor at Hiawatha Davis. When I mentioned the men in the card room, it sparked a memory for him, prompting Dave to reflect on the elders from his own time as a supervisor. "Hiawatha Davis was the only place in the city that you could see older African American men gather to just be. To play pinochle, to play dominoes, to talk shit, to watch TV. To me, that space is unique, especially within our system." Dave's portrayal of a place for

African American men to gather to "just be" recalls Black scholars and authors who have written on the challenges Black people face navigating white spaces—their sense of being constantly on guard and the need to constantly convince others of their respectability and worthiness.[9] Elijah Anderson writes about a Black person's "deficit of credibility" in white spaces and how they must explicitly demonstrate that racial stereotypes do not apply to them.[10] Ethnographies of Black drinking and nondrinking establishments describe them as gathering places for leisure—places to "just be."[11] In these spaces, middle-class and working-class people escape the burdens of the white spaces they frequently occupy during the day.

Trapper intuitively recognized the need for older Black men to have a place to "just be." He had lived in the neighborhood since his teenage years and finally moved to Aurora in 2000 to pursue his version of the American middle-class dream: a comfortably sized suburban home at the end of a picturesque cul-de-sac. He retired two years after the move. Despite Aurora's visible Black presence, Trapper found himself surrounded by white neighbors. Most evenings, he returned to the center:

> I keep coming back here, Steve, because this is like home for me. They got some new centers over there, don't get me wrong, but they don't have dominoes in them. They got brand new centers where I go and exercise sometimes. I go swim. I go get the hot tubs and all of that. It's a lot better than this center here, 'cause all that stuff out there is new. But the reason I come over here every week is because most all these old guys, you know they're Black, and I kind of grew up around them.

But as Alim finds, Black residents can come to feel like "'strangers in their own land' due to the silent, yet sweeping, process of gentrification."[12] Donald, a seventy-eight-year-old regular at the card room, echoed a strong desire to socialize more within a Black space. He reminisced about growing up in Five Points, eventually moving to northeast Park Hill, and still longing for the days when he could mingle in one of its many Black bars and nightclubs, now closed. He spoke of Park Hill's soaring home values and the involuntary displacement of longtime neighbors. Donald described how the influx of young white residents shifted both the demographics and the atmosphere of these neighborhoods. Then, with a half-smile, he abruptly ended our conversation with, "Someone had the bright idea to integrate." It was his turn to join a game.

*Finding the Card Room*

As he explained it, Mr. Hall and most of the elders came to the card room for a singular purpose: to have fun in a place filled with other older Black men. "We come here every day, I ain't saying all of us, but 95 percent of us come here to have a good time, and laugh and joke, reminisce, cuss a little bit, talk about where you from, your background, where you're raised in. You have those laughs, then you go home."

The men tell me that the card room, a nondescript twenty-by-thirty-foot rectangular space, hasn't changed since Hiawatha Davis Recreation Center first opened its doors. The original commercial carpet squares still grace the floor. Two circular tables in front of the television serve distinct purposes: one is for pinochle games, the other doubles as a convenient spot for storing the TV remote and an assortment of snacks. That same table provides Derek a spot to rest his bare feet. A framed photo of former mayor Wellington Webb—Denver's first Black mayor—hangs on another wall, presumably in homage to his effort toward rebuilding the center. A small bulletin board holds a Denver Broncos football poster, Parks and Recreation announcements, a Chicken Shack menu, and funeral programs that rotate as men die. The television in the card room, which is always on, mostly plays basketball and football. If anything can momentarily divert attention away from a domino game, it is the collective thrill of watching the Denver Broncos score a touchdown or the Duke Blue Devils sink a winning basket.

Mr. Carr explained that the card room was one of the last remaining spaces for them to go for entertainment:

> Ain't nothing else to do. All the private clubs is gone now. There's not no more Masonic Lodges, the Elks, and the Masons. They used to have all kinds of activities going on, those guys. That's what my old lady don't understand. It'd just be boring. I'd probably stay home all the time, wouldn't go nowhere cause ain't nothing to do. See people don't do like they used to. I had friends you know, you go to his house and visit, just to play cards or visit the house, you know. But

FIG. 9. Barbershop. Steve Bialostok, photographer.

they don't do that no more so if you don't go to the center, you ain't got nothing to do.... Right now, the guys are really afraid that if we don't go over there, they'll wind up taking that room away from us. Where we won't have no place to play. Because you go to one of these other centers, you don't have no room like that.

Before joining the card room, many of the men had played dominoes in a Black barbershop down the block from the center—the kind that had red, white, and blue striped barber poles painted on the window.[13] The shop looked just as it did when it opened in the 1960s, offering haircuts during the day and dominoes after hours. When I began my research in 2015 no one cut hair there anymore, but dominoes continued there for several more years. Mr. Taylor remembered the first time he visited, encouraged by his ex-wife's suggestion after he stopped drinking and was searching for new social circles and something to do. He described what happened when he peered inside. Two barber chairs were visible in the front room, aprons draped over each chair. He looked past them to the small room in the back.

[There were] all these people, and they were all Black, and I was looking in the window and thinking, "Wow!" [Laugh] I hadn't seen that many darkies in a long time! [Laughs] And they all talked shit! "Come on in here and let's play some dominoes!" Now, I didn't know how to play dominoes. Nobody ever believed that. Nobody can believe that, being a Black man, you don't know how to play dominoes! They said, "You're Black. It's impossible for a Black man to come who doesn't know how to play dominoes." But a Black man don't have to be good at dominoes.

Having watched his first wife and her family play dominoes on a daily basis, Mr. Taylor already "knew the basics" by "sitting around and lookin'. You're gonna learn somethin' by lookin'." But the men in the barbershop were far superior players. Undaunted, he returned regularly, spending far more time standing and observing than playing. "If you lose that game, you may not play again for another hour or two. You may not play but two or three games a day. So," he laughed, "you better win." Some of the men had regular partners. But players who needed a partner "took a chance" on Mr. Taylor (much in the way that he took a chance on me). He realized that there was much to learn and felt it was his job to carefully observe the best player in the room, the one man who won game after game: Mr. Hall. "I said I'm gonna learn from him. I gonna figure why was he doing this? I didn't ask him nothing. Just watched him. . . . If you were interested in the game, you get interested in one player. At least *I* did. Instead of all four. I was interested in seeing what he was doing. Because he was winning most of the games. I don't wanna know what you done over here if you're losing."

Mr. Taylor saw the card room for the first time only after bringing his daughter to Hiawatha Davis to swim and run track. "You know how you guys come in there to look?" he said with a big grin, referring to me and my white brethren. "And you see a big room of colored folk? Loudest people in the building." He recalled George inviting him after spotting him outside. "Come on in here and play cards!" Despite his considerable amount of domino playing experience, pinochle remained Mr. Taylor's area of expertise. "The cards come automatically. You don't forget that game." It was only much later, when George needed a domino tournament partner, that Mr. Taylor partnered with him. Compared to the barbershop, the card room offered a more laid-back and enjoyable setting for domino play—one that still centered Black male presence and connection.

"We own that room," Mr. Taylor and others often reminded me. "We need a center in Colorado that's got a Black room. Think about that."

> STEVE: What does that mean to you?
>
> MR. TAYLOR: It means that we kind of forced our way in there. The reason we forced our way in there is Mr. Simmons [George] and all of the big employees when they first built this center. Swimming pool was outside. You remember?
>
> STEVE: Yeah, the swimming pool was outside. Yeah.
>
> MR. TAYLOR: And glass and debris and all that. Well, none of the white centers had the pools outside. People fought to get this stuff done, all of the work done, around here. They fought for it. They also fought for the control of that one room. And that was a good thing.
>
> STEVE: Well, that is important.
>
> MR. TAYLOR: It is because if you walk in there, you can see all of the track stars and things, and athletes, that have come through here. They actually built this place. They built it. They made it what it is. We should have some place to go that we can relax. . . .
>
> STEVE: What would happen [if you lost this]?
>
> MR. TAYLOR: What would happen? I hate to think of what would happen! 'Cause them people over there, they don't give a damn about us. They'll want it to be a little bit different. They'll want to be able to go in there, sit straight and erect, and everybody is: [imitating white people] "How are you?" "It's your move, Johnny." "Is your card game here?" "I'll play that one." They would like that. They don't want the flamboyance. We have rights, too, you know. We have, we don't have the right to say all the things we say, but we have the right to express ourselves the way that we are used to, accustomed to.

If the card room constituted an important space for the elders, there was no more important time to be in the card room than during the annual domino tournament.

## The Domino Tournament

As I mentioned in chapter 1, the annual domino tournament is the highlight of the year. The laughter, playfulness, and banter in the card room reach a crescendo during this monthlong spring event. It becomes a bustling hub, filled with nonregulars from all over the city who return to their old stomping grounds. The regulars greet these familiar faces by name, and the camaraderie among the men is infectious. The enthusiasm is palpable, with the sounds of dominoes slamming and playful trash talk echoing throughout the space. Some participants even arrive a week early to get in extra practice.

Coordinating the tournament is no small feat. Mr. Cummings cofounded the event in the 1960s and takes on the organizational heavy lifting. He reaches out to potential players, arranges teams and schedules, secures external funding, and coordinates the awards ceremony luncheon. The tournament resembles a domino version of NCAA college basketball's March Madness, complete with brackets indicating which teams move forward. The tournament is so important to the men that Mr. Cummings told me, "I don't care what's going on—[Denver] Nuggets could be playing basketball, Broncos could be playing football—dominoes gonna be playin'. No matter what. Somebody would say, 'What happened?' I'll see in a minute."

I observed my first tournament in 2015 during my first year at the center. A month before the tournament was set to begin, Denver Parks and Recreation shocked and dismayed everyone by transferring Dave, the much-beloved supervisor who had served Hiawatha Davis for nine years. A neighborhood resident since the 1970s, Dave had cultivated a family-like atmosphere that defined the center's identity as a genuine community hub where people cared for each other. Dave had also worked behind the scenes to ensure the annual domino tournament ran seamlessly. Together with Mr. Cummings, he created the illusion that nonpaying tournament participants could simply raise two fingers in the air to bypass the front desk and gain direct access to the card room. In reality, an annual contribution from a local nonprofit covered the entry fees for nonmembers, as well as the trophies and food expenses for the awards banquet.

After Dave's departure, Jerry, a seasoned Parks and Recreation employee, became the new supervisor. Jerry came in with a reputation for being difficult. His first mission was to formalize the informal system that Dave had run for years—not only for the tournament but for all aspects of the locally run center.

With Dave gone, Mr. Cummings found himself tasked with managing the tournament's logistics alongside an oppositional Jerry. During one meeting, I watched the two feud across the front desk—Jerry standing behind the counter and Mr. Cummings standing on the outside. Paul, a sixty-year-old card room regular, joined Mr. Cummings for support and tried to serve as a diplomat. But Jerry remained aloof and dismissive, preoccupied with accounting for each nonmember who walked through the door and how the room rental would be paid. Mr. Cummings tried to explain the funding source, but his explanation only seemed to confuse Jerry. Convinced that Jerry wanted to undermine the tournament, Mr. Cummings responded with anger and impatience. In the end, the two reached an impasse. Mr. Cummings and Paul returned to the card room, fuming in front of the packed room where regulars and many nonregulars were busy preparing for the upcoming tournament. It was a Tuesday, and someone had brought in a few buckets of Popeye's Chicken.

Mr. Cummings's account of the unsuccessful meeting transformed the atmosphere of cheerfulness and banter into an unusual silence, although dominoes continued without interruption. Then, a wave of collective anger swept over the room. "Jerry disrespected Mr. Cummings," Paul called out. "He called him an 'old man.'" Mr. Cummings let Paul talk. Paul's voice was high-pitched, hoarse, and animated. "He's doing it on *purpose*. Saying that we can't come in without a membership." Someone from across the room yelled, "I ain't paying for a membership for just two months." "We ain't never had to pay to come in," added someone else.

Paul explained how the nonprofit distributed funds: "The lady gives us the money. All he got to do is let her handle it."

"That's it. She's already been here," Mr. Cummings added. "Put things on the computer. That part is done."

"Just let her handle it. You know she know who to talk to," someone suggested.

"I just want to know what you guys think," said a disturbed Mr. Cummings. The tournament was only a couple of weeks away.

"We still playin'. He ain't runnin' nothing. He ain't changing nobody," said three men. Others offered similar reassurances, their concerns momentarily taking priority over their games. "It's a simple domino tournament. It's getting paid for," one said. "He's just making it difficult. That's all he's doing," said another.

"They can't come in unless they buy a card," said Paul.

Then Mr. Buford voiced the sentiment that led the others to *uh-huh* and nod in agreement: "They're trying to take this room."

"They always be trying to take this room from us."

After that declaration, most of the men resumed their games, while others collectively recalled the center's history:

"Shit. This place used to be our babysitter. I used to play football up here in this rec center before they changed the name."

"This is *Skyland*. It wasn't no Hiawatha Davis. That's how long I been coming in."

"We been coming here since we was kids."

"I came here since '65. That Black man up there just *got* here."

"Hey, man. Do you remember when they had the swimming pool outside?"

A determined Mr. Cummings came to a decision. "I'm gonna tell you guys right now. Here's what I'm going to do. We're gonna still have it."

Jerry had managed to complicate a straightforward issue with unnecessary bureaucracy. Once Parks and Recreation responded to multiple complaints, the tournament went on without Jerry's supervision. But the misunderstanding had exposed the elders' latent concerns about encroachment and change and their concerns over the future of the card room. The men reacted similarly, echoing a shared sentiment: *This used to be my place. I used to fit in. I used to be an insider. Long ago, I felt I belonged.* Even their references to the center's name change—from

Skyland to Hiawatha Davis—suggested a sense of removal. Despite the nourishment and refuge the card room provided, it could not fully resolve their fears and the reality of displacement. As Moten puts it, "The whole point about escape is that it's like an activity; it's not an achievement. You don't ever get escaped."[14] I watched as the elders worked hard to preserve the mental and emotional "escape" the card room provided. But they knew change was all around them.

*Demographic Changes at the Center:*
*Further Erosion of Black Space and Community*

These changes occurred so gradually, especially from 2018 onward, that they initially went unnoticed by me. But the all-male, middle-aged staff working behind the front counter noticed. They had a special fondness for the young people who came in, often buying them after-school meals with their own money. They intervened during conflicts, occasionally coached basketball in the gym, and enjoyed games of pool and ping pong in the nearby youth lounge. The staff expressed concern about the shrinking number of young people and the simultaneous reduction in youth sports programming. They also noted that interactions with white patrons, while polite, felt more formal and, as Eli put it, "not as fun." Like Bob, staff members wondered what had happened to the men who used to show up in the weight room around five o'clock. They also observed a growing trend of predominantly white patrons using the ellipticals, bikes, treadmills, and rowing machines. In my ceramics class, Linda bemoaned the removal of rap music from the weight room, supposedly due to complaints from white patrons. But the weight room didn't actually have a music system. Linda's concern, though inaccurate, revealed the significant role that Black music played in helping her affirm her identity and engage in Black placemaking. It made her feel like she belonged.

A minor uproar followed when Parks and Recreation replaced Michael, the Black Silver Sneakers instructor, with a white instructor. Though she was skilled at guiding older adults through exercises, on her first day she chose Neil Sedaka's "Love Will Keep Us Together" for the warm-up. Within a year, attendance shifted to mostly white participants. I felt a sense of loss when an older gentleman in the locker room, who used to sing rhythm and blues songs while changing, stopped singing altogether as more white men filled the space. I missed his rendition of Etta James's "At Last."

As the number of white members grew, it became evident that Black and white patrons perceived the center's purpose differently. As in Bob's depiction, the Olympic-sized swimming pool became a symbol of personal enjoyment. Similarly, white members showed up for exercise, their children's swimming activities, or sports participation—mostly with an individualized focus. Conversely, Black patrons regarded the center as an extension of their social lives—a space for community—even when visiting for a specific purpose. This was particularly evident among the elders who, while intending to play dominoes, also highly valued social interaction. Like the "yelling" and "hollering" that Bob heard in the weight room, the noise in the card room was an audible expression of the intricate interplay of personalities, ideas, and emotions—this unique symphony that fostered community life.

But the room also became the constant object of the white gaze. Grover brought this to my attention when he said across the room for everyone to hear, "Steve! You notice that white people walk by and look in, but they never come inside?" Until then, I had not noticed how frequently white individuals cast brisk glances inside, whether while passing the always-open door or briefly peering through the windows. The observers slowed down just long enough to glance inside (as I had once done), but they refrained from entering. The only exception was when a young white man paused at the door to catch a glimpse of the March Madness finals on TV. He resisted several repeated offers to watch from inside. "I'm fine," he said, standing at the door. However, to obtain a better look, he took one giant step inward, keeping his other foot tethered to the entrance. "Come on in," Grover insisted. The man repeated that he was "okay" and left a moment later. No one saw him again. The men thought that his refusing to enter was dismissive but laughed off his behavior.

The awareness of being observed was not a novel sensation. During the decades when the men played dominoes in the kitchen, beginning in the 1960s, a comparable trend had surfaced. White patrons who had exclusively frequented the (then) outdoor swimming pool had also perceived Skyland Recreation Center as divided. One evening I spoke with several elders who, like Mr. Cummings, had been Skyland domino pioneers. "White people would come in here and be gone just as fast as they could swim," Tom said. Marlen, a longtimer, added, "We wondered, why is it that Black people come in and go left [toward the kitchen, weight room, and basketball court] and the white people come in and go right?" Edward concurred: "We saw it all the time. They were going to the pool. They didn't wanna hear all that noise that we was talking about." Frank recalled that the management had grown increasingly concerned about how loud they sounded slamming their dominoes and talking shit. "The city wanted all commotion, loud disturbances, anything, away from the front door discouraging the paying customers," he remembered. "One evening the center's manager came in and told everyone, 'Quit slamming dominoes or you're going to have to leave.' He said they needed to quiet down for the members. 'That means white people, right?'" Edward described how the men became defiant and resisted. "Every motherfucker that played was slamming dominoes after that, just to make a point. That didn't work at all." Management eventually placed the men in the arts and crafts room at the back of the building—which, Edward said, "was really small. The room only had long tables. They finally changed the tables out so you could have more than one game at a time. They closed the door. You had to close the door." Shifting the men to the back room conjured an image, as Frank told me, "Like putting us to the back of the bus."

*Conclusion*

The city of Denver has experienced significant racial shifts throughout its history and into the twenty-first century. Just like neighborhoods that were once segregated as white-only, then became majority Black and are now undergoing gentrification, the Skyland-turned-Hiawatha Davis Recreation Center at the heart of the Holly is shifting as well. The older Black men who helped found and protect the card room and its activities—including the annual domino tournament—are engaged in the ongoing practice of Black placemaking: a dynamic effort that not only confronts the historical legacies of oppression they have faced but also propels them toward self-determination and collective empowerment in their struggle for belonging in their own spaces.

The card room was something they had fought for—an anchor against the tides of change reshaping their neighborhood. The men didn't always know each other's full stories, but the space itself held a shared sense of belonging—sustained by the rhythms of domino games, the slamming of bones, and the constant exchange of playful talk. One of the most beloved among them was Mr. Carr, whose life reflected many of the same struggles and triumphs that shaped the community around him. In the next chapter, I turn to Mr. Carr's story—not only as a reflection of one man's journey, but as a window into the enduring presence of Black spaces like the card room. Then, in chapter 8, I shift focus to one of the card room's central and most enjoyable practices: talking shit. This verbal play offers more than amusement—it serves as a crucial daily ritual through which these Black men build community, navigate resilience, and claim space for themselves in a city that continues to change around them.

# 7    Herman Carr

The Carrs and I lived so close that I'd occasionally drop by unannounced. I was always graciously welcomed. One afternoon, Mrs. Carr pointed to the spare bedroom, where Mr. Carr sat at the head of the bed with his feet on the floor, watching football on a small television. With no chair in the room, I sat on the edge of the bed, noticing the medicine bottles scattered across the dresser. Whether Mr. Carr's longevity and mental clarity were thanks to those pills or the genetics of his mother—who had lived to 112—was anyone's guess. Eventually, I grew uncomfortable and slowly reclined on my side. There I was, chatting with Mr. Carr in bed.

But more often, we spoke at his dining room table, usually with his wife. They had lived in their cozy North Park Hill home, which was filled with framed family photos scattered across small tables, for six decades. Mrs. Carr always set out bowls of fresh fruit, though she'd often say, "Herman barely touches any of it." She knew that when her husband went to the center, he ate pork rinds, whole bags of Cheetos, and cans of salted peanuts. But how could you complain about the dietary habits of a man who was still alive at ninety?

*Glory Road*

The first time I saw Mr. Carr, I found his looks dazzling. He was much stockier than I imagined a ninety-year-old to be. A knee operation had reduced his 6'2" frame by a couple of inches. That and his slightly slouching walk were his most obvious signs of age. His smooth skin resembled that of someone much younger. He tried to color his wavy hair silver, but it always came out purple—inspiring his card room nickname, "Purple Rain." Yet his sideburns remained an age-appropriate gray.

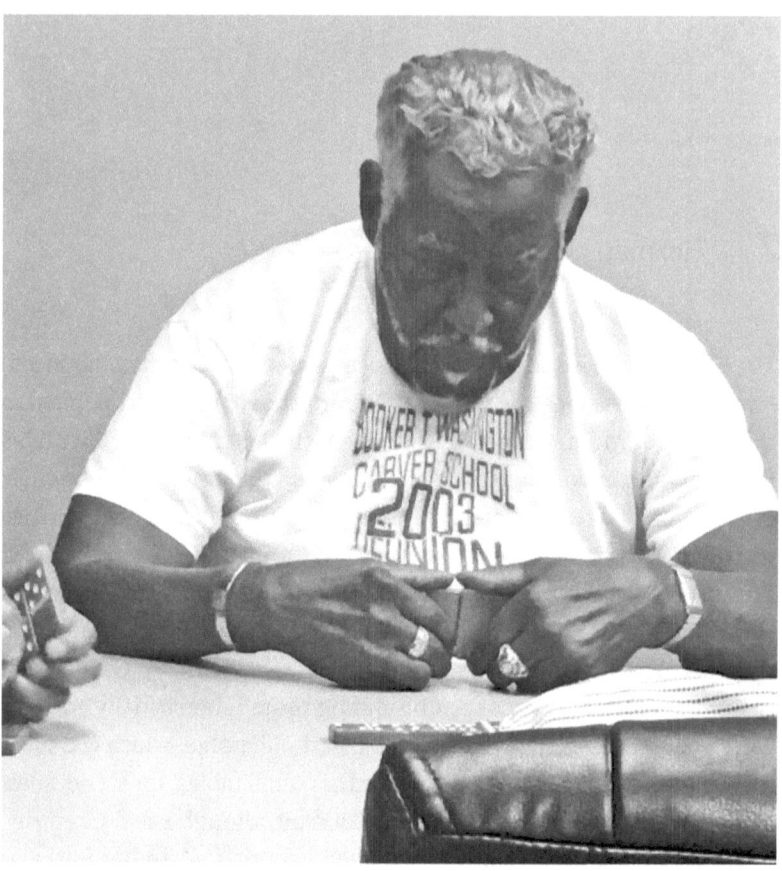

FIG. 10. Mr. Carr. Steve Bialostok, photographer.

Mr. Carr's slightly arched posture belied his youthful basketball physique, which I could see in photos on the walls. Don Haskins, the famed basketball coach for Texas Western (now University of Texas at El Paso), spoke of their high school friendship in his book *Glory Road*: "Herman . . . could not only outjump and outrun me, but outthink me on the court. . . . Herman Carr was the best basketball player in Enid."[1] At fifteen, Herman Carr had befriended the future coach at a feed store where they both had summer jobs. Haskins described their early friendship as filled with contests over who could lift more hundred-pound sacks.

Haskins went on to tell Mr. Carr's story: "No one named him All-Star, no colleges came to recruit him, because he was black. This was

1948. It was as if he didn't even exist. Yeah, I had no idea how this could happen. Herman was plenty smart enough to go to college."[2] Mr. Carr responded matter-of-factly when I read him that passage. "It [going to college] never dawned on me. *Never* dawned on me."

Haskins's sole Black high school friend contributed to his perception of the players he later trained. The white coach made sports history by starting five Black players in a championship game against an all-white Kentucky squad, and he brought Mr. and Mrs. Carr to many events related to his book. Haskins wrote that he "didn't recall a lot of overt racism in Enid back then" in that there "weren't any lynchings or anything like that."[3] But his sentence that "the town was segregated" doesn't approach the depth of the racial segregation that Mr. Carr recalled: "I was in high school when I met Don and I don't know, it's a funny thing, when nobody be on that school ground but just me and him, we'd be up there playing basketball, we'd be playing one-on-one and we just communicated. He'd know, he knew I was Black and he was white and we wasn't supposed to associate with each other."

I was curious about what Mr. Carr thought about the way Haskins had recognized him in his book. "He credited me for a lot of stuff in that book," he said. "Yeah. Well, I don't know. He had to let you know he wasn't prejudiced, too." Mr. Carr wanted me to understand that despite the friendship that had extended into adulthood, their profoundly different backgrounds meant Haskins couldn't truly grasp the experience of growing up Black in Enid.

*Herman Carr's Enid*

Descended from a family that had been enslaved, Herman Carr was born in 1928 on a cotton plantation in Arkansas where his father was a sharecropper. Five years later, an uncle brought the entire family—his mother, father, an older brother, and two younger brothers—to Enid, a town of about twenty-seven thousand in northern Oklahoma. Mr. Carr's mother lived with and worked as a cook for a white family who owned both a dairy farm and an oil company, and she spent her entire life in their service. Herman would eventually have six brothers and a sister. His parents separated when he was twelve. The boys lived with their father, who worked at a filling station.

Oklahoma passed eighteen Jim Crow laws between 1880 and 1957. Mr. Carr recalled the warnings, the signs, the segregation of his school, the "white" and "colored" water fountains, people he could and couldn't look at walking down the street:

> I got it from conversations, and my parents. "You ain't supposed to go here," and "You ain't supposed to do this here," so that if you walkin' down the sidewalk, you move right away and let them, let the white people by, you know, and now they call you a nigger, you just ignore it. . . . But the kids didn't do that. It was the grown-ups. . . . [S]ome white people was pretty good. If there weren't no good white people during that time, it wouldn't have been no Black people, 'cause they'd have killed them all.

Herman Carr was twenty-seven years old when Emmett Till was brutally murdered in Mississippi after an encounter with a white woman who, on her deathbed, recanted her accusation that he had flirted with her. Herman understood the consequences of even being friendly to a white girl, let alone flirtatious, in a state where interracial marriage was illegal.[4]

In the seventh grade, the tall, athletic teenager began playing varsity basketball, which continued throughout high school. He also made the all-state football team. But after graduating, he was eager to leave his hometown, and the U.S. Army made that possible, drafting him in October 1949. Leaving behind a child he had fathered while in high school to the care of his own mother, Herman departed for basic training and was eventually shipped to the Japanese island of Okinawa.

## Military Loyalty and Old Wounds

"I *liked* the service," Mr. Carr told me proudly. He often displayed evidence of his four years on Okinawa during the Korean War. On the back of his windbreaker, "United States Army" was inscribed above the American eagle logo. But talking about that period of his life also brought to the surface wounds of racial injustice.

> I got busted from staff sergeant to private. They took all of my stripes and they busted me for inefficiency. . . . Well, because me and the lieu-

tenant got into it, tell you the truth, that's what started it. He was a master sergeant and he goes out on this road once.... [W]e marching behind everything, and he got a flashlight turning on by the step, you know? He told me, "Sergeant Carr, somebody's out of step." And you can't even see it 'cause it's dark. I said, "Go fuck yourself." I did. He tell me that I ain't gonna see the light as long as I'm in this outfit.... They said I showed disrespect toward an officer, and when I went out, I slammed the door.... They couldn't put me in the stockade, but they bust me from a staff sergeant to a private E-1. I left as a private E-1 but I transferred out of that outfit.... I made PFC back in the other outfit and I was up for corporal before I got discharged.

One might view the outcome as typical for the military. However, Mr. Carr framed the incident in racial terms—a conflict between a Black staff sergeant and a white sergeant. The proof, he argued, was that he would have been promoted to corporal after being transferred, had he not been honorably discharged.

*Marriage . . . and Hanging Out*

Herman returned to Enid after leaving the military and worked there for several years before his cousin, a Denver resident, visited and suggested that they go to Denver together. "I wasn't doing nothin' but runnin' wild," he said. So he moved to Denver to seek a new life. His mother continued to raise his young son alongside the boy's mother.

Herman enjoyed his early days in Denver, especially Five Points. However, Mrs. Carr offered her own explanation for his decision to move there. They had met in an Enid restaurant when she was sixteen. "Well," Mrs. Carr said, "I didn't think he was as old as he was and he thought I was older than I was . . . and somebody else told me how old. I couldn't believe it. Twelve years older than me." After graduating from high school, she moved to Denver to be near her sisters. "You *followed* her?" I asked Mr. Carr, recognizing that Mrs. Carr was a charmer in her own way. "He wouldn't admit that if he had a gun to his head," she said.

The two married in 1959 and rented an apartment in Northeast Park Hill, close to Holly Square, and then moved to a nearby subdivided home. Nemiah Wilson lived next door when he played football for the

Denver Broncos. In 1970, after working eight years for the post office, Mr. Carr decided "to get me a house, and it's gonna have a basement." North Park Hill fit the bill.

During those years, Herman enjoyed socializing around Five Points. Shooting dice and "after hours" drinking were key forms of recreation, as Useni Perkins noted in *Home Is a Dirty Street*. The "streets"—corner bars, clubs, pool rooms, after-hour joints, and so forth—formed a social institution "in the same way that the church, school, and family are conceived as institutions."[5]

But when you're ninety, the International House of Pancakes is among the best places to hang out, and that's where Mr. Carr, Mr. Taylor, and I regularly ate breakfast together. One morning, over pancakes and bacon, Mr. Carr reminisced about his days working graveyard hours at the post office as a maintenance supervisor. He then went on to discuss what Anderson J. Franklin described as "brotherhood rites of passage and activities."[6]

"I'd get off work at 7:30 a.m., then we'd go open up the liquor store at 8:00. Then I'd drink till I got tired, and then I'd go home and go to bed."

"Did you drink to go to sleep or just because it was fun?" I asked.

"I call myself socializing. Socializing!" Mr. Carr insisted. He thoroughly enjoyed the clubs on Welton Street, once the central hub of Black culture and commerce in the Rocky Mountain West. By the time he was hanging out in his friend's shoe-shining parlor, Five Points was in decline. But Welton Street, with its bars, clubs, and some remaining retail, remained a Black destination. White bars outside Five Points were hardly welcoming to Black patrons, deemed to be "bodies out of place."[7]

After he turned fifty, Mr. Carr began joining his wife at church regularly. "I tried to be a gentleman and got baptized and went to church every Sunday. Quit drinking. Later on, I quit smoking." The Carrs attended a nearby church where he still served as a deacon. I asked what he thought of his lengthy marriage. "See," he explained, "I been with my wife for sixty years in March. Sixty years with one woman in March. Now, I ain't gon' say *with* one woman. I've been *married* sixty years to one woman in March."

*Heartbreak*

Mr. Carr also spoke of his son Shelton's brief life. Shelton Delano Carr was born in February of 1966 and died in July. They found the infant lying face down in his crib, not breathing. "Herman crawled on the floor," despondent, Mrs. Carr said in a separate conversation. Mr. Carr confessed, "I didn't go to work for a week. I drank every day, man. Even down at the funeral. At the funeral, I was drunk."

A framed photo of Shelton rested on a small end table in their living room, nestled among other pictures. In the photo, a healthy-looking Shelton sat propped up by a fluffy white pillow, wearing white pajamas decorated with panda bears.

Mr. Carr mentioned Shelton's name in the present tense. "Our son's name is Shelton Delano Carr." "I just can't imagine how you feel," I said, though I could tell it was too painful for him to discuss. He quickly shifted the conversation, talking about his other children. If Mr. Carr's drinking escalated after the sudden and unexpected tragedy of losing a child, he evidently got it under control. If their marriage suffered, the loss of their child didn't lead to its collapse. A sign affixed to their front door read, "Warning: This property is protected by JESUS CHRIST." Shelton's death didn't shatter their faith.

*Herman Carr and Don Haskins*

Mr. and Mrs. Carr happily recount the many places they've traveled in the United States, but their trip to Washington DC remains the most memorable. "Do you want to have dinner at the White House?" Mr. Carr asked Mrs. Carr one day while she was at work. He had just finished a phone conversation with Don Haskins. It was 2006, the year the Disney movie *Glory Road*—based on the book—was released in theaters, forty years after Texas Western made college sports history. The team, the first to win the NCAA title with five Black starters, was featured on a Wheaties cereal box. Haskins and the remaining team members had been invited by President George W. Bush for dinner and a screening of the film. In the Carrs' living room, a framed photo of the two with George and Laura Bush sat on a small table among other pictures. The Carrs were dressed to the nines.

Haskins and Mr. Carr remained in touch over the years. When Haskins died in 2008 at the age of seventy-eight, a National Public Radio sports correspondent reached out for comments from Mr. Carr, who reflected on Haskins's true racial awakening. "When it really hit him, you know, is when he found out that I couldn't drink out of the same water fountain that he drank out of."[8]

*The Card Room: Competition and Friendship*

After years of playing dominoes at the barbershop, Mr. Carr was introduced to the card room by a coworker. "I looked around, and I see one guy I know, and see another guy that I know in there. I just joined."

Mr. Carr split his time playing dominoes between the elders and the youngsters. He enjoyed the card room's sociability, but he appeared slightly more competitive than the other elders. He wanted to "figure out how to beat someone that can beat me." His only complaint about the youngsters was all the talking they did. "I like to concentrate on what I'm doing when I'm playing dominoes." When asked if he was one of the best players, he replied modestly but confidently, "I think I can play as good as anybody." Mr. Carr remembered details from games long ago—just as he recalled dates, names, events, and his favorite egg-salad sandwich from his twenties at Sanford's drugstore.

It's nearly impossible to think of Mr. Carr in the card room without Mr. Taylor. The two first met playing dominoes at the barbershop. "We was playing," Mr. Taylor told me, "and I started teasing him and it starts up. 'Where'd you get that funny-looking hair?' He was *known* by that purple hair. But we never got into any arguments. We just started teasing each other."

Mr. Carr rarely talked shit during a game, but he and Mr. Taylor often exchanged shit talk between games, especially while Mr. Carr relaxed in his high-back chair. These moments seemed perfect opportunities for Mr. Taylor to publicly get under Mr. Carr's skin in a way that he never did with other elders. One evening, Mr. Taylor taunted him by claiming to be the superior player.

"George taught me everything," said Mr. Taylor, looking at the TV.

"George taught *you*? He didn't teach you much," Mr. Carr replied, munching pork rinds.

Insult hurled; insult reciprocated. Several men sitting within earshot burst into laughter.

One night, when the three of us met at the nearby Popeyes Louisiana Kitchen, Mr. Taylor told a story about their recent emergency trip to Walmart for Mr. Carr's asthma inhaler. "The other day, he called me. He says, 'I've got one puff left.' I asked him, 'Well, why don't you hurry up and take it!?' He started laughing and says, 'I need to go to the store!' I drove the truck right up in the damn Walmart. And that's how he got his puffs." Mr. Taylor's story was revealing, indicating that their relationship was built on mutual comfort, trust, and care.

"He wanted *you* to take him," I said to Mr. Taylor as we sat later in his home, the television blaring *Gunsmoke*.

"Yeah, but that's too close," said Mr. Taylor. "One puff left?"

"Sometimes," I replied, "I think if we have a close friend, they mean more to us than maybe our most immediate family." At the time, Mr. Taylor rebuffed my observation, claiming instead that "something I'm very short on is friends."

*"I'm Very Short of Friends"*

On the morning of March 23, 2019, Mr. Taylor sent me a text: "Mr. Carr passed away sometime yesterday. I hope to visit the family later today." After he called to say that Mrs. Carr had asked if *I* knew, I decided to head over to their home. "I'm so sorry," I said when Mrs. Carr answered my knock. We hugged, and she explained what had transpired. On Wednesday morning, after noticing his abnormally swollen legs, she had called 911 against his wishes. An ambulance rushed him to the hospital, and he died that afternoon.

I had imagined that Mr. Carr was generally healthy, but Mrs. Carr said, "He had a lot of things wrong with him." She kept repeating, "It's still hard to believe he's gone . . . I was so sure he was coming back home . . . we were married sixty years on the third of this month . . . it seems like a bad dream." I started to speak, but my voice broke. "I'm sorry, Steve," she said. "I didn't know what I was gonna do with 'im. I dunno what am I gonna do without 'im. I really don't. He's been my life. So many years."

I returned the following evening to find the house filled with family. Mr. Carr's two sons from Oklahoma had flown in. We talked about

FIG. 11. Author and Mr. Taylor, pallbearers. Photographer unknown. Courtesy of author.

dominoes. "Did he teach you to play?" I asked. "Yeah," one son replied, "and we're good. Dominoes was something the family passed down."

Mr. Taylor would be one of the pallbearers. I was asked to be the sixth, and while I said that I would be honored I also felt that others had known him longer. But Mr. Carr's family insisted. His youngest son told me, "I just want you to know that you were one of the very, very few people who would come and spend time with him."

A couple of days before the funeral, I stopped by the card room. The only sign that Mr. Carr had passed away was the sympathy card Trapper had brought for the men to sign and send to his wife, whom they had never met. "May God bless the family, our brother, gone home," someone signed. "May God give you the strength. He was a great man," someone else wrote. Other comments read: "Rest in Heaven"; "Sorry for your loss. God Bless"; "So sorry. My heart is broken for you." As the card was being passed around, Derek walked in. "Who died?" he asked, and when he heard the answer, he stood frozen. "Herman?" he repeated, as if trying to convince himself it wasn't true. "Herman dead?" was all he said. He asked no further questions. Eventually, he sat in his usual spot in front of the television, staring off a bit vacantly. A half-hour later, Derek left. No one said anything more about Mr. Carr's death. The men just went on playing.

On the morning of the funeral, I parked across from the church. Funeral home attendants joined the family and the pallbearers in the lobby, then directed us to begin the slow, synchronized procession down the aisle. Three hours after the service began, mourners lined up to say goodbye to Mr. Carr. I passed by my friend one final time. There he was, dressed in the same cream-colored two-piece stripe suit he'd worn at the Carr family reunion that I attended a year earlier—a classy dresser to the end. As I write this, my eyes still well up with tears. I cared about him in a way that I could never have imagined when I began my research.

Mr. Carr's burial was scheduled for Monday, but since that was my teaching day, I couldn't attend. That afternoon Mr. Taylor sent me a text. "I'm very short of friends," he wrote. "You pointed out to me that I have one, and it was Mr. Carr. I struggled with accepting him as a friend, but now I know in my heart that we were truly friends."

"I'm certain he knew that," I wrote back. "And I know how painful this is for you."

"Thanks," he responded. "I will keep that in mind as I travel a difficult path."

# 8   Talking Shit inside the Card Room

Ethnographers are often drawn into their research topics, and while I was interested in the elders' games of pinochle and dominoes, I became especially fascinated by the shit talk that accompanied their play. The men's rhythm, stress, and variations in pitch captured my attention. I was struck by the articulatory stress of certain words. For example, in the often uttered, "That's how you make ten," they emphasized "that's" rather than "ten." The way they chose to stress the word "that's" emphasized their power and their agency. Before long, I found myself paying close attention to the men's linguistic interactions, noting how what sounded (to me) like rough-and-tumble exchanges could suddenly shift to laughter. Their fast-paced energy and palpable camaraderie was mesmerizing. In this chapter, I seek to unpack and celebrate the joy, pleasure, nostalgia, and spiritual rhythms embedded in shit talk. I examine it as a repository of cultural heritage, verbal tradition, and social cohesion.

*Rhetorical Features of Shit Talk*

Talking shit is a well-established social activity in many Black speech communities and has garnered attention from folklorists, sociolinguists, and sociologists.[1] Some scholars, such as Henry Louis Gates, place *talking shit* within the broad genre of *signifying*, which involves using indirect language or gestures to convey underlying meanings or messages.[2] Talking shit, especially with its humorously confrontational, vulgar, and sometimes sexualized insults, is a verbal practice that upholds traditional notions of male competitiveness and bravado.[3] It also showcases stereotypical masculine traits like toughness, resilience, and the ability to withstand pressure. The concept of having a "tough skin" aligns with these expectations and with the cultural ideal that a "real man" can face

FIG. 12. Mr. Carr, Mr. Taylor, Mr. Buford, Grover, and D-Ray. Steve Bialostok, photographer.

adversity head-on without allowing external critiques to undermine his self-confidence or provoke him to show emotion.[4] In this context, laughter—rather than taking insult or getting agitated—is always the best response.

As the elders accompany their game of dominoes with shit talking, most voices grow loud and confrontational, but their interactions lack genuine tension. Like other similar verbal rituals, shit talk carries deep cultural and social significance and plays a crucial role in shaping the card room as a Black place. Even a cursory analysis of their exchanges reveals the elders' "jousting" as playful. However, for their talk to function effectively as play, "there must be a sense of threat arising from the 'real' and 'serious' world of behavior."[5] Just as in real jousting, verbal barbs mimic an attack. Their play treads the boundaries of reality, evoking a sense of threat, and skillfully conveying the impression—through near-perfect simulation—that the unfolding scenario is authentic, despite its nonserious nature.[6] To explore the significance of their banter and give shit talking the proper analysis it merits, I include here transcriptions of recorded interactions in the card room.[7]

Here is a typical example of shit talking among Mr. Hall, D-Ray, Mr. Buford, and Grover:

MR. HALL: Pass.
D-RAY: His little fat—
MR. BUFORD: Five.
GROVER: Bitch.
D-RAY: That ain't nothing.
MR. BUFORD: He grabbed.
D-RAY: Like he got something.
MR. HALL: [Placing tile] Twenty-five.
D-RAY: I got some nuts over here. You wanna grab some nuts?
MR. BUFORD: You grabbing motherfucker. Pull out your teeth.
GROVER: Pull out the what?
MR. BUFORD: Pull your teeth out and start gummin.
MR. HALL: [Laughs]
D-RAY: Y'all got y'all's laugh for the night. I'm through with it.
MR. BUFORD: Come on, gumming motherfucker.
GROVER: That's a young man, man. He got all his teeth, man.
MR. HALL: Domino!

While all the men in the card room embrace talking shit, my five participants each bring a distinct style to the table. Mr. Buford and D-Ray most consistently use language that would be considered obscene. On the other hand, Mr. Hall, though he derives great pleasure and laughs heartily at the banter, mostly refrains from using such language himself. Instead, he focuses on game-related language such as declaring points and announcing wins. However, an emphatic declaration of "domino" carries significant weight. By calling out "domino," Mr. Hall not only decisively ends the game but also effectively closes the play-frame, signaling the close of their shit talk.

Talking shit is part of a verbal tradition that blends spontaneous self-expression, spirited intensity, humor, and sociability.[8] As part of a ritual interaction, it follows a repetitively rehearsed sequence with predetermined expectations, even as participants improvise. Talking shit is characterized by two simultaneous rhetorical features. First, there is a noticeable increase in acoustic intensity. This heightened volume might be followed by a moment of silence, which is then followed by collective laughter. Second, speakers are rewarded for comments that are provocative, clever, and off-color.[9] Some exchanges can be described as adjacency pairs, where two turns are produced by different speakers placed adjacently, where the second utterance is dependent on the first. For example:

> MR. TAYLOR: These guys are as easy as Sunday morning.
> JAMAL: Like Sunday morning.

At other times, a single spontaneous playful utterance is shared out loud but directed at no one in particular. In the example below, as Mr. Taylor narrates the game he is playing, he refers to himself in the third person, squealing with delight: "Now, he come all around the back route again. He didn't want to take his money. [Seventeen-second pause] Watch him. Watch him. Watch him. WOW. HOO HOO. HOO HOO HOO HOO. LOOK AT IT. LOOK AT IT [ecstatic voice pitched high, nearly squeaky]. Do you see what I see? See what I see?"

Much shit talk is delivered indirectly, even when the intended target is sitting right there.[10] In the next two examples, Mr. Buford refers to D-Ray, sitting across from him, in the third person. Then, Trapper speaks indirectly to Mr. Hall, who is playing immediately to his left:

> BUFORD: D-Ray can go fuck himself and an old sideliner can go with him.
> TRAPPER: Charlie Hall trying to rob something that don't belong to him.

Not every verbal assault elicits a direct response. Although D-Ray responded to Mr. Buford, Mr. Hall's face showed no reaction. It is also important to note that not all talk during a game qualifies as shit talk. To simplify, I identify shit talk as anything that carries a playful tone, while anything lacking that tone isn't considered tough talk. For example, the following exchange between Trapper and Mr. Taylor is *not* shit talk. Trapper looks over the tiles on the table, verbally determining his next move. There's no obvious reason why Trapper refers to Mr. Taylor specifically, other than he always directs his remarks to an opposing player. Trapper's talk is grounded in the real world, as if he momentarily steps out of the play-frame to think aloud about his next move. There is no "playful" tone or intent involved:

> TRAPPER: I'm gonna see it like this, Taylor. No, I better not do that. I'm just set up, that's why I play it like that. I hate to play it like that, I'm gonna get off anyway. [Places tile]
> MR. TAYLOR: Right there? [A subtle *Do you know what you're doing?* or *Why you gonna fuck things up with that?*]
> TRAPPER: Yeah.

Mr. Taylor once drew a parallel between the colloquial term "talking shit" and the traditional Black verbal game known as "playing the dozens," which involves exchanging insults about one another's family members.[11] During a game of dominoes, however, there is little reason or occasion to directly insult someone's family. Nor is talking shit competitive in the same way as playing the dozens. The elder's fundamental purpose when talking shit is general amusement. To repeat Grover's assertion, "It's no fun if you don't talk shit." Despite the absence of familial insults, the spirited banter involves plenty of pointed and teasing verbal jabs. But even when things get intense, because the men frame it as play, I never observed their banter to escalate into confrontation.

Johan Huizinga's *Homo Ludens* suggests that during playful encounters, participants create a "magic circle" that marks certain actions as nonserious within a designated space. In other words, within this play-frame, elders engage in a unique form of ritualized play, with the card room serving as their designated playground.[12] The elders' shit talk can be seen as a series of "playful nips," exchanged purely for the enjoyment of the interaction.[13] They eagerly anticipate the absurd and enthusiastically embrace the unconventional dialogue. Within the play-frame, where concerns from everyday life are largely excluded, shit talk fosters a camaraderie built on familiarity and trust.[14] Even as the elders insult each other, they subtly convey, "We understand each other."

*When Youngsters Talk Shit*

Although the elders were my primary focus, I occasionally engaged with a few of the younger players, such as Grover and Freddie. Like Grover, Freddie is in fifties. I first encountered Freddie as I walked my dog past his home, two blocks away from mine. He had resided there since the 1970s, when North Park Hill was predominantly Black. Freddie had a robust, muscular physique adorned with tattoos. Whenever I saw him, he wore a sideways cap and a T-shirt. His full, graying beard complemented his confident, strong everyday voice. When Freddie talked shit, his voice transformed into an amplified version of itself, exuding a vibrancy that might be daunting to those unaccustomed to his expressive capacity. In contrast, Grover, taller than Freddie, kept a clean-shaven look and, true to his trademark style, wore his black cap backward. Grover always exuded a casual demeanor. He had a quick wit, an easygoing nature, and an ability to attract attention. His everyday speech, softer than Freddie's, often involved smart-ass remarks, punctuated by his signature cackle.

The excerpt from Freddie and Grover's domino game that follows exemplifies the distinctive style of play and banter among these younger participants. Freddie adopted what Anderson terms a "cool pose," characterized by a deliberate and conspicuous demeanor that conveyed fearlessness through his speech, gesture, stance, and other physical expressions.[15] In contrast, Grover appeared more relaxed, frequently smiling and ready to engage in banter. Both men projected a tough exterior. In this particular domino game, Grover and Freddie found themselves on opposing teams, with Will as Grover's partner and Lonnie as Freddie's, though Lonnie remained silent during this exchange. The excerpt unfolded after the game commenced, with Will confidently slamming down a domino tile and assertively declaring the total: "Five." Unable to match any domino on the table, Freddie leaned in, placed his elbow on the table, turned to Grover, pointed his finger at him, and glared.

> FREDDIE: Yo *play*. [As if Grover was not acting fast enough]
> GROVER: Did you pass? [Surprised]
> FREDDIE: [Looking at Grover directly in the eyes and motioning with his hands] Do you have that many dominoes that you can't

play? [Sounding accusatory] You got *two* dominoes. [Holds up two fingers]

GROVER: You passed.

FREDDIE: Pass. [Gestures with his right hand that it's now Grover's turn]

GROVER: Okay, then why are you still talkin' to me? [Sarcastic and spoken as Freddie grins dismissively and turns away. Grover turns to Freddie's partner sitting on Grover's left] Your play. *Get* to the table. [An order]

Napoleon—in his late seventies and a semi-regular—sat at the adjacent elders' table playing dominoes with Mr. Hall, Mr. Taylor, and Mr. Buford. In response to his own play, he uttered a satisfied, "Yeah-eah . . . eah . . . eah," spoken between Grover's "Your play" and "Get to the table." After Will passed, Freddie slammed down a domino with a force to match the intensity of his voice.

FREDDIE: [Directed toward Freddie's opponent, Will, sitting to his right] Fifteen. Shut up. It don't matter what he got. Where's your goose leg now, chump?

WILL: I just took that.

FREDDIE: What's the score?

WILL: One-one.

FREDDIE: Oh, okay. [As Grover studies his hand] What is wrong wichoo?! What is it that we have to do to get you to play?

When I presented a video of Grover and Freddie engaged in a game of dominoes to my predominantly white mainstream university students, they were surprised to learn that the two were actually close, rather than mere adversaries. Freddie and Grover skillfully blurred the boundaries between real aggression and play, which Gregory Nikon notes is the point: for their play to successfully function *as* play, "the most constant message must be the deeply ambivalent one: this is play—is this play?"[16] Their shit talk not only kept the players in the game connected but also entertained everyone in the card room, as "public play."[17] Grover demonstrated his desire for a larger audience when he turned his body away from the game focusing on Napoleon ten feet away, and said loudly with his usual grin, "Napoleon, take that raggedy-ass hat off." Napoleon, his back still facing Grover, did not remove his hat, but two tables of men laughed—exactly what Grover had intended.

Once the game ended, the play-frame dissolved. The four domino players could now be heard summarizing their moves and discussing their strategies, all smiles and laughter, without the insults. Freddie's voice softened slightly. Grover and Freddie called across the room to Paul and D-Ray to "come on over" to play. Privately, some elders express antipathy toward the youngsters' shit talk, which they feel sounds more aggressive than fun. But even when talking shit may sound overly confrontational, even within the play-frame, it also fosters social solidarity and a strong sense of connection among participants.

*The Elders Talk about a Whole Lot of Nothing*

While it sometimes sounded like the men were reinterpreting the famous verbal confrontations between the prize fighters Mohammed Ali and Joe Frazier (marked by resilient banter), the elders employed distinct forms of talking shit. As Mr. Taylor aptly put it, their talk was often "a whole lot of nothing." This phrase captures a straightforward description of sociologist Georg Simmel's concept of sociability and the role of play in society.[18] Simmel saw sociability through conversation as a fundamental form of leisure—a "pure form" of society that may appear mundane but holds significant importance. Sociability, characterized by basic human connection, brings liveliness, joy, and relief. Though these effects are often subtle and may go unnoticed by participants, the act of talking itself becomes an end in itself, reaffirming people's trust in one another.

Shit talk involves little meaningful exchange of information beyond the conveyance of insults or barbs. Instead of focusing on substance, these verbal performances are meant to entertain. Unlike "the dozens," shit talk doesn't have a clear winner, and no single contribution is considered superior. It's less about competing for individual status and more about fostering *communitas*—a shared sense of unity, connection, and joy that comes from participating in a collective experience. This experience includes the men who sit around, watch, laugh, and collectively enjoy the experience. In fact, shit talk is framed in a distinctive way, in part to be displayed for an audience.[19] While winning domino games undoubtedly brings satisfaction, successful shit talk can produce authentic delight.

In the following excerpt, Mr. Taylor makes the obviously absurd claim that in the South, hamburger patties are formed when women put chunks of meat under their armpits to flatten them. To demonstrate, he places his hand under his armpit and flaps his arm like a bird.

MR. TAYLOR: They do that down South down there!
MR. HALL: [Laughing] How'd he think of that thing right on top of his head?
MR. BUFORD: [Laughing] I don't know. He's somethin' else!
MR. TAYLOR: [Places a domino] Fifteen.
MR. HALL: How does he think of stuff like that?
MR. TAYLOR: They do that down South. Them big women back down there in the woods.
MR. BUFORD: Damn!
STEVE: [Confused] What do they do? What?
MR. TAYLOR: Make hamburger patties.
MR. HALL: Listen to him, Steve. Go ahead and tell 'im.
MR. TAYLOR: You know you roll out—you make 'em up in your hands.
STEVE: Hamburgers.
MR. TAYLOR: Hamburgers. And you pinch you off a big—
STEVE: Yeah.
MR. TAYLOR: Slap it on the arm pit. And do like that.
MR. BUFORD: Flattening it down.
MR. TAYLOR: Slap it on the stove. [Cackles]
[Buford laughs]
MR. HALL: What'da think, Steve? [Taylor cackles] I see why you come down here all the time.
GEORGE: How comes you guys—
MR. HALL: How he comes up with a story like that—every day.

FIG. 13. Mr. Taylor, George, and Mr. Carr. Steve Bialostok, photographer.

The elders' laughter featured prominently throughout the game. Mr. Taylor's playfulness was fully supported. He seamlessly executed his verbal explanation and pantomimes with the same finesse and energy that he used to slam a domino. His claim was relaxed and sociable, allowing the other men to enjoy an interaction constructed as informal, friendly, and ever-so-slightly transgressive. Mr. Taylor is an accomplished teller of tall tales, and Mr. Hall eagerly includes me as part of the audience. The content of their talk may be a "whole lot of nothing," but the social work they are accomplishing through such talk matters.

In the next excerpt, the men maintain their comfortable and friendly banter that flirts with homosexual masculinity where dropping one's drawers suggests "fucking" or "getting fucked."

MR. TAYLOR: Is it my play?
GEORGE: Yep.
MR. HALL: No, I just played.
MR. TAYLOR: You played that, Mr. Hall?
MR. HALL: Yes, sir.
MR. TAYLOR: Well, how come you didn't drop his drawers?

[Buford laughs]

MR. HALL: I did. I dropped 'em.
MR. TAYLOR: I'm gonna go with you?
GEORGE: [inaudible]
MR. TAYLOR: I'm gonna go with Mr. Hall.
MR. BUFORD: Ah, man. You sure enough done mess me. Five.
MR. TAYLOR: I know you wanted it.
MR. BUFORD: Didn't want it.
GEORGE: Ten.
MR. TAYLOR: George wanted it. He kept it. [Laughs]
MR. BUFORD: Yeah.
MR. TAYLOR: [Cackling] He killed it. Goll-y. What kind of deal— what's the [inaudible] in that? Six?
MR. HALL: [inaudible]
MR. TAYLOR: I'm gonna kill this one.
MR. GEORGE: Blank-secuter! [Scores]
MR. HALL: Six?
MR. TAYLOR: I had mine and didn't know it.

When Mr. Taylor seemed intent on emphasizing everyone's masculine identity, Mr. Hall readily joins in (*I dropped 'em*), whereas Mr. Buford doesn't play along (*Didn't want it*). Nevertheless, the group's social stability remained intact. Then, Mr. Taylor shifted from the sexual violence involved in dropping one's drawers to that of "killing." George, who had been mostly silent, suddenly sprang to life, scoring with a blank/six tile and simultaneously introducing a new compound word. This inventive combination, merging one side of his blank tile with "executor," secured his victory in the match, as confirmed by Mr. Hall.

Like all shit talk, theirs is performance within a play-frame where, in this case, the men's fictionalized sexual intimacies (mediated through humor) foster their interconnectedness and simultaneously allow them to maintain their hegemonic masculinity as "real men." None of what they say is touchy-feely. But "a whole lot of nothing" talk safely conveys a range of affectionate emotions that otherwise are never directly expressed—chiefly their deep sense of affection and enjoyment in being together.

*Negotiating the Play-Frame*

After this last exchange, there was a brief silence. Despite their spirit of socialization, their talk should not be confused with indifference to the game or interpreted as suggesting that the game was secondary. The elders balanced lighthearted banter with fierce competition that fully engaged their minds, bodies, and emotions. Sometimes they were, to use Mihaly Csikszentmihalyi's expression, "in flow": so engrossed in their play that nothing else seemed to matter.[20] A lengthy and pragmatic pause allowed for decision-making without distraction, offering bursts of time to assess their situation and plan their strategy. After an eighteen-second pause in the conversation and banter, they returned to the game's final moves:

MR. TAYLOR: Mm-mm [no]. I'm going on the other side. [Referring to the other end of the domino skeleton on the table]
MR. BUFORD: All right. Talk to him, partner.
GEORGE: Five.
MR. TAYLOR: I didn't have a one to play with.
GEORGE: I'm surprised—
MR. BUFORD: Five.
MR. TAYLOR: You're killing. He killed the damn thing. That's ten.
MR. BUFORD: No, it ain't. My partner in there. What was that? Oh shit. [Lays down a domino] Shoulda played that a while ago.
GEORGE: I played the wrong thing.
MR. BUFORD: No, you didn't.
GEORGE: Yes, I did.
MR. BUFORD: My play.
GEORGE: Wait a minute, hold it.
MR. TAYLOR: Hold it. *Hold it.*
MR. HALL: [Singing] Hold that ti*ger*.
MR. TAYLOR: Goll-y. Aces and Treys and good-lookin' babes. If there ain't no aces, you gotta have babes.
MR. BUFORD: Twos and fo's and good-looking hoes.
MR. TAYLOR: Ten, for me and my friend. [Taylor has dominoed. Taylor and Hall win the game]

MR. HALL: Ten, all the way.
MR. TAYLOR: That's a *hard* ten.
GEORGE: Thank you. Ten!
MR. TAYLOR: Wow, wow, wow. It's over. It's over!
MR. BUFORD: You got it.
MR. TAYLOR: Hey man. I told you. You all were laughing. He ain't got nothing at the bottom.
GEORGE: What'da call down there?

Mr. Buford's encouraging words, "Talk to him, partner," addressed to the aging George, portray George as a player who still possesses prowess. George's subsequent actions, exemplified by phrases like "Hold it," which Mr. Taylor humorously echoed, further illustrated George's enduring skill and presence on the field. Mr. Hall, an avid college sports fan, gave his rendition of the "hold that tiger" chant from the *Tiger Rag* as performed by the Louisiana State University Tiger Band.[21] Then, Mr. Taylor brought the talk back to the topic of his more traditional masculinity in a variation of his recurring chant (*Aces and Treys and goodlookin' babes*), which Mr. Buford (and everyone else) already knew by heart. Mr. Buford recited Mr. Taylor's "original" version (*Twos and fo's and good-looking hoes*). The game ended when Mr. Taylor announced his definitive and final ten—a nontraditional declaration that emphasized the collaborative nature of winning (with Mr. Hall: *Ten all the way*). Mr. Taylor then reasserted the victory as if peace were being declared (*That's a hard ten; It's over. It's over.*)

Mr. Taylor—who had dominoed—reshuffled the tiles, and the conversation continued. The new game had not yet started. It was during this interlude that the men suspended the play-frame talk. Instead of shit talk, the ornery Mr. Buford registered a legitimate complaint to his partner sitting across from him:

MR. BUFORD: George, you keep steppin' on my foot and pushin' it. Pushin' my foot all the way. I'm tryin' to raise it up.
GEORGE: [Says something to disagree but unclear]
MR. BUFORD: No, you keep—you done did that thirty times. And you tryin'—

MR. HALL: Partner.
MR. BUFORD: Yeah, he tryin' to reach his partner and kick.
MR. TAYLOR: He kickin' you on the foot.
MR. BUFORD: Yeah man. You got long legs, man. I got it right there.
[Unintelligible crosstalk]
MR. BUFORD: He tryin' to kick his partner and he done whammed my leg up.
MR. TAYLOR: Let's be for real here. That's a whole lot of foot.
[Buford laughs]

Mr. Buford intended his protest about George's legs to be mildly playful (true as it was), but it didn't elicit the confrontational response he had hoped for—the kind that would have made for a satisfying exchange. Unfortunately, George was no longer capable of quick, defiant retorts. But Mr. Taylor came to rescue him: *Let's be for real here. That's a whole lot of foot.* Their exchange continued as the game went on:

GEORGE: Five.
MR. HALL: Fi-EEVE.
MR. TAYLOR: Oh man.
MR. BUFORD: That's for Mr. Hall. Ten.
MR. TAYLOR: Golly.
MR. BUFORD: Ah man. He'll do anything for ten. I'll kill that mother.
MR. GEORGE: Ten.
MR. BUFORD: Don't talk like that.
MR. TAYLOR: I'll *kill* that mother.
MR. BUFORD: Ah man.
MR. TAYLOR: Fifteen! That's what I wanted to see.
MR. BUFORD: I know it.
GEORGE: Fifteen.
MR. TAYLOR: That's what's going on right there, man. [Then, exaggerated] That's what's happening, maaan.
GEORGE: I think I go down there right quick?
MR. TAYLOR: Where you going?

[Here I omit a short section where George talks about where he plans to eat after he leaves. Mr. Taylor expresses an aversion to that restaurant]

MR. TAYLOR: Fifteen! I gotta have it, man. If you give it to me, I'll take it.
MR. BUFORD: Go ahead. That fifteen?
MR. TAYLOR: I don't know.
MR. BUFORD: Okay, partner.
MR. TAYLOR: Twenty! This could be.
MR. BUFORD: Mr. Taylor, you ever seen two squirrels fucking?
MR. TAYLOR: Squirrels.
MR. BUFORD: Squirrels. The little old—
MR. TAYLOR: Oh *yeah*. I got two of them *horny* motherfuckers.
[Buford laughs]
MR. TAYLOR: In my backyard.
MR. BUFORD: Man, they be—
MR. HALL: [Joking] Stop that!
MR. BUFORD: Boy, he roped that tail and he hit it tum, tum, tum. [Laughs]
MR. HALL: [Announcing his score] Twenty days in the county jail.

Why Mr. Buford asked his squirrel question at that moment is anyone's guess, though it was entirely in line with his sense of humor. He was well aware of his role as the feisty and cantankerous group member who made outrageous and vulgar comments for a laugh. He needed a good verbal opponent as much as he did a competitive domino opponent. Mr. Taylor was the obvious choice—someone who could confidently hold his own, and he did not disappoint. Mr. Taylor's response only reinforced his image as a self-assured, quick-witted, and slightly naughty humorist.[22] Their mutual enjoyment of skillful banter cemented their bond and fostered a sense of community for everyone around them.[23]

*Fun* was the precise term Mr. Hall used each night to describe their time together: "We had fun tonight," he usually said just before leaving, and the others would agree. In an interview, Mr. Hall told me, "Every day I've had fun. I laugh, and I listen to jokes. Guys make different comments and stuff." Mr. Taylor, like most of the men, repeatedly told me that talking shit is "good-natured fun." As D-Ray emphatically observes, "It's all in fun, man. Shit!"

It's easy to take "fun" for granted, but daily fun in the card room is no trivial matter. A "euphoric state of sociability" helps strengthen group cohesion and provides significant benefits to the elders.[24] Denver Parks and Recreation supports the "active older adult" program "to engage adults 50+ in wellness, exercise, and leisure activities that support healthy aging." Despite the mental acuity and physical coordination required for their play, none of the men would describe dominoes or shit talk as ways to keep their minds active or support healthy aging. They would, however, acknowledge that their "fun" together has helped maintain their commitment to frequenting the card room for so many years. Nevertheless, science journalist Catherine Price argues, "Fun is not just lighthearted pleasure. Fun is the secret to feeling alive."[25]

The laughter that permeates their shit talk also wields a profound and subversive power. In a society structured by systemic racism and oppression, the joyous laughter of Black men disrupts narratives of marginalization and subjugation. It defies the attempts to diminish their humanity and agency, reclaiming spaces for authentic self-expression and cultural identity. Steeped in resilience, this laughter becomes a defiant assertion of existence and a celebration of survival. It challenges the status quo, offering moments of liberation and solidarity amid the weight of historical injustices. Through laughter, the elders assert their right to joy and autonomy, carving out spaces of resistance in a society that often seeks to silence and erase their voices.[26]

*Music as Memory and Collective Identity*

Mr. Taylor once told me that their talk was like the improvisation in jazz. "Every instrument got in a little solo. Everybody got their own little thing, right? This guy over here in the clarinet, he got his little thing, and they'll go, 'Do do do do do do do,' to keep up with him. And then this guy over here going to break out. It's the same thing. Everybody got a solo that they want to get across, and everybody just humming at it along with them."

Indeed, the men's shit talk operates like a jazz band. Jazz is often described as conversation—a genre based on innovation in compositional style, improvisation, and communication between musicians, where players build on each other's ideas. I am struck by how the men never seem to interrupt each other. Instead, they show sensitivity toward each other's contributions and intuitively adjust to the tempo. Their "scales" (their script of interaction) are always in mind, but there is always room for improvisation. Mr. Buford is ready to be outrageous; Mr. Taylor is impish; Mr. Hall serves as the band leader, neither controlling the conversation nor letting it spiral out of control. It is evident that their interactions are finely tuned and well synchronized.[27] But their talk is only part of the card room's soundscape.

Music also shapes the card room as a Black place. The television was often blaring, but the music never failed to drown it out. If the card room were a movie, the old music played would be its soundtrack. Donald was the first person I saw bring in music. It was mostly old-school R&B and soul, with occasional bursts of funk, even as Napoleon and Trapper started downloading and streaming tracks to share. Earth, Wind & Fire—the band rooted in Denver—always brought out wistful smiles. The younger men never brought in music that might appeal to their own generation or musical tastes. Instead, most appreciated the old style, often whispering or silently mouthing along with the songs.

One Tuesday night, I took careful notes on the music and the mood. Johnny Nash's "I Can See Clearly Now" came on first; then "Before I Let Go" by Maze, followed by "I Hope That You're Okay" by Toni Braxton and Babyface, and then the Isley Brothers' "Work to Do." The music seemed to reconnect the elders to their past, and songs like the Platters' "Smoke Gets in Your Eyes" even elicited physical responses: D-Ray closed his eyes, while Mr. Hall swayed. The elders' unabashed and sentimental musical attachment could transport them into a dream state. Mr. Cummings and George, standing next to each other, closed their eyes and swayed to the rhythms of Sam Cooke's "Send Me Some Lovin'." Mr. Hall, smiling from his chair, cupped his hands and rhythmically moved them back and forth in front of his face. Mr. Buford turned to Mr. Taylor and quietly remarked, "That takes me back," followed by the predictable remark that the music was "getting me hard." Even Derek, who had been watching basketball, turned to Mr. Buford and said, "I feel like holding your hand." For a moment, he seemed lost in a memory. As soulful melodies and rhythmic beats permeated the room, the music transported the elders to the sounds of eras past, prompting feet to tap and bodies to sway with the exuberance of youth once more. Even Mr. Taylor and Jamel's earlier exchange—"These guys are as easy as Sunday morning; Like Sunday morning"—echoed the Commodores' 1977 hit "Easy," taking the two back to their youth, parties, and relationships of a different time.

Sitting with the youngsters, Ray and Grover played on opposite teams. Ray slammed down his domino: "Fifteen." "Fucking bitch," Grover responded. Then, caught up in the emotions of the music and without missing a beat, Grover softly joined the chorus of "Natural High." It was common for the men to talk shit and then, as D-Ray did, immediately join half the room singing along with Sam Cooke's "You Send Me." The music often sparked one elder's recollection of the time of the song, which in turn inspired another to reminisce. As Mr. Hall noted:

> It takes me back. I've been right there, and it makes me happy all over again. Yeah, I'm seventy-six, but it puts me back at sixteen, eighteen, twenty, twenty-five years old, because back then you got to get the feeling of the music. You heard the word "soul"? Well, it gets into my soul. Muted words. That's soul music. It always got a story to it. But it takes me back personally when I was dancing with the pretty girls, dancing with the ugly girls, laughing and talking. To this day, I don't do it anymore, but I got all those stacked up. All that music played in there, I've either got an album or a dish at the house. I don't play it much, but when I come down here, I've got my friends and stuff, and it makes me like I was when I was young.

Scholars have explored the significance of Black music—both religious and popular—for its intended Black audience. Historian Douglas Henry Daniels writes, "In predominantly white universities, black professors and administrators and staff often play radios in their offices, listening to black music as if it were their lifeline to the world from which they are temporarily insulated by white institutions."[28] Writing about the centrality of Black music in Ralph Ellison's *Invisible Man*, W. J. Schafer argues that in the novel, "we are never far from the blues and the astringent humor of Jazz."[29] Early blues music had once been the primary medium of communication—for joy, sorrow, loneliness—and an expression of Black community, solidarity, and identity.[30] I wondered if, beyond the elders' obvious affection for these songs, the music also provided them with lifelines and a sense of connection and stability, especially as so much around them had changed both inside and outside of the Hiawatha Davis Recreation Center. At the very least, the card room offered the elders the chance to hang onto their music and their ways of talking.

*Conclusion*

In a world where older adults are often assumed to focus solely on their medical concerns, medications, or discussions about their trips, children, and grandchildren, the elders' shit talk defies these social conventions and expectations. It forgoes conventional politeness. Early in my research I assumed (incorrectly, as it turned out) that older Black men who lived through different eras of race relations and racial politics in America would quite naturally discuss current issues of racial violence and anti-Blackness, especially as it played out in the media. But I learned that shit talk is rarely overshadowed by current events. The elders' shit talk persists regardless of the state of the world or the events in their past and present lives. Even the death of family or friends fails to disrupt their rhythm, as they continue to share in the joy of their time together.

In the heart of this gentrifying neighborhood—once a bustling hub of Black life—the card room stands as a defiant testament to the endurance of a community. Within its walls, this group of elders gathers nightly, not just for the ritualized game of dominoes and camaraderie, but as an act of resistance. Their shit talk, their music, and their boisterous laughter echo through the room, serving as a powerful reminder that even elders are not passive bystanders in the face of change. The dominoes they slam, the melodies they hum, and the verbal repartee they engage in are not mere pastimes but acts of cultural preservation. The noise that spills out the door is a joyous assertion of their right to exist, to be loud, and to be human. The card room is more than just a place; it is a testament to the power of Black community, the resilience of their spirit in the face of adversity, and the determination to claim their rightful place in the world despite threats of erasure.

Beyond its sophisticated rhetorical structure, talking shit forms social bonds that require trust and build connection. It also serves as a democratic leveler. Yet talking shit is only one dimension of how the elders in the card room cultivate resilience and connection. In the next chapter,

I focus on Mr. Buford Yarborough, whose life story reveals the deeper roots of this resilience. His history—marked by racial injustice, personal loss, and perseverance—provides a fuller context for understanding the power of these nightly exchanges. From there, in chapter 10, I return to the card room to examine what I call *the business of intimacy*: the subtle, sometimes hidden ways the men care for one another through play, banter, and presence.[31]

# 9   Buford Yarborough

"I could tell ya stories that would make you cry." Mr. Buford and I were having breakfast in a booth at the Village Inn, his favorite restaurant. All the waitresses knew his name. Each time we ate there together, a different one served him his coffee and then confirmed, "Do you want the usual?" (Eggs over medium, bacon crispy, and sausage patties well done on both sides on a bed of potatoes). They knew to bring his pancakes later because they would otherwise get cold. It was a lot to eat, but he'd wrap up the leftovers and take them home for dinner. He now lived alone with no one to cook for him.

"How ya doin', baby?" The waitresses laughed at Mr. Buford's "old man" flirtations, even as they made me squirm. "Baby" was not the worst of his lines: "Now, *she's* my girlfriend," he would comment. Another time I heard him order, "Coffee and a large water with some lemon and come over here and give me a kiss or something like that and I'll get some of that lipstick off you." He consistently replayed a version of himself as a young man: the tall, handsome, smooth-talking ladies' man who, I once joked to him, "had lots of little Bufords running around the country." He laughed and said, "Yeah, man, I got kids scattered all over, well, you know." At "almost ninety," Mr. Buford maintained much of the slender physique of his youth. He wore steel-rimmed glasses, and one of the baseball caps from his large collection covered his full head of hair. He liked to be complimented as a "good-looking man" and sometimes added, "You know, back in the day they thought I was pretty cute too. And I didn't look too bad."

*Forging Resilience: Buford Yarborough's Early Years*

Buford Yarborough was born in Arkansas on January 21, 1932. He grew up on a pig farm in rural Oklahoma with his grandparents, father, and

FIG. 14. Mr. Buford. Steve Bialostok, photographer.

siblings. One of ten children (three boys and seven girls) who "worked in the fields," Mr. Buford described himself as like his father—both were "raised up picking cotton." His parents never married. "That was something against the rules back in the old days," he said, without expanding. He never spoke about his mother. In 1942 his father was drafted for the war, leaving his grandparents "stripped of help on the farm." His father's departure meant that the quiet, tall, "skinny-as-a-rail" but apparently muscular ten-year-old was left to lift bales of cotton and hoist them on the bed of a flatbed truck. Billy, as he was called, was "out of school half of the time," trying to help with the crops so he and his siblings could make a living. He jokes about all of the school he missed as a child: "That's why I'm so stupid now!"

After the death of his grandmother, Billy went to live with his father in Denver's Five Points. However, Billy soon felt the move had been "a big mistake." Life in the city was different from the country where he had spent his days hunting with his cousin. His father, a train porter, traveled extensively. "He was gone a lot." The woman his father lived with was not motherly or supportive. "She never liked me for some reason." Furthermore, Billy had to start attending school regularly, and he felt out of place in classrooms filled with all white classmates.

Buford's advantage over the rest of the boys was his speed and strength and apparently—as he enjoyed punctuating all the tales of his life—that he had a way with the "ladies," even at eleven years old. He summed up his situation with a grin: "The girls started comin' around and talkin' to me, and then the boys didn't like it." They began to bully him.

> I been chased by them little white boys. "Try to catch that nigger. Try to catch that nigger." But I was fast as a kid. I was lucky enough. I could run fast enough I never did get caught and beat up and all that shit, you know. That's why you take a lot of that stuff. They just, people calling you and throwing rocks out there and hitting you, and you have to keep walking or run. You can't fight back. You know better than to fight back.

Mr. Buford added, "I been called the n-word a million time." I asked if he ever fought back, being so feisty and strong. He said no. "They would kill you."

Buford avoided fights by skipping school, easily accomplished with a father working elsewhere and a relatively indifferent stepmother. Most of the time he stayed home "reading comic books all motherfucking day."

In high school, Buford discovered he could earn money playing dice. "I used to play dice and make enough money for my food. . . . I made enough nickels and dimes and I'd save them up." Other opportunities were limited.

> We didn't have a goddamn thing to do. We didn't have no jobs for the Blacks and shit like that. We throwed papers on a paper route. White kids had all the damn jobs. We stuck with each other, wrestling and holding each other's arms and arm wrestling and all that shit. Well, I was already pretty strong. But I was trying to help these little old weak-ass guys. Because they wanted to be strong like me. We catch them Western movies. . . . You could get in the theater for twenty-five

cents.... I started stealing bicycles.... [We'd] go out in the white neighborhood and find a bicycle, steal it, and we could take a bicycle and run as fast as the goddamn bicycle could go down there. So we was fast and shit like that. Sometimes find a old bicycle in an alley somewhere that people were throwing away, we'd take the good ones and fix them up and shit like that. And that's how we got our bicycles.

When I told Mr. Buford my first bicycle had been a Schwinn, he said, "A Schwinn? Man, that was an upgrade. That was a goddamn BMW or Mercedes or something. Riding a Schwinn. Shit. Riding a goddamn Schwinn." He laughed, "You lucky to be white." I got used to hearing this refrain from him.

Once his father discovered the stolen bikes, he told Billy to "be a real good boy, and I'll get you a bicycle." "I was the only kid on the block had a new bicycle," Buford recalled. When his father had enough money to take him shopping for other items, Billy experienced racism in a way that was common in Denver outside of Five Points. "My dad took me downtown to buy me some clothes and stuff like that, and so we would go to little old store. I seen this hat, a brown hat. He said, 'You like that? That's a nice hat.' And so I tried it on. Then the clerk told my daddy, 'You *got* to buy that hat that boy done tried on.' I *had* to buy the hat because I tried it on." Then he reiterated, "See, you lucky to be white."

By the summer after Mr. Buford's junior year, with academics a distant priority, his father returned to Denver and grew tired of "taking care of the shit that I done got into." He gave the teenager an ultimatum: "I was still fucking up, running with my buddies and shit like that, wasn't doing things I was supposed to do, and so he told me, 'You got to get you a job, go in the service, do something instead of getting in a truck on a seat [just driving around].'"

In 1950 he was drafted into the Army. "I didn't know I was gonna get called. I would never have got married. I was having too much fun to go into the service by then." Off he went to Ft. Leavenworth, Kansas, the induction center, then to Arkansas for basic training. "I ran into all that racism shit. For a long time, I wouldn't even talk to nobody about all that crap. It was bad for the Black man. Shit. It was doubly bad." He recounted his first encounter with racism in the military:

Down there in Arkansas I went to town with a white kid. We did our training and they let you go into town if you'd been good, and you get a pass; you can go to town and go see a movie. We got down there. We were standing in line with a lot of white soldiers there. So we stand in line and going to get the ticket. We got the tickets, and my friend was allowed to enter, but when I got to go in, she about had a fit. So one of the white guys in line said, "You can't go in here. Don't you know you can't go in there? Go call your daddy." She told the white kid to come around, but I couldn't go in. I had to go up to the loft. We said, "The hell with it." We went across the street to the bus station. I said, "Let's go over there to get some coffee and a donut" and stuff like that. They brought the other kids food. They didn't bring me none.

You know, to go through that shit, and you in the Army fighting for the same cause and you can't do shit. It was real bad. Yeah. They wouldn't serve me. So this other white kid, he was from Missouri, he shoved a coffee and shit over off the counter. I said, "Man, let's get out of here. You all gonna get my Black ass." I'm in the service now with my Army suit on just like them. And man, I tell you it was tough. . . .

They were supposed to be integrated. I never seen such a mess. Them white kids didn't want to be in the barracks with the Black kids. It wasn't nothing but a bunch of bullshit all the time. I remember I was taking basic in Arkansas. We went out to the firing range. They teach you how to shoot. One of the Black kids and the white kids get into a scrap. We kept our weapons. You put them on a big rack when you came in the barracks. The white kid was still pissed at the Black kid and he got after him with the gun. The kid went around the side of the barracks. The gun was so powerful he done shot through the side of the barracks to catch him on the other side. He shot and killed one of the officers. . . .

There was this white guy. I think he was from Oklahoma. He couldn't take it. He was sleeping in the barracks. They had bunks. You sleep on this bunk, and the white guy sleeps on the other bunk. And he couldn't stand sleeping aside of a Black man. It was that bad. I'd seen so much shit, man you wouldn't believe it.

Although the Korean War "was hot," the military lottery worked alphabetically so "by the time it got to me [Yarborough], they'd had enough soldiers and didn't get to me. So I went to North Carolina where I stayed in that son of a bitch hell, damn near a year." From there, the Army shipped him to Germany near the Russian border. "It was bad," he said, "sleeping in them bags in the woods," where Russian soldiers would cross over to shoot at them.

His superior was "another racist white officer from Mississippi" who "caused hell" for the Black soldiers, "treating the Blacks bad and the whites better." He described restrictions on Black movement; white soldiers eating before Black soldiers and with better food; fears of white soldiers "going to get my Black ass." The racism was worse than anything he had experienced in Denver and crueler than in Oklahoma. Again, he reminded me, "Man, you lucky you turned out white. If you were Black your ass wouldn't have made it."

Mr. Buford returned to Denver after three years of service, where finding work proved nearly impossible for Black folks. "I went around here for I bet three months before I could get a decent job. When I *did* get a job, they didn't pay a damn thing. We had to survive." Occasionally he would go hunting in Wyoming with his cousin.

> They used to have that private hunting, and we could go up there and kill the rabbits for the farmers. Me and my cousin, we was up there, and we stopped at a little old place to get us some coffee. So, we walked in the damn place, me and my cousin, and I'll be damned, I bet you can't think of the song that starts in there. "Bye Bye Blackbird." My cousin damn near went crazy, and man, there was maybe twenty-five or thirty white people in there half drunk. Shit, and you see what they done said. When there's the song on, "Bye Bye Blackbird," that mean get your ass out of there. And he starts, "Man, them goddamn peckerwoods, God help them." And I said, "You bring your ass on outta here." Man, we ran, got in the car, and he still, "Them son of a bitches." I said, "You son of a bitch, you are gonna get us both killed."

He eventually got a job at Denver's Lowry Air Force Base and held it until the Air Force moved all the jobs an hour south to Colorado Springs.

Then he worked several positions at the Public Service Gas Light Company (later, Xcel) until he was transferred to small appliance repair. From there he moved on to repair cars. "I had several jobs for thirty-six years, a whole bunch of jobs running around. Bullshit jobs, but I was finally making a little money when I retired."

"You really have an interesting life," I told him once.

"Yeah, I had a hell of a life," he answered. "If I can get down and deep in some of that stuff, man you'd be crying."

*Mr. Buford's Personal Trials and Triumphs*

Over a period of two years, the two of us got together regularly for breakfast or visited at his home. Mr. Buford eventually told me life stories that got "down and deep." Upon returning from the service, he discovered that his wife had been cheating on him:

> I should have known that she ain't going to put no muzzle on that cotton for three years. So, anyway, when I come back she had some old guy she was going with, he's a taxi cab driver or something like that. He had money and the money that I was sending her, hell, she was doing real good. I didn't know I was going to go in the Army. And when I come back, that hurt me real bad. I done sent money back. That woman fucked off all my money that I done sent back, I gambled and shit in the Army and made all that money and sent back here. A hell of a lot of money. You could go for a pretty long while before you spent a hundred dollars unless you was a fool. I was going to buy me some apartment buildings and live in one unit, and take care of the rest of them, because I was young and could do all the manual work around there. I come back to the goddamn woman and I sent the money back, she done spent all the money. And, now that's the time I had tears down to my motherfucking knees.

Though he acknowledged his own prolific sexual escapades while serving in Germany, he obviously still suffered from an unhealed wound of sadness and anger about his first wife's infidelity and her flagrant spending of the money he had sent home for their imagined future. He knew this was not a therapy session, but he wanted to tell me more.

> That was some hard times, man, that was some hard times. And we tried to make it for a little while and it wasn't working then. It take me a long time to get over that shit. I went down there one time and she was in one of them clubs with this guy, and I asked her to come on home and talk to her and the guy said something and then I had to whoop his ass all the way across the street. So the motherfucking police put me in jail. And I'd go home and, goddamn it, "Why you do shit like that?" But at a young age, you don't think about that, you know? That was one of the things that brought tears to my eyes, a lot of times, man, I got a lot of bullshit, you know? Trying to get over that shit.

He had also experienced heartbreaking loss in his life when his adult son, from another woman he never married when he was young, died of liver cirrhosis in his forties.

> It's a hurt feeling. You know family. That's family; that's a hurt. It's a hell of a hurt feeling. When I found out about it, his girlfriend came over to my house and told me about it. Oh, man. It's a hell of a feeling. You don't get over it. No, you don't get over it. I still don't get over it. And like I said, shit, for years I'd go out there and put flowers on the damn grave and shit like that, you know. You can have ups and downs with your son or your daughter but when something like that happen, oh man. Shit, it'll tear you all up.

Mr. Buford also shared a story about his last wife at his large home in the white section of Aurora, Colorado, where his family had moved in 1993 after his retirement from thirty years in public service. It was a long way from Park Hill. "I liked my house over there in Park Hill. Shit, we'd been there twenty-five years, I think." But gangs were negatively influencing his children and "fucking with my car and shit like that.... We had so much problems with them kids and gangs. Goddamn Crips and the Bloods." Once, he chased a young gangster who had vandalized his car in the middle of the night.

> If I'd have had my clothes on I'd have caught him. But I was out there in my drawers. I had my pajamas on but no top. And I came back up

the street and the police was there and I couldn't hide my gun. I didn't have no motherfucking where to put it. That man said, "What in the hell are you doing? Running up and down the street shooting in the city limit. Don't you know I could take your ass today?" He talked to me just like, "I take your ass to jail right now." But he went to school with my other daughter. And they talked to me for a long time. And he said, "Don't do that." He said, "You'd get charged for shooting in the city limits and then shooting at a . . . whatcha call 'em . . . another person or something like that."

We sat on comfortable recliners across from each other in his home while talking. Mr. Buford glanced back and forth from watching the news on the large television hanging on the wall and talking to me, sometimes both at the same time. "This is what I do. Sit here, pull this chair back sometimes, and put my feet up and go to sleep, watch TV and sleep. A lot of times when I'm watching a good movie, go to sleep and don't see the end of it. Goddamn it! I wasted time. Shit."

When I complimented the art he had hanging on the walls, he smiled. His wife was "into that Black art stuff," he said. They had been married forty-one years.

MR. BUFORD: I had a hell of a life, man, you know? I'd fuck everything I could.
STEVE: Is that true?
MR. BUFORD: That's true, yeah. I'm not gonna lie to you.
STEVE: So you learned to calm down?
MR. BUFORD: Oh, I calmed down a bit.

He met Patricia in his late thirties at his aunt's funeral in Vallejo, California, and soon learned she was "raised up there in Alaska, around *you* folks." "*My* folks?" I asked. "*White* folks," Mr. Buford said. After two years of long-distance dating, Patricia moved to Denver with her two young children, and Mr. Buford "raised 'em as my own."

Mr. Buford reminded me, again, that one day I'd hear stories that would "make you cry." I asked again for him to share just one, but he answered, "You don't really ever get used to it. After you been together for so long. See, I stay with her longer than anyone. Say, this is going to be it, Jack. We had some good times."

"She had a hard road of it," he said of her three-month illness. Before Mr. Buford would tell me about his wife's death from cancer, he asked that I turn off the recorder. An awkward silence filled the room after he finished his story, so I asked for a house tour. After complaining about my forcing him out of his recliner, Mr. Buford showed me around his large and well-furnished suburban home. The living room, family room, multiple bedrooms, and two cars in the garage presented a study in contrast compared to his rural days in Oklahoma, "coming up" in Denver, or even living in a much smaller home in North Park Hill. Nothing had changed since his wife died. Every piece of furniture, pillow, sofa cushion, chair, and table appeared as if the house had been staged for potential buyers. Patricia must have been quite a woman. After they became a couple, "I straightened up to the point where I said, 'when I get married this time, I'm going to try to find one of them fucking women that I think I can deal with.' Because I done went through so many women." Their life in the suburbs was one they built together to create a particular type of household that Mr. Buford could finally settle into. Mr. Buford loved that "Patricia's mommy was crazy about me. I used to say, 'Come here you pretty thing.' She was old and she loved that." And he drove the kids around from activity to activity like a soccer mom.

To write about Mr. Buford required rereading hundreds of pages of interview transcripts, recordings, and notes. Despite all the "data," I found myself confused about some matters and reflected on Mr. Buford's refrain: "I got to take you so slow. You're hard-headed and can't get nothin' through your goddamn thick head. Shit. Man, I got to keep repeating myself over and over. And I'm old and I forget half the shit. You know, you're a trip."

The "ladies" of his youth were attracted to him, and they approached him in bars. He especially liked to talk about how they enjoyed playing with his curly hair. "I used to have real nice curly hair until them goddamn women got their hands on it," he reported. "That's where them bald spots came from . . . where them son of a bitches take and jerk the whole goddamn root out! Shit!" Mr. Buford told tales about various children who *emerged* from encounters with women: the daughter and grandson who Mr. Buford only discovered when the daughter turned fifty-one; the woman whose abortion he paid for; his relief about another woman's baby who was *not* his. He had stories.

"You can't tell by looking at him?" D-Ray said after telling me that Mr. Buford was "part Indian." Mr. Buford's skin *was* lighter, but I had never thought about it. If true, could that have been the reason that nobody in the Yarborough family ever spoke about his mother? Was this another story that would make me cry?

"What is it about me that you like?" Mr. Buford asked me. "Or *do* you like me?"

I felt too shy to admit my enormous affection, so I kept our conversation formal. "Of course I like you," I said. "Why would I spend so much time with you if I *didn't* like you? Plus, you have great stories to tell."

He smiled and looked directly at me. "I think you like my constant bullshit. I ain't nothin' but just an old joker that's trying to make it."

"Because you have great stories."

He gave me that same grin that I'm confident charmed the ladies over the years. "Oh," he said, looking down. "I don't want to tell you *all* of them."

# 10   The Business of Intimacy

While I was drawn into the card room by the sounds of loud laughter and the fast-paced energy of the men talking shit, I came to appreciate and value the emotional depth of the elders' seemingly superficial exchanges. The elders did not just play dominoes and verbally spar in the card room; they worked hard to develop and maintain significant social connections and engage in what I affectionately describe as "the business of intimacy." Mainstream American understandings of platonic intimacy—what many might consider close friendships—generally include a mutual sharing of personal information or experiences that generate a sense of connectedness.[1] Richard Sennett contends that intimacy is characterized by "warmth, trust, and open expression of feeling."[2] But elders in the card room tend to avoid personal matters: they don't discuss their families, the events of their days, or their health, and the only emotions they share include their animated exchanges, the energetic slamming of dominoes, and a lot of laughter. Yet behind the faux fighting and the lack of personal details shared, the men were building critically important interpersonal relationships. In this chapter, I show how the elders build intimacy—a sense of connection, comfortable familiarity, and closeness—as they spent time together in the card room. Through shared life experiences and their familiar nightly routines, they conveyed the unspoken message, "I know you. And you know me."

*Shared Experiences of Racism*

One rare moment that shifted the elders' playful talk into something more serious occurred in 2018, when they overheard a television news report about a racial profiling incident at a Starbucks in Philadelphia. The story involved two Black men who were arrested while waiting for a friend—without having made any purchases—after a store manager called the police, accusing them of trespassing. The story prompted Mr. Buford, without looking up from his domino hand, to recall events from decades earlier. "Yeah, I remember them days, man," in a tone I had only ever heard when it was just the two of us—not during a domino game.

> MR. BUFORD: Shit, it was tough. That stuff's for real. Shit, fuck. When I was in the Army I went down there in Arkansas, them son of bitches wouldn't let me go into the movies.
> NAPOLEON: Hell no, you can't go in the movie. I don't know what your problem is. Shit.
> MR. BUFORD: I didn't know nothing about you couldn't go in the goddamned movies.
> NAPOLEON: No, you couldn't go in the movies.
> MR. BUFORD: No, you couldn't go in.
> NAPOLEON: Domino! No you can't go in the movies, shit. You couldn't go into a café no nothing. Shit.

As they reassembled the domino tiles to shuffle and play again, Mr. Hall recalled that when white people allowed Black people to enter movie theaters, Black people were relegated to the balcony. From there, he gleefully described throwing ice down on the white people who were sitting below. Mr. Buford, Mr. Taylor, and Napoleon enthusiastically recalled this same practice as if they had all gone into the same theater together and collectively organized the rebellion. Mr. Taylor said an usher once came up with a flashlight, and "he start shining the light down on you and say, 'Who threw that ice?'" "And don't nobody know nothing," added Mr. Hall.

> MR. TAYLOR: No, no, no. Somebody's gonna tell.
> MR. BUFORD: Somebody's gonna tell. They start whooping ass.
> NAPOLEON: You can get back at them. Every once in a while you get a chance to get back at them a little bit. That way you can kinda get back at them.
> MR. TAYLOR: You go to jail. Or you gonna get your ass whooped before you go to jail.

MR. BUFORD: You get your ass whooped up *there*.

MR. HALL: And then that white man gonna go tell your parents, and you gonna get another ass whooping.

NAPOLEON: That'll damn near kill ya.

MR. BUFORD: [Back to the game] What is that? A big six?

MR. HALL: I'd rather have 'em whoop your ass than have a white man kill ya.

MR. BUFORD: Yeah, they'll kill you over nothin'.

NAPOLEON: Yeah.

MR. TAYLOR: I remember in my senior year, one guy got all brave and said he was gonna date a white girl. Take her to the movies. He was gonna go on the white side. We went in this door; they went the white folks door. [Laughs] And that ticket agent come out with a club that long, he said, "You ain't going in there!"

They laughed momentarily, then their voices grew solemn.

NAPOLEON: Yeah, it was terrible.

MR. TAYLOR: Boy, I tell you.

NAPOLEON: Yeah. Terrible.

MR. HALL: Terrible times.

NAPOLEON: [Affirming] Mmhmmm.

MR. HALL: Put five on it.

NAPOLEON: You go to town, and you know they have like a Sears and Roebuck or something like that, you couldn't go through the front, you had to go around to the back.

MR. BUFORD: Yeah. Every time, man.

NAPOLEON: Everybody coming in getting waited on before you, you have to wait till there wasn't nobody in there or wasn't nobody coming in and then you could get whatever you want.

STEVE: What do you think of those two guys getting kicked out of Starbucks?

MR. HALL: It's coming back. It's coming back. Everything goes in a—

NAPOLEON: Circle.

MR. HALL: Three-sixty. I think I pass.

STEVE: Then two guys got kicked out of LA Fitness in New Jersey.
NAPOLEON: Just for being Black. It's an uprise now, now that the presidency is what it is.
MR. BUFORD: What about the Black guy that got shot . . . in Sacramento? When that guy got shot all in the back—
STEVE: At his grandma's house.
NAPOLEON: Give us five, sir.

"Do You Love Me" by the Contours played in the background. Mr. Napoleon joined in the chorus of "Do the twist." The game continued. Mr. Hall, his competitor, threw down a domino. "You're a mean man, Mr. Hall," Napoleon said.

MR. BUFORD: Go 'head.
MR. TAYLOR: Look at him! Look at him. Watch him now.
MR. BUFORD: Go 'head.
MR. TAYLOR: Watch him rock the baby.

Then their dialogue shifted back to memories of racism:

MR. TAYLOR: They used to hang them where I come from and then they'd make they children go jump on they leg. Pull them down. Break they necks. Sometimes your neck don't snap.
MR. HALL: Yep. It'll paralyze you if you live.
NAPOLEON: Mm-hmm. [Affirmative]
MR. TAYLOR: But if you get there in time, you can cut them down.
MR. BUFORD: But you can't get there because they gonna wait until he's dead.
MR. HALL: Yep.
MR. BUFORD: Yeah, you can't get there, you cannot.
MR. TAYLOR: Yeah, but these boys, they didn't kill, these little old boys. They wasn't the real Klansmen. They were just boys having fun. They call that fun.
MR. BUFORD: Just a bunch of white kids. Yeah. Yeah.
MR. TAYLOR: Some of them you knew. Some of them you worked for.

MR. BUFORD: Yeah.

NAPOLEON: Yeah, but they talking pretty hot with them sheets though. Yeah, you could see all, that was the sheriff, that was town mayor, that was the councilman.

MR. BUFORD: They all was helping.

NAPOLEON: You know who it was. You better not go to the town. You better not go to them yelling, "Sheriff! Sheriff! Sheriff! Sheriff!" If you go to the sheriff, he's wearing that damn sheet.

MR. BUFORD: Steve, don't worry. We're good to you.

[Laughter]

The elders' collaborative narration here constitutes a "retold story" of lynching as recalled from when they were young and living in the South.³ They were not direct witnesses to these events, although Mr. Taylor told me in a separate conversation that sometimes wandering through the woods, he would come across a dead body hanging from a tree. But they needn't have all directly witnessed this legacy of racial terror to feel its full effects. The elders also recognize that had the situation been differently configured, *they* could have been victims.

The author Richard Wright, born near Natchez, Mississippi, knew of two men who were lynched: his step-uncle and the brother of a neighborhood friend. In his memoir, *Black Boy*, he wrote, "The things that influenced my conduct as a Negro did not have to happen to me directly; I needed but to hear of them to feel their full effects in the deepest layers of my consciousness. Indeed, the white brutality that I had not seen was a more effective control of my behavior than that which I knew."⁴ Wright's prescient comment captures how people often retell stories from the past that they did not actually witness. Speakers can frame past events as if they had just happened, making them relevant to teller and audience. A common way a speaker does this is to project himself backward into the event of the narrative, recounting past events as if he or she had been present.⁵

Collective memories are also passed down beyond the lifetime of the original witnesses. These retellings in the card room ensure that collective memories endure and emphasize their shared nature. In their extended discussion, the men take up similar perspectives in how they choose to narrate these stories, including and even highlighting harrowing physical descriptions: the positions of lynched men's bodies, the methods used to kill them, and the amount of time it took. They know these intimate details because lynchings—if anything—were meant to spread fear. Those who heard the stories, even at a young age, remembered them. The fact that the men narrate this retold story as if it were a shared firsthand experience points to the indelible impression these brushes with racial terror left—but also to the intimacy created among survivors. This violence did not happen to them. But they all knew it intimately, and they use these shared emotions and experiences to create intimacy among them.

Mr. Buford's final line—intended humorously—points to another intimacy, between the narrators and *me*. It seems an attempt to differentiate me from the white men mentioned in the story and to place me, however temporarily and symbolically, outside this fraught Black and white dynamic. I could not share in the joint telling of their painful and deeply felt narrative, but they would allow me to listen.

*Intimacy and Care in the Card Room*

It was 3:50 in the afternoon, and *Jerry Springer* happened to be on television. A half dozen men in the card room watched, riveted, as a young man proposed marriage to a woman, only to discover that she was a lesbian. The men hooted and hollered along with the studio audience as the woman's girlfriend walked on stage, and the two kissed passionately. D-Ray watched but kept an eye on the clock. Mr. Buford had yet to arrive, and it was already four o'clock. D-Ray left the room to wait outside. Finally, at 4:15, Mr. Buford's car pulled into the handicapped space in front of the center. By 4:25, the men in the card room were treated to a live show far more entertaining than Jerry Springer's.

> D-RAY: You won't crawl in there no goddamn more with your faggot ass.
> MR. BUFORD: Your finger all in my face. Your finger smell like pussy.
> D-RAY: What is the business, what is the business?
> MR. BUFORD: This is the business, you big-head motherfucker. I'm tired of being nice to you, man.
> D-RAY: You a liar.

In "A World of Black Intimacy at the Card Table," poet and cultural critic Hanif Abdurraqib explores the journey of a group of friends through the American South, using the game of spades as a vehicle to show the deepening of their fellowship and connection.[6] He writes, "Oh, friends—I most love who you become when there are cards in your hands. How limitless our love for one another can be with our guards down."

To illustrate the expressions of platonic affection and intimacy over dominoes in the card room, I focus on the spirited exchanges between D-Ray and Mr. Buford. No other elders exhibited the level of intense and consistent engagement that D-Ray and Mr. Buford shared. And no one drew an audience like they did, both reveling in sublimely provocative language. But behind their jest and banter, trust and warmth permeated their exchanges. Their interactions offer a valuable opportunity to explore the underlying dynamics of camaraderie, care, and intimacy at play in the card room.

*It's All in Fun*

Mr. Buford described how he and D-Ray initially crossed paths—three decades before my research. They were initially drawn together by their verbal performances:

> See, I mess with D-Ray. He mess with me. He's the only one in there that I fool with. I never had nobody to talk to like that, even when I was in the service. I didn't talk to none of the guys like I talk to D-Ray. D-Ray actually, matter of fact, the only one I ever *did* talk to like that. I'll tell you how that started. He started messing around, having to do shit with me, so that got started. It got bigger, bigger, and bigger. Some people you can talk to and they can tease you and tease you. And you tease them and get away with them. They get mad. I found out that D-Ray wasn't that way. And so that's how I started talking to him. And he's the only one. The other day I went in there, walk in there and say, "D-Ray, my friend, sweet motherfucka." Real loud.

There is a comforting predictability in the outrageous contributions of D-Ray and Mr. Buford—ritualistic performances that never fail to entertain. Their exchanges, full of sharp wit and bravado, have become as much a part of their bond as any shared history. But beyond the sheer entertainment value, these rituals serve a deeper purpose. The more D-Ray and Mr. Buford engage in their unique brand of shit talk, the more they cultivate a heightened sense of intimacy. What might seem like playful banter on the surface actually creates a space where vulnerability and care can flourish, where resilience is built through mutual understanding. Through these moments of back-and-forth, the two men not only affirm their bond but also strengthen it, weaving humor and affection into the fabric of their relationship. The following examples illustrate how their dynamic—rooted in playful insults and deflections—becomes a subtle, yet powerful, means of connection.

"D-Ray, sweet mothafucka, eyes like a frog. Leap to me, and I'm gonna fuck you like a dog." Mr. Buford recited these words to me, standing in the Village Inn parking lot next to his car, as if performing an old-fashioned choral reading, with its characteristic melodic rhythm, exaggerated vowels, and a rising and falling intonation. He summed up the effect on the rest of the men: "Boy, everybody cracked up." Cracking everyone up, of course, was always the goal.

D-Ray said he first heard of Mr. Buford from the brother of a golf buddy who hung out with him at some of the Five Points bars. One night, someone bestowed upon Mr. Buford the nickname *Pretty Buford*. The moment the two met at the center, D-Ray teased him about it.

> Buford say, "Don't start that shit, man." He look at me funny and say, "Who telling you this shit, man?" I say, "Word getting 'round about you, Buford." He'd be cussing and shit. I'd be laughing. It was all fun. That's when I first started messing with him. You know how you say [using a raspy voice], "Yeah, that's my baby there. You my bitch." That's how all that junk got started. One day we start doin' it. And it ain't never stop.

In a previous conversation, D-Ray had made the following observation about the dynamics of shit talk: "It's all in fun. We *know* how far to take a person. You know what I'm sayin'? You could tell how far you could push a person before you say stop and cool off and leave it alone."

Although their shit talk can be linked to the exaggerated bravado, masculine posturing, and competitive elements found in the verbal tradition of playing the dozens, a competition of ritual insults, the two elders do not take their exchanges seriously. Their somewhat theatrical performances of humor, sarcasm, and quick wit reinforce communal bonding, all the while affirming a positive, albeit stereotypical, masculine identity that conforms to the group's expectations. There's a comforting predictability in their sometimes outrageous contributions, like ritualistic performances that never fail to entertain. Similarly, in a study on rituals within relationships, Judy C. Pearson, Jeffrey T. Child, and Anna F. Carmon found that couples who share more rituals tend to experience a heightened sense of intimacy.[7] The following section illustrates how Mr. Buford and D-Ray's shit talk cultivates intimacy, care, and resilience within their relationship.

*Talking Shit as Gift Exchange*

In one game in March 2018, with light snow falling outside, Paul and D-Ray teamed up as domino partners against Mr. Buford and Mr. Hall. Anticipating a show, three other men took seats around them. They didn't have to wait long. D-Ray and Mr. Buford are both strong believers in Newton's third law of physics: every instance of shit talk causes an equal and opposite retort. Neither yields, and their banter normally lasts for most of the game. Antagonistic and sexually charged remarks are highly preferred.

> MR. BUFORD: I dominoed.
> D-RAY: You're a liar.
> PAUL: No, you didn't.
> D-RAY: You're a liar.
> PAUL: D-Ray gets fifteen.
> D-RAY: Spank his ass.
> [Three men laugh]
> MR. BUFORD: Bitch.
> D-RAY: You get your stanking ass to moving.
> MR. BUFORD: Wait a minute.
> D-RAY: You ain't nothing but a tramp. [Slams down domino] Five! Tell me, what is Buford over there blowing about? Buford over there blowing like he's some kind of bitch.
> [Three men laugh]

MR. HALL: Better quit talking like that. I mean it.

D-RAY: You don't want a person blow like this. What is he telling you?

MR. BUFORD: I'm tired of your ass.

[Three men laugh]

D-RAY: He want to blow you, don't he?

MR. BUFORD: I'm tired of your ass.

D-RAY: He want to blow you, don't he? What is it then?

MR. HALL: I ain't heard nothing.

D-RAY: You ain't heard him breathe. All the whistling over here? [Slams down domino] Ten. With your punk ass trying to get fours in my business. You better get you a life, man, and get the hell away from me.

Watching D-Ray and Mr. Buford sparring, I began to think of their reciprocal taunts as a discursive exchange of gifts. They gave each other the "gift" of words and attention. In Marcel Mauss's seminal work, and in anthropological explorations of gift-giving and the gift economy, scholars study the interplay between individuals and material items, arguing that these gifts forge ties that reflect the interdependence among individuals.[8] Mauss, in particular, delves into the profound ways in which people establish connections with objects and, by extension, with one another. As Mr. Buford and D-Ray shared words, I saw them solidify their bond to each other through very personal and intentional exchanges. In these moments of verbal sparring, their attention was trained solely on each other, and all others could do was watch and occasionally chime in.

The ability to build intimacy through talk in this way draws on the history and significance of call and response. This verbal tradition originated within African rituals and is now integral to modern Black culture, particularly in religious and informal settings.[9] Call and response is characterized by a reciprocal dialogue wherein the speaker's statements or "calls" are punctuated by responses from the listener, thus blurring the lines between speaker and audience and requiring active participation from all parties involved.[10] Thomas Kochman further explains call and response as a cyclical pattern where each response triggers the next call.[11] While traditionally rooted in gospel oratory in the United States, call and response has transcended its religious origins and now permeates everyday interactions. In secular settings, it fosters a sense of connection and community among participants.[12]

Often the speakers appeal to the emotions—or pathos—of the audience. In the case of the card room, this includes the men seated at and around the table, who chime in and laugh along. Calls and responses typically occur in close succession, generating a sense of energy and urgency. D-Ray "calls" to his intended audience ("Spank his ass"), and Mr. Buford responds ("Bitch"). Then later, D-Ray only pretends to be talking to Mr. Hall: "He want to blow you, don't he?" In reality, he is "calling" to Mr. Buford, who understands that he is D-Ray's target and quickly responds, "I'm tired of your ass." While shit talk prefers sacrilegious assertions, it creates shared, communal experiences that draw individuals and a group together, as in Black churches, where preachers call to the congregation and expect them to respond.

*Intimacy and Communal Experiences*

Even the subzero temperatures and icy roads of November 2018 couldn't reduce the crowd in the card room. Since Mr. Hall traveled this time of year to visit his mother, Mr. Taylor stepped in as Mr. Buford's partner. Quick-witted as he was, Mr. Taylor's shit talk never quite reached the levels of D-Ray and Mr. Buford's bellicosity and hyperbole.

In this example, D-Ray and Mr. Buford are positioned across from each other. Shortly after the first domino is played, Mr. Buford transitions rapidly from silence to verbal dueling, as if a switch has been flipped.

> MR. BUFORD: D-Ray can go fuck hisself and an old sideliner can go with him.
> D-RAY: Sideliner?
> MR. TAYLOR: A side*winder*.
> D-RAY: Sideline *this*.
> MR. TAYLOR: Sideliner or a sidewinder?
> D-RAY: Get out of there! [Throws down a domino]
> MR. TAYLOR: [Laughs] I know [unintelligible]

D-RAY: I'm tired of—
MR. BUFORD: [Slams the domino] Five!
D-RAY: He was gonna hold that goddamn blank.
MR. TAYLOR: Where will he hold it?
D-RAY: [Rapidly] What's that? What's that? What's THAT? That dog son of a—[Lays down domino] Give me ten.
MR. TAYLOR: You're taking it all. I can see it.
D-RAY: Here we go again.
MR. TAYLOR: I can see it.
D-RAY: Running off crying. You could have fell a minute ago.
MR. BUFORD: You can bend over now.
D-RAY: You bend over. I'm really gonna ram you, boy.
MR. TAYLOR: He's talkin' that game.
D-RAY: That's what he doin'. Gonna buckle his though, when I hit it.
MR. BUFORD: The man don't domino. What the fuck you talking about?
D-RAY: See that fool in the butt, boy. I'm gonna get you drop down. You know your ass gonna drop.
TRAPPER: Don't make it drop down on—
D-RAY: Whose play is it?
PAUL: Yours.
D-RAY: No.
PAUL: Yes.
D-RAY: Okay then, ten.
MR. TAYLOR: Man, they taking all the money. That ain't fair.
D-RAY: Man, put Buford in bad shape man. Didn't I just take that off?
MR. TAYLOR: You took it off.
MR. BUFORD: Stop talking the game, you one-eyed motherfucker. Shut up that talk the game a big head son of a bitch.
D-RAY: I just took it off.
MR. BUFORD: Don't you people know what you're doin'?
D-RAY: You're ain't gonna do a damn thing. You come here.
MR. BUFORD: Come over here and get it.
[Room laughter]

As Gail Jefferson, Harvey Sacks, and Emmanuel Schegloff have noted, one way to increase the level of intimacy in an interaction is through humor, sexualized language, and banter—elements that convey a sense of informality, relaxation, and unguarded communication.[13] Deborah Cameron and Don Kulick have also found that "intimacy is often achieved, at least in part, through the transgression of public taboos."[14] Their breaking of sexual taboos, especially through the hint of homosexuality, is jointly constructed. Mr. Buford does not expect a comment like *You can bend over now* to be met by silence. When D-Ray inevitably responds, they engage in what Jennifer Coates calls "conversational dueting."[15] In these exchanges, ever more outrageous responses are tolerated and even expected, and the only incorrect rejoinder would be to fail to respond at all.[16]

Energy is generated through these exchanges, which also allows others to chime in with their own rejoinders, as Mr. Taylor and Trapper do through laughter. This laughter, too, signals the end of the exchanges. A sense of contagious joy creates a synchronized connection among the elders. Emile Durkheim describes this type of intensity as "collective effervescence."[17] These assertive and expressive linguistic patterns represent culturally meaningful ways of framing what might otherwise be considered posturing and aggressive speech. This interactionally produced play turn performances into forms of entertainment and recreation while still accomplishing important social goals of solidifying relationships and fostering group cohesion.[18]

As the elders frequently reminded me, the card room stands as one of the only remaining Black safe havens in Denver for the men to come together, play dominoes, and talk shit. They treated the space as special, and they did not violate its rules: If family talk was not permitted inside the card room, I never witnessed the elders talking shit while conversing in front of the recreation center. Married elders claim they refrain from talking shit in the presence of their wives. Established for these men, the card room offered a safe, private, and celebratory space where intimacy and familiarity were recreated through ritual practices like talking shit. This highly charged discourse helped construct the social and emotional significance—and benefits—of the physical space.

*Building Intimacy*

Scholars who study conversational dynamics recognize laughter as an official conversational activity, not merely an accompaniment to talk.[19] Coates argues that laughter *is* talk, often a consequential response to a prior remark.[20] Though the transcript seems to end with Mr. Buford's *Come over here and get it,* the group laughter at the table should be understood as the response to his call. The laughter as a response encourages another call, which fosters sustained involvement in the play-frame. Paul does not normally say much. But his distinctive and robust laughter keeps him audible and relevant. The men's laughter conveys that what is being said is *intended* to be humorous, as part of a play-frame and not to be taken seriously. It is also important to note that the laughter arising from the play-frame is often *shared* group laughter. The men laugh at the same utterance, and they laugh at the same time, in the same way. The men's joint attention reinforces shared views, shared identities, and a strong sense of group membership. Laughing together, each audibly declares how comfortable they feel in that space and with the people around them.

Soon after Mr. Buford and Mr. Taylor won the domino game, D-Ray sat to Mr. Buford's right. The play-frame had ended. Mr. Buford turned toward D-Ray. Since I sat to Mr. Buford's left, I heard Mr. Buford say quietly to D-Ray, "We all right." It seemed as though he was acknowledging that the characters that they had just played on stage, which resembled the antics of cartoon wrestlers vying against each other in a ring, may have inadvertently caused harm. D-Ray quickly reassured Mr. Buford. "Yeah, we all right." Nothing more needed to be said. The brief and discreet exchange between them unfolded as a tender and private moment, briefly acknowledging that their performance that evening might have surpassed even their standards.

On the one hand, D-Ray and Mr. Buford both embody the metaphorical roles of sexual dominance (in gay lingo, both are "tops"). Their semi-structured performances allow them not only to verbally spar with one another but also to communicate to their audience that they should not be perceived as feminine in any way. Buford's "we all right" was the most intimate statement I ever heard anyone utter in the card room, suggesting that hidden within their loud battles for linguistic control were tender male relationships.

*The Intimacy of Goodbye*

On January 1, 2019, I received a group text from Mr. Buford's son.

> 2019 Blessings to all!!
>
> THIS MESSEGE COMES WITH A HEAVY HEART TO INFORM YOU ALL THAT BUFORD YARBROUGH MY DAD HAS PASSED AND WENT HOME TO BE WITH THE LORD LAST NIGHT. WHEN WE AS A FAMILY HAVE MORE INFORMATION ABOUT SERVICES WE WILL SEND IT OUT TO ALL. HE WILL TRULY BE MISSED AND TOUCHED SO MANY LIVES WITH HIS LOVE AND PERSONALITY.

I was taken aback, though not entirely surprised. Mr. Buford had exuded confidence when he called on Christmas Day, cheerily wishing me a "Merry Christmas, y'ho-ho-ho" and boasting about feeling much improved on his new medication. Just a few months prior, he had greeted me in the card room with his customary warm handshake and his usual quip, "How you doin', man?" followed, predictably, by "Steve, you ever been with a tall, leggy woman?" As per usual, I failed to respond other than with a shy smile or head shake. Embarrassing me was generally the point. Later that same evening, as I helped him into his car, Mr. Buford leaned on me for physical support, a need that became a nightly routine until his visits ceased altogether. Then, on the Friday night before Thanksgiving—after a three-week absence—I stepped outside the card room to call him. I was relieved when he answered. He shared that he was spending time with his daughter and grandchildren. Mr. Buford was curious who was present in the room that night. I replied, "It's Mr. Taylor, Mr. Hall, Mr. Carr, and D-Ray." He then tasked me with delivering a message to them, which I dutifully obeyed. "Say hi to Mr. Taylor, hi to Mr. Carr, hi to Mr. Hall," he instructed, before adding, "And tell D-Ray he can go fuck himself." The group erupted in laughter when I relayed the message. Mr. Hall chimed in, "You know he meant that," while D-Ray, doubling over with laughter, pounded his fists on the nearby cabinet.

The day after Christmas, I arrived at the center earlier than usual and found D-Ray already there, watching television. With nobody else present in the room, I took the opportunity to bring up Mr. Buford's recent phone call from the day before. D-Ray shared with me that Mr. Buford had undergone triple-bypass heart surgery seven years ago. Sensing D-Ray's concern and forcing the issue a bit, I suggested he reach out to Mr. Buford and offered him my phone for the call, placing it on the table and activating the speakerphone for convenience.

D-RAY: Is this sugarloaf?
MR. BUFORD: What the hell do you want?
D-RAY: Look man. I'm telling you. You ain't got no days off. I know Christmas was over, but you better get back on the job.
MR. BUFORD: [Unintelligible but characteristic grumble]
D-RAY: Because if I need to walk you up on that stroller up there, I got plenty of gas to watch ya.
MR. BUFORD: [Says something about being short of breath] I went up to the doctor's for a check-up.
D-RAY: Did your doctor stick his finger up your ass?
MR. BUFORD: What?
D-RAY: Did your doctor stick his finger up your ass?
MR. BUFORD: No, they wanna know why my dick's so big.
D-RAY: You're a damn liar. [Laughs] I see you feeling pretty goddamn good. If you can joke, you're good. [Laughs more]
MR. BUFORD: They brought me some peanut butter. And it got smooth, smooth. [Referring to anal lubricant]
D-RAY: But you're doin' all right though.
MR. BUFORD: All righty, man. I hope you had a merry Christmas.
D-RAY: We'll probably see you on the first of the year.
MR. BUFORD: Hey man, I'm telling everybody. I'm through wichoo [with you]. I'm through wich your ass.
D-RAY: You know, Buford. You can't say nothing nice, can you?

Blurring the boundaries a bit, D-Ray and Mr. Buford continue their shit talk beyond the card room and venture into the topic of Mr. Buford's health. Once again, the deep connections between talking shit, mascu-

FIG. 15. Mr. Buford's funeral. Steve Bialostok, photographer.

linity, and intimacy surface as D-Ray offers a welcome diversion from Mr. Buford's ailments. D-Ray calls on Mr. Buford's mental strength and masculine resilience and encourages him to come back and play. In contrast to a pity party, D-Ray forces Mr. Buford into his boisterous and outrageous posturing. Leaning into the energy and the bravado of shit talk, D-Ray tries to stoke Mr. Buford's fire for life, urging him to rekindle their verbal sparring as a means of spiritual (and hopefully physical) rejuvenation. This was the last time they spoke.

*Mr. Buford's Homegoing*

Two weeks after Mr. Buford's passing, a procession of limousines and automobiles brought his family to the small, Black-owned funeral home for his homegoing celebration. Following the service, they would transport Mr. Buford to Fort Logan National Cemetery for a full military burial. In the chapel, a single row held seven men from the card room, though D-Ray, Mr. Hall, and Mr. Taylor were notably absent. Up front, an American flag adorned Mr. Buford's closed casket.

Although not the churchgoing type, Mr. Buford would have likely appreciated the numerous eulogies. His children spoke first, followed by the grandchildren, with an open invitation extended to other speakers. A young man from the family shared a fond memory of Mr. Buford teaching him to play dominoes. "I'd go back to school [college], and I taught my friends to play dominoes just 'cause he taught me. Then I'd take their money." Laughter filled the room.

To my surprise, Trapper stood up next. He walked down the aisle and approached the podium. Trapper was not typically characterized as someone radiating warmth and sensitivity, but it made perfect sense for him to represent the men. Whenever an elder passed away, Trapper brought a sympathy card for the men to sign. He organized the money collection for Mrs. Carr and made sure it was enclosed in the card. He did the same when George's son died and brought flowers to the home of the bereaved. Now, Trapper delivered a heartfelt eulogy.

> I met Mr. Buford, gosh, I don't know how long. It's been over twenty-five [years] I know. And we played dominoes. And he was one giant human being. Once I got to know him, he was like a father figure [pause] to me. And I got a chance to meet his grandson. I got a chance to meet his daughter one afternoon. But I don't recall their names. Mr. Buford had a lot of friends that played bones with him daily. And I was one of them. I don't have a whole lot to say. But I just want the folks, the family, and the friends to know that there's a lot of guys at the service. And I just want them to stand up. And give them a hand. All the guys that play at Hiawatha Davis. Dominoes. There's more. A lot of the guys didn't show today. I'm just saying to his family and all of his friends—you know, he was a giant of a human being.

The following day, D-Ray and George sat together at the table, watching television. George, who had known Mr. Buford longer than almost anyone and was about five years older, remarked, "Buford beat me out of here." D-Ray turned toward a few men gathered nearby and said with concern, "We need to keep an eye on George." Little O walked in carrying enough food from the Blazing Chicken Shack to feed everybody. "We lost a soldier," D-Ray somberly noted.

*Mr. Buford's Poetry*

During the summer of 2020, I had a phone conversation with D-Ray when the COVID pandemic led to the closure of all recreation centers. "About 90 percent of the time I stay home," he shared. Although D-Ray still played golf occasionally, securing tee times had become a challenge. Sadly, he had lost two friends to COVID. I read Mr. Buford's "poetry" to him—the lines I had recorded him saying:

> D-Ray, sweet motherfucka,
> Eyes like a frog.
> Leap to me,
> And I'm gonna fuck you like a dog.

Listening to Mr. Buford's common refrain jogged D-Ray's memory. "That's what he do. That's what he do. He start laughin'. I say, 'You son of a bitch.' You don't take it as an insult or nothin' cuz I know he's playin. He go [D-Ray lowers his voice to imitate Buford's raspy voice], 'Hey baby, how you doin' today?' I say, 'Bring your ass in here. I'm feeling to dust it.'"

D-Ray recalled several stories about times they would sit around the table and discuss people who walked in. "Buford'll tell you who he don't like," he said, using the present tense. "He'll say, 'Man, I don't like him. But I put up with his ass.' 'I don't like him either, Buford.' That's just the way it was between me and him."

*Conclusion*

Every evening from Monday to Friday, the card room at the Hiawatha Davis Recreation Center echoes with the sounds of dominoes being slammed and spirited shit talk. But the men who gather there share more than just space at plastic tables. Over the course of these hours, they forge relationships that go far beyond the surface. Intimacy and care are deeply woven into their interactions.

We often think we "know" people when we are privy to personal details about their families, daily lives, or struggles. Yet there are other, more subtle signs of intimacy that reveal the true depth of a connection—like the elders' shared laughter, the jokes they tell, or the way a player places a tile on the table when winning or losing. Knowing others and feeling known are fundamental human experiences. These small gestures speak volumes about mutual understanding and trust.

The level of intimacy shared by the elders in the card room disrupts the hegemonic narratives that continue to dehumanize Black people in our society. Through their nightly rituals, they enact countless moments of care, affirmation, and mutual support. In doing so, they recognize each other's worth and dignity—creating a space that honors their humanity. Within this safe, Black enclave, the bonds they forge transform them into embodiments of resilience and collective strength.

## 11   D-Ray Edwards

"How ya doin', D-Ray?" I asked. D-Ray was standing outside the recreation center.

"Hanging in there, Stevie. You know that."

D-Ray came dressed in color-coordinated exercise outfits, this time blue sweatpants with white stripes, a matching white T-shirt with Adidas on the front, a blue hoodie with a cotton-white hood, a blue baseball cap, and blue Adidas sneakers. He wore a gold bracelet, and a gold ring on his right-hand ring finger. Gold caps covered five teeth on the bottom row in front.

I discovered that the best time to talk with D-Ray was when he was smoking a Marlboro Light in front of the center, sitting on a retaining wall, or standing on the sidewalk. D-Ray never stood outside alone. His posse usually included Grover, Freddie, and Paul. D-Ray had mentored Grover and Freddie ever since they were at Glenarm Recreation Center, where D-Ray began his career as the Sports Program coordinator. Working for several recreation centers in the same underserved neighborhoods made D-Ray the ideal historian. He knew the names of nearly every kid who participated in youth sports, and their parents' names too. In other words, D-Ray was one of the longest-running and most consistent "participant-observers" of the neighborhood where he lived as an adult. "It was fun up here," he said, pointing across Holly Street from Hiawatha Davis.

> See where those lights is back over there? That was the liquor store. Right next to that, there was something, a beauty shop or something else. Next to that was a church. . . . The Hope Center was over there. Library wasn't even there. . . . Down on Dahlia we had a McDonalds.

FIG. 16. D-Ray. Steve Bialostok, photographer.

33rd and Dahlia we had a skating rink. And a bowling alley. A little bar. The old Dairy Queen turned into a Capris Chicken. Man, you see the change right in front of your face. And you can't do nothin' about it.

D-Ray's succinct reflections offer his observations and life lessons: change, regrettably, is inevitable; one must concede and adjust to it. Places, like people, have identities that transform over time. Buildings disappear; stakeholders erect new ones. These buildings serve new purposes for new people: "Library wasn't even there." Eventually, there will be new place memories. But the inevitability of change threatens longstanding and formerly durable attachments. To D-Ray, who first put down roots here after college, Park Hill symbolized home—the place where his soul was rooted.[1] It held memories, both comforting and painful. And even though he now lived in the suburbs, Holly Square remained his home. Despite the confidence he sometimes projected, you could almost see him grappling with the loss of a changing community and its recreation center. He lit another cigarette and reminisced about a past era, a time when staff genuinely cared about youth and youth sports. "We had a good thing going, man. You can ask anybody. Sent a lot of kids to college. I guess they don't want that anymore. We had eight to ten teams back then. Same for baseball. And basketball. We was going all over. We had a lot of teams, man."

D-Ray supervised sports when youth sports were channeled through the local recreation centers. Neighborhood staff coached and knew the kids. They worked closely with the community, and this was crucial to Skyland's (and later Hiawatha Davis's) central philosophy. When Denver Parks and Recreation took away much of Hiawatha Davis's local control, the neighborhood staff were let go. The visible replacement of residents angered the community and left a gaping hole. Local programs were discontinued. D-Ray realized that the community's needs were being phased out, so he and several others sat down with the central administrator in charge. "We told her about all the great people who came out of [Hiawatha Davis]. 'You know what?' she said. 'We're not here to produce those kind of people.' And we said, 'How are they going to get an education past high school?'"

D-Ray paused, then sounded angry and frustrated. "It ain't about a community center or a rec center anymore. It's about a cash cow they trying to bring in to make themselves look good. This ain't even Skyland, this is something else. The real one ain't here."

There it was again—*Skyland*. Decades after Skyland was officially rebuilt and renamed, D-Ray's deep sense of place underscored the tension of a metamorphosis from "the way things used to be" to today's "superficialities," capturing the inexorable character of change in a single placename.

D-Ray had learned to play dominoes at Glenarm, but after work, he regularly joined the men at Skyland in the old kitchen. Five years later, they moved into the card room. "All of them dead, man," he says, referring to the names he easily recalls. D-Ray once drew a rough sketch for me to see what the inside of Skyland looked like.

"Do you wish this place was like the old Skyland?" I asked.

"It was good fun up here, man," D-Ray said with a smile.

*From Texas to Colorado*

Born Donald Ray Edwards in 1948 in the tiny town of Franklin, Texas, D-Ray relocated to Denver in 1953 together with his family—by then, five girls and five boys. At the time, they hoped that Colorado's dry climate would cure his father's asthma. D-Ray still refers to "the projects," a neighborhood adjacent to Five Points where he grew up. There, D-Ray's brothers nurtured his athletic passion and his competitiveness: "Anything that was a round ball involved, I'd follow it." He excelled playing baseball but recalls having to tolerate the racial slurs yelled at him from the crowd. But it was D-Ray's successful career in high school basketball that earned him a full college scholarship. At the end of summer 1966, off D-Ray went to Seattle, leaving behind his girlfriend and a one-year-old son he had fathered at sixteen. While D-Ray was away at college, his son developed cancer. D-Ray traveled back and forth for his son's chemotherapy. Then one day, he got the call and returned to Denver soon enough to hold his son in his arms as he died.

After graduating with a degree in political science, D-Ray returned to Denver. Basketball remained his passion, so D-Ray pursued the professional leagues. Despite repeated tryouts, he rediscovered a lesson he had already learned in college: being a star in high school didn't make you a star later in life. "Man, I tried. . . . And then, you know how reality hits you? You got to make a living." D-Ray turned to his friend, Harry Hollins, the former University of Denver basketball star and all-American, who worked for Denver Parks and Recreation. Hollins hired the college graduate to work at Glenarm Recreation Center. "See, me working with inner city kids . . . I was brought up in that environment." This first job turned into a lengthy career working at several recreation centers, and he eventually retired from Hiawatha Davis.

*A Place at the Recreation Center*

A small group of youngsters in the card room share a deep respect for D-Ray—some due to his lengthy history working at Denver Parks and Recreation; others, for his influential role at Denver Parks and Recreation during their formative years; all, because of his fame as a high school basketball player. But of those career milestones, D-Ray was most proud of his basketball record of fifty years earlier. To hear him talk about it, one would think he had graduated only a week earlier. D-Ray's bravado made him an easy (and responsive) discursive target for the men who admired him and talked shit as one way to readily express their affection. In one instance, D-Ray roared angrily when Grover dared to question D-Ray's claim about his basketball team's legendary status. Said D-Ray, "I can't name nobody that was ranked higher than *we* was!" Paul declared that it was a different high school that went undefeated. "No, it *wasn't*," D-Ray shouted. "Quit *lyin'*!" These events from nearly half a century ago seemed extraordinarily trivial to me, but eventually I realized how seriously D-Ray took that record. "You stop lyin'! Mr. Callaway will *tell* you they wasn't as good as us," he said, resurrecting from the dead his high school principal to come to his defense.

Paul and Grover laughed and continued challenging D-Ray's memory. But D-Ray didn't crack a smile. Instead, he attacked Grover's high school basketball team's standing: "Where was George Washington [High School] and Grover ranked?" "Number one, bitch!" Grover cackled in response. When Paul returned to questioning his high school rankings, D-Ray responded at the top of his raspy voice, "You're talking about the history of my high school, man. I've got the history of that!"

With his competitive spirit, D-Ray playfully upped the intensity of every domino game. He and Paul had been playing a good hand, and D-Ray followed their win with a husky and enthusiastic: "Oh we *fuckin'*, we *fuckin'*, oh, we fuckin' *now*. Oh, we stickin' it in him. Paul, we stickin' it in him. He doesn't know whether to shit or go blind right now." D-Ray's eyes twinkled as his head cocked slightly downward to the right. As the game continued, with a crooked smile, D-Ray inserted more of the typical outbursts from his repertoire: "Get your stinking ass out of here." "Fuck you." "Quit lyin'." "Shut up." "That's what I'm *telling* ya."

It was 7:00 when D-Ray, Mr. Buford, Mr. Hall, and a fourth player I didn't recognize began a game. Two men sat out, one keeping score. Grover sat alone at a separate table while four of the youngsters played at a third table and several others waited their turns. Derek had his feet up on the round table as he watched television. The dominoes had been mixed and selected. D-Ray initiated the game with one of his standard openers.

D-RAY: Who you trying to play hard on, bitch?
JOHN: Who's playing?
D-RAY: Your piece of one-ass play.
MR. HALL: I pass.
D-RAY: What'd I tell you? Didn't I tell you I was gonna kill him?
MR. BUFORD: Suck my dick.
D-RAY: Shut up!
GROVER: [Newspaper in hand, pretending to read a headline] It says here. "She-Ray got married to Trapper. It was free. Down there at the Webb [City] Building." Come and shake D-Ray's hand. Come and shake Trapper's hand. They got the marriage license.
PLAYER: Which one is the male?
GROVER: I don't know. I can't speak to that. Which one of y'all is the female?
D-RAY: You're a goddamn liar. Five.
GROVER: It says right here. She-Ray.
D-RAY: No, no, no. Something there says, Grosetta. [Making fun of Grover]
GROVER: What's it say right here? *She*-Ray.
D-RAY: Grosetta.
GROVER: It says right here, "Better known in the center as She-Ray." That's what it say.
D-RAY: No, Dick-Ray. Ask Buford about it. He been stuck with it a few times. Oh yeah.
MR. BUFORD: You sorry motherfucker.
D-RAY: That son of a bitch passed me that thing.
MR. BUFORD: Ten! Domino!
D-RAY: It's supposed to snow tomorrow.
PLAYER: It was seven below last night. It set a record.
D-RAY: It was minus twenty-two at the airport last night.

Here, D-Ray begins playfully, but it doesn't take long before Grover instigates another round. But the game keeps D-Ray largely within the play-frame, and D-Ray talks shit right back. Had Grover declared him "She-Ray" outside the game, without the protection of the game's "magic circle," D-Ray would have easily fallen into Grover's trap once again. In this instance, however, once Mr. Buford calls domino, the play-frame ends, and D-Ray immediately discusses the upcoming weather.

### Talking Shit and Belonging: Levert

In spring 2020, after decades of employment at two recreation centers, Levert, a physically and cognitively disabled employee, lost his job. Like D-Ray, Levert was a significant institution inside the center. For regulars, Levert's venerable presence linked Hiawatha to memories of Skyland and to the heartbeat of this Black community. Despite all the bureaucratic changes, Levert's presence helped preserve a sense of place. Levert belonged there, as did they.

But Denver Parks and Recreation had abolished jobs at his level. Elevating him to the next level would have increased his wages from $7.00 to $18.00 an hour but required tasks he could not perform. Hiawatha Davis's supervisor at the time had no interest in keeping Levert. So, instead of the administration figuring out how to maintain him at $7.00 an hour for a few hours a week, Levert was terminated. No one was angrier than D-Ray, who had known and worked alongside Levert for forty years. "I didn't like how they done him up there at Hiawatha. You don't had to cut his job, man. Just cut his pay, put another title on him. Come on. You know, that little bitty bullshit you giving him. He ain't been working but two days a week there. For what, two hours? So what? You got tired of filling out the paperwork?"

D-Ray had supported Levert's initial employment when he was hired back in the early 1960s. Several months after Levert was transferred from Glenarm to Skyland, Keith arrived. It took Keith three years to realize that Levert was an employee. Levert had created his own job description, which he took quite seriously: "Watch the kids and keep them out of trouble." Even when the kids were in school and the quiet and near-empty center felt like a tomb, there was Levert, admirably carrying out his duties.

After his termination, Levert was angry, but he returned regularly, still keeping the kids out of trouble. He would push his walker into the card room to socialize or play checkers with any willing participant. One afternoon, as I was interviewing D-Ray and waiting for the other men to arrive, Levert came into the card room. It was just the three of us. I asked Levert if he knew why he had lost his job. Cutting in before he could answer,

D-Ray, who knew about Levert's termination, began talking shit to him. D-Ray asserted that Levert had been "too busy flirting" instead of working. (Levert's card room moniker was "Levert the Flirt.") What's more, D-Ray claimed, Denver Parks and Recreation had selected *him* (D-Ray) to replace Levert. D-Ray's no-holds-barred approach was on full display. In a feisty and rapid exchange, where Levert held his own, D-Ray alleged that Levert "never did anything" around the center. Levert responded:

LEVERT: What did I do around here before I got fired?
D-RAY: Nothing!
LEVERT: You ain't doin' nothing 'cuz you don't know what I was doin'.
D-RAY: You don't do nothing around here. You don't work here. You know what's wrong with you?
LEVERT: I see why they cuss you out.
D-RAY: You don't want to admit that I'm a better man that you.
LEVERT: No, no, no. You're an old, old dude.
D-RAY: You old, too. Shit. But you know, I got it going on.
LEVERT: Stop it.
D-RAY: I can't hear you.
LEVERT: I'm not talking to you right now. You're just jealous.
D-RAY: Jealous a what?
LEVERT: That I'd be doin'.
D-RAY: Like what?
LEVERT: Ladies.
D-RAY: No, no, no.
LEVERT: I said, 'Ladies.'
D-RAY: Don't you start that. You a fruit cake.
LEVERT: In your mind.
D-RAY: In *your* mind. See, I'm trying to get you straight.
LEVERT: You can't get me straight—
D-RAY: *Listen.* Let me finish *my* speech. I'm trying to get you straight. So you'll be able to call yourself a ladies' man.
LEVERT: Your name is D-Ray.
D-RAY: When I ask the women, they say, "*What* Levert?" They don't know you. But you wanna be like me, don't cha?

LEVERT: [Laughs] No, oh, no. Don't even go there.
D-RAY: You wanna be like *me*.
LEVERT: Don't go there.
D-RAY: Flirt, come clean. [To Steve] He wants to be like me.
LEVERT: No.
D-RAY: You just *said* it.
LEVERT: No.

In the remaining verbal dueling, D-Ray provoked Levert with, "Have you kissed a girl?" Levert stared at him with a silent and sarcastic look. D-Ray responded to Levert's momentary silence with, "That's what I'm talking about."

I followed Levert out the door to ask what he thought of D-Ray's comments. "He be joking," Levert said. "D-Ray and I know each other a long time. We were together at Glenarm." An outsider overhearing their exchange might easily interpret D-Ray as being verbally abusive, especially given Levert's condition. But D-Ray, and the other elders, consider and treat Levert as one of them. Levert is no neophyte at talking shit, so D-Ray and Levert's banter accomplishes the social purpose of conveying camaraderie and belonging. But being fired is being fired. The popular assumption is that men who lose a job can experience that loss as a loss of masculinity. The *content* of shit talk—which rewards masculine bravado—provides an accepted means to construct and reconstruct traditional masculine normality. Just by participating, by being targeted and keeping up, Levert can rightfully lay claim to masculine toughness. This, I believe, was D-Ray's goal all along. D-Ray hurls the gay pejorative, "You a fruitcake" and "I'm gonna get you straight," just as Grover playfully had hurled "She-Ray" toward D-Ray. *I'm gonna get you straight* might be interpreted metaphorically as being honest and moral (on the straight and narrow), but D-Ray suggests that modeling his own behavior will strengthen Levert's masculinity—no matter how much Levert might protest ("You can't get me straight"). Without his intervention, D-Ray implies, Levert will remain hopelessly single (or the non-straight homosexual). Levert, however, holds his ground, performing his own masculine identity in real time, with D-Ray and me as his audience.

*D-Ray: Witness to History*

People tend to associate "witnesses to history" with those who have survived wars, the Holocaust, apartheid, and other unbearable catastrophes. We can also bear witness to changes that wash over neighborhoods, observing the evolution of city blocks and the impact on long-standing establishments. D-Ray was born witness to the loss and erasure of the greater Northeast Park Hill neighborhood, the Holly, and the recreation center specifically—and has spoken out against the racial injustices that include fewer opportunities for Black youth in his community. As he watches these changes unfold, D-Ray questions the new names, values, and ways of doing things that no longer foreground the needs of residents and community members. He laments that "they only care about the bottom line." The bottom line is responsible for Levert's wrongful termination. D-Ray struggles with his inability to protect his community from the forces of change. He fears that little by little, their Black place will be squeezed out.

# 12  Endings

Death took its toll. During my five years of research, three elders died. Their absence was a punch to the gut of the card room. Mr. Cummings died on October 2017, at eighty-five, a year after we first met. He had already started to organize the domino tournament, but it was obvious that his health had taken a turn for the worse. Mr. Cummings—the spry, sharp-minded man who claimed to be the first Black resident of his Northeast Park Hill street in 1962 and worked as a medical technician for "thirty-five years and ninety-nine days"—now advanced his weakened frame at a snail's pace. The sarcastic wit that once roused an entire room to laughter was now voiced just audibly enough to make his presence known. Sadly, the man who established the domino tournament in an old and decrepit kitchen in the mid-1960s could no longer take part in a single game.

No one knew what was wrong. No one even had his phone number. Only Walter, who grew up down the block from Mr. Cummings and attended school with his son, paid him regular visits. Sometimes I saw Walter walking back from Mr. Cummings's home when I stood outside talking with D-Ray. He never had any specific information to share, although we conjectured it was cancer. Mr. Cummings himself didn't seem to know what was going on when I paid him a visit in early fall 2017, or maybe he didn't want to say. On that day, he lay in bed watching football, "in more pain than I've had for a long time." He told me to pull up a stool. As tactfully as possible, I asked if it was cancer. He responded, "Nobody's ever said that to me." A friend had taken him to the center the previous week. "My friend stopped and said, 'Well, are you going in?' I put one foot on the sidewalk and couldn't move."

But Mr. Cummings didn't really want to talk about illness. He wanted to talk about the domino tournament. "What's going on?" he wondered, although I didn't have much information to provide. He anticipated that "they ought to be finishing the playoffs" that week, and he still didn't trust "the new guy that's taking over the center." He seemed reassured when I explained that participants without memberships now had a sign-in system. "That's great," Mr. Cummings said, his voice so faint I had to lean forward to hear. "They seem to want to change things around. We've been doing this for years. Nobody's ever given us a problem." Mr. Cummings asked how my domino playing was progressing. "I play more, but I'm not any good." Then he seemed to find some untapped energy. "Let me tell you something. You can play that game forever. And it depends on who you play with and how good you do. It depends on how good you play and how good *they* do. Just a funny game." He planned to attend the tournament banquet for the singular purpose of talking shit to everyone. "I'll come in there and tell everyone, 'Shut up . . . Say *what*? . . . Shut up and sit down and let me tell you this.'" For a moment, he was himself again.

But Mr. Cummings never made it to the tournament.

His death, two months after we spoke, was met with as much apprehension as sorrow. *Maybe* tournaments would continue in the future, but organizing them was time-consuming and no one wanted the task. More importantly, Mr. Cummings was the soul of the room, the figurehead, the protector who fought for their right to carry on the mantle of the annual tournament. And in doing so he contributed mightily to the protection of this historic Black place. Among those who had been present the longest, memories of him initiating the tournament were fondly shared. Others recounted his unwavering commitment to collaborating with Denver Parks and Recreation to establish their cherished room.

Yet even before Mr. Cummings took ill, change had troubled the men, especially when they found out that the recreation center's supervisor had insulted Mr. Cummings. During a disagreement related to the tournament, the supervisor had called Mr. Cummings an "old man." The elders complained that the new front-desk employees no longer greeted them respectfully. They imagined that the recreation center would soon go the way of Holly Square. Vince recalled the time "when Skyland was Black." Trapper offered his garage, with its central heat and air conditioning, as a place they could all gather and play if needed.

Toward the end of 2019, the number of men showing up to play dwindled significantly. Mr. Buford had passed at the end of 2018. Mr. Carr had died in March, just a few months later. George's senility worsened, and he stopped coming altogether. D-Ray appeared only once every few months. Then came another shocking loss: thirty-year-old Shawn, the youngest of the men, was crossing Colorado Boulevard on an electric scooter when he was hit by a car. After two months in a coma and hospitalization, he died. There were times I would walk in to see only Mr. Hall and Mr. Taylor playing against each other.

*Domino Tournament Awards Ceremony*

Mook volunteered to coordinate the 2020 tournament, but despite his efforts, so few competed that I didn't even realize the tournament was taking place. Nevertheless, the award ceremony and banquet were held, as always, in the Hiawatha Davis multipurpose room on the afternoon of Saturday, March 7, 2020. The room, which seats seventy-five, felt larger with only seventeen men attending, half as many as in the past. They sat at one of four eight-foot folding tables. Mook stood in front and announced that this year's tournament had been "smaller, it wasn't much attended, but it was less hassle because it *was* smaller." After the men's laughter subsided, he continued. "Saying that, I don't know *what's* gonna happen next time. We'll have to talk about that at a later date. I don't know how much participation if people want to do this again. If we get enough participation—" "We start asking now," someone interrupted. Trapper suggested a meeting in June: "Let everybody meet up, and we'll figure out who all wants to participate. And try to bring some new members in."

Someone recommended that "we make up fliers." Mook said, "Think about how we can make this better—or do we want to continue—whatever ideas anybody's got about doing this. I think that we might have fun. It's a good time for me. I like dominoes. I know a lot of other people who do. It's something to do, to get you to meet other people." Someone joked, "Get you away from home," and Mook completed that sentence with, "For a minute." Not so long ago, no one could have ever imagined that low participation would end the tournament, much less that they would need a recruitment plan that included fliers and a justification for why playing dominoes was a good thing to do.

Happily, they pivoted to declare winners "just for first and second place." "That's cold," complained the player in third place. Mook announced that Mr. Hall and Mr. Anderson had secured first place. Mr. Anderson could not attend, but Mr. Hall was all smiles as he walked up to the front and was greeted with applause, hoots, and talk. He proudly held up the two 2020 first place champion trophies. Engraved on both were "Ed Anderson and Charles Hall." Mr. Hall spoke: "First of all, I want to thank every last one of you guys. I want to thank Ed for being my partner. I want to thank Mr. Mook. Last but not least, I want thank each and every one of you guys that participated. You did a great, great job. I met some beautiful and wonderful people. We want to keep this going. Thanks, guys. I appreciate it."

There was applause. Before the catered buffet of brisket, chicken, baked beans, coleslaw, and potato salad, Little O led everyone in prayer.

*Post-COVID Reopening*

The men never convened to discuss how to save the domino tournament. Not long after the awards banquet, all of Denver's recreation centers closed due to COVID mandates. In May 2021 I learned about the reopening from Linda, my ceramics instructor, in a text to her students:

> Ceramic Students, I'm very sad to announce that Hiawatha Davis Recreation Center has discontinued the Ceramic Class. Everyone it was fun while it lasted. I'll miss you all! Y'all stay safe.

I texted Linda to find out what happened, after twelve years of her tenure there. She wrote:

> No one even called me. I heard that the center was open, so I called, and they were like, "I'm glad you called. We boxed everything up." I just told them to throw everything out, except for my paints. I have nowhere to store anything.

During the closure, Denver Parks and Recreation took administrative measures to centralize all of Hiawatha Davis's local programs, a bureaucratic process that had begun prior to the pandemic. Hiawatha

Davis wasn't unique in this regard; it had just managed to control local programming and facilitators longer than other recreation centers. Everything now had to operate under one of the five "Core Programs." Designating an activity as a "club" guaranteed it an official day, time, and space. Ceramics, now under the core program of Arts and Crafts, was assigned an official Denver Parks and Recreation instructor. The men's play now fell under the "Card and Board Room Club," a designation under the core program of Active Older Adults.

*To Be Old*

When Trapper explained why he kept returning to the card room from his home in the suburbs, he spoke of "these old guys." Trapper and the other elders were once young domino players, and they had all experienced that great conveyer belt of life. None were thrilled about their various age-related ailments, but in the card room, they never complained or talked about their health, despite the multiple medications scattered across their bathroom countertops. Whenever I discussed their health with them, a few elders expressed confusion and uncertainty about the purpose of certain medications or medical procedures. During the summer of 2021, one elder set up a medical visit, and together we reached out to his doctor and discovered that a biopsy was needed.

Over the years, the elders recalled others who had died. When explaining the origins of his nickname, Trapper spoke four times of the death of one friend: "I'll tell you who really gave it to me. The brother's dead now. He actually gave me that name. We used to play right here. When I was little. He started calling me Trapper. Cuz I been trappin' him all the time. You know, in the domino game. That's the way the name really originated from. Was with Lonnie. He's dead. Me and him was really close friends. He died of bone cancer."

"What a fine man," Mr. Hall would often say of Mr. Cummings. When Mr. Carr's name came up, his memory was celebrated with laughter about my near mental breakdown as he, frustrated with my domino playing, repeatedly corrected each move I made. Mr. Taylor and Mr. Hall recalled with amusement Mr. Buford's exchanges with D-Ray: "He and D-Ray went around and around with each other." Mr. Hall smiled, and Mr. Taylor added, "They were crazy about each other."

In graduate school, I learned that anthropologists try to learn how others (often racial Others) think. This is, of course, an exercise in imagination. Nobody can get inside the head of the people they observe. Over the years I hung out with the elders, I often thought about the elderly Jews in Barbara Myerhoff's classic 1980 book *Number Our Days: A Triumph of Continuity and Culture*. Her elders told stories so they could be remembered. I, too, would like to be remembered. And I want to honor the memory of the elders.

In Ezekiel Emanuel's article, "Why I Hope to Die at 75," he writes that by seventy-five, "creativity, originality, and productivity are pretty much gone."[1] But seventy-five is younger than the elders' average age, and I saw them remain creative and productive. I watched them cultivate all of the positive health-enriching social effects of the card room as they drew on the continuity of social and cultural practices, forged critical social connections, and sustained durable and stable relationships. In the card room, men worked past personal losses and their declining physical health to make all of the room's participants feel valued, relevant, and irreplaceable. They knew how deeply they mattered to each other.

*Surviving Racism*

Mr. Hall, Mr. Buford, Mr. Carr, Mr. Taylor, D-Ray, and the other elders had worked together to transform the card room into a distinctly Black place that fostered their ability to be emotionally tough and resilient. They have physically survived the toll racism takes on a body, and they were painfully aware that anti-Blackness endures in contemporary America. Mr. Taylor was especially aware of the disproportionate number of Black people dying of COVID when he told me, "They're trying to kill us." Responding to the recent wave of voter suppression laws, Mr. Hall remarked, "Feels like nothing has changed." Mr. Buford's pronouncement echoed in my head. "You lucky to be white."

Trapper was the most outspoken. In his home office, decorated with an homage to Barack Obama, he opened up about the challenges growing up in Jim Crow Jonesboro, Alabama, a mill town founded during the Civil War in the center of northern Louisiana. When Trapper was

FIG. 17. Trapper. Steve Bialostok, photographer.

born in 1946, the timber industry, papermills, sawmills, and a canning company fueled the local economy for the three thousand residents. By 1960 one-third of Jonesboro residents were Black. In 1964, when Trapper was eighteen, integration was almost an afterthought afforded to Trapper's woefully inadequate and unaccredited school. The school library was barren of books; classroom textbooks were outdated and worn; the gym had been burned; and there were few drinking fountains and no landscaping. Ten years earlier, in May 1954, the United States Supreme Court had ruled in favor of public-school integration in *Brown v. Board of Education*. But in Jonesboro and across the South, enforcing the ruling would be, at least through the 1960s, spotty at best. Even the landmark 1964 Civil Rights Act made only slow inroads into the Jim Crow South. The police not only disregarded the federal law; they also opposed it. A litany of crimes was committed against Black people in Jonesboro, including church burnings, police harassment and brutality, and "unbridled Klan violence."[2]

A small group of Jonesboro residents, including barbers, mill hands, factory workers, church deacons, and World War II and Korean War army veterans, founded a group called Deacons for Defense and Justice in response to KKK terrorism and police complicity. The Deacons defied the nonviolent policies of the mainstream civil rights movement, arguing that armed protection was the only way to combat the Klan's violence in Jonesboro's Black neighborhoods. Trapper, then a recent high school graduate, joined them.

The last time I spoke with Trapper was in August 2021. He had just returned from Louisiana, having spent time with his older brother who was hospitalized and in intensive care. I asked for more details about his Civil Rights experiences, but he had tired of talking about it. "Look at the country sixty years later and what have we got?" he said. His words were raw and heated. "Forced to live in a world that is hostile to us."

On November 26, 2024, I received word from Mr. Taylor that Trapper had passed away from a heart attack. Mr. Hall later said that Trapper had been playing with them several weeks prior. His obituary notes that "he was an avid player of dominoes, dating back to playing with his late father."

To the extent that the elders cultivate joy and create a space for themselves and their traditions, the younger Black generation would say they are "keeping things real," a phrase that Mich Nyawalo traces to a variety of Black cultural sources in the early twentieth century.[3] The meaning of the phrase varies slightly, but hip-hop artists keep things real by rapping "about undesirable or hard-to-hear truths about black urban street life." To *keep it real* denotes a refusal to sound white or racially assimilate and offers an affirmation of one's cultural and racial authenticity.[4] The elders' practices in the card room reflect the intimacy of shared resistance to white expectations of Black people who are forced to occupy white spaces.[5] As gentrification takes over Northeast Park Hill and in turn the center, the elders pound dominoes and talk shit to call attention to their vitality and their continued presence.

One late afternoon in 2020, five years after I had first stepped into the card room, my customary entrance triggered the room's motion detector that turned on the lights. It felt eerie to stand in a silent and empty room. Just then, Mr. Taylor walked in ready to play. His eyes opened wide as he gazed at the empty chairs and tables.

"What do you think?" I asked, hoping for some inspiring, optimistic words. I should have known better.

"The writing is on the wall," he said. He pulled up a chair next to mine.

"What do you mean?" I asked, but Mr. Taylor could only repeat his pessimistic idiom, now extending it to a geography lesson: "Look around you. Look around."

"It's kind of depressing," I responded.

"Why? Why is it depressing?"

"It's not obvious? It's change," I replied.

"Change always happens," he said.

I recalled the day after Mr. Buford's funeral when I confided in Mr. Taylor about my sadness. "Why?" he asked then as now, seemingly incredulous. As we sat next to each other in the empty room, it seemed as if the card room itself was having a funeral. At that moment, Mr. Taylor appeared to accept the "death" of the card room calmly, but, ironically, nobody was as devoted to, or as pessimistic about, its future as he was. "They want to take it away from us," he'd been telling me for the past five years. Even when it went unsaid (and occasionally denied), I understood what this Black place and these people meant to him. The card room with its group of domino regulars offered evidence "of what it means for individuals and groups to feel and provide care, survive, and even dare to thrive in environments that challenge their very existence."[6]

In February 2022, more than a year after Hiawatha Davis had reopened and following a lengthy absence on my part, I passed by the card room on my way to work out—just as I had done seven years earlier. The room was packed. I walked in. Twelve men sat at three tables. Shit talk and raucous laughter fell through the open door. Stevie Wonder's "Part Time Lover" played directly from someone's cell phone, and two men sang along. The only men I recognized played together at a second table: Mr. Hall, Mr. Taylor, and Paul. Troy, Mr. Hall's partner, remembered me from "when

FIG. 18. Card room sign removed. Steve Bialostok, photographer.

you used to come in." Mr. Hall, resting a COVID mask just underneath his lower lip, offered a familiar smile, and a COVID-friendly fist bump. As I sat next to their table, Paul shared a funny memory of something Mr. Carr had once said. Mr. Taylor, his beard climbing around the corners of his mask like a vine, talked about something he read or saw on the news: "Poor people are buying Lobster at Safeway with food stamps. Can you believe it?" No one said much else. Troy bragged that at eighty-five, he was "the second oldest person in the room." At ninety-five, Vince, sitting at the table across from us, was the oldest. "How old is George now?" Paul asked. "Ninety-five," answered Mr. Taylor. George apparently still lived alone in the same apartment. Thirty minutes before closing, Troy said he had to leave but was easily convinced to stay.

At the end of the evening, Mr. Hall, Mr. Taylor, and I slowly exited Hiawatha Davis. I held the door open for Vince, who impressively rushed past us with a smile and a "thanks." "You still going to Wyoming?" Mr. Taylor asked, remembering my teaching schedule. "Yeah," I said. "But on Tuesday I got up as far as Cheyenne and 80 was closed. High winds and blowing snow." Mr. Hall reminded me, as he had many times before, "You be careful," he said, his voice soft and his expression serious. He repeated, "Be careful." There was a pause. "What's today?" Mr. Hall asked. "Friday," answered Mr. Taylor. "Let's see," said Mr. Hall. "I'm not gonna see you on Saturday and Sunday. I miss you guys on the weekends." Off he went to his car.

"Where did you get the idea that poor people buy lobster with food stamps?" I asked Mr. Taylor. "And even if they do, does it matter? A long time ago lobsters were *only* fed to poor people." There I was again, debating with Mr. Taylor. "Did you ever notice that all the Safeways are in poor neighborhoods?" he said. "There's a Safeway less than two miles away," I argued. "It's not in a poor area." "You can read it [the article] yourself," he said, and with that he left to make dinner "for me and my wife and whoever else is there."

Two weeks later, in the morning, I walked by the card room and noticed that the "Card Room" placard had been removed. None of the men I asked that evening had noticed. The newest supervisor told me the next day that a "Classroom" sign would be installed in its place. My face must have registered disbelief. "There are a lot of activities that go on in the room now," he said. "The guys still play dominoes there on Monday, Wednesday, and Friday. And if there isn't another activity going on, they can also play Thursday evenings." I nodded, then walked to my car thinking that Mr. Taylor's prediction had been accurate, at least on one level. I thought of endings, about gentrification, cultural erasure, and racial displacement, and about how the card room exists somewhere between then and now.

# Notes

## Notes on Transcription

1. Ochs, "Transcription as Theory."
2. Bucholtz, "The Politics of Transcription."
3. See Rickford and Rickford, *Spoken Soul*.
4. There are also regional differences between forms of AAL. See two excellent dissertations: Charles Farrington's "Language Variation and the Great Migration" and Taylor Jones's "Variation in African American English."
5. Alim and Smitherman, *Articulate while Black*; James Baldwin, "If Black English Isn't a Language, Then Tell Me, What Is?" *New York Times*, July 29, 1979; Kirkland, "Black Masculine Language;" Smitherman, "Black Language."

## 1. Beginnings

1. A note on capitalization: White supremacists and other hate groups have long capitalized the term "white" to give it the respect they think it deserves. My choice to capitalize only Black, and not white, intends to confer dignity, power, and racial equity and follows the lead of many African American writers and scholars today.
2. I discuss this further in chapter 4.
3. Anthropologists' paramount responsibility is to those they study. Among the protections that anthropologists must provide participants is the right to remain anonymous. I asked each participant (recorded and unrecorded) whether they would prefer that I use their real name or a pseudonym in the book. If someone was discussed in a conversation or interview, or came into the recording only briefly, I used a pseudonym. While I offered anonymity to the five participating elders, I mentioned that it was their choice and that using their real names might mark and honor their presence in the card room. All five chose to include their names. I refrained from using pseudonyms for the neighborhoods and the name of the recreation center because delving deeply into Denver's racial history was essential to their stories.

4. In "African-American Language Use," linguist Arthur Spears prefers the term "uncensored speech" as to not prejudge the actions of the users of such speech.
5. Alexander, "Racializing Identity," 17. Alexander suggests that offering dap is more than a mere choreographed hand dance; it's a request for intimacy.
6. Dominoes boasts a rich and diverse history, spanning centuries and continents, making it one of the world's most beloved pastimes cherished by cultures from the Far East to the Caribbean. Evidence suggests early versions were played in regions like China during the twelfth century before spreading to Europe in the eighteenth century. European colonizers brought dominoes to the Caribbean, and the game quickly became a favorite pastime, enjoyed in local bars, community centers, and even on the streets. Tournaments and competitions are common, reflecting the competitive spirit and enthusiasm for the game among Caribbean communities. Nasir and de Royston, "Power, Identity, and Mathematical Practices."
7. This version of dominoes is sometimes called "All Fives." Other variations and rules are common.
8. Abrahams, *Talking Black*. Rituals of insult are playful verbal exchanges often among peers or in cultural traditions like "the dozens," which I touch on in chapter 8.
9. Chapter 8 is dedicated to the topic of talking shit.
10. All the station's correspondents at the time were white.
11. Bourdieu, *The Logic of Practice*; Bourdieu, "Social Space and Symbolic Power," 19.
12. Grieser, *The Black Side of the River*. Space and place are related but distinct concepts, although scholars often conflate them. Many scholars take space and place for granted, only acknowledging it as a backdrop where something happens. Space is generally understood as the abstract or physical category (see Low, "Towards an Anthropological Theory of Space and Place"; Low, *Spatializing Culture*), whereas place—following cultural geographers—refers to spaces that have been imbued with meaning, significance, and a sense of attachment. See Ryden, *Mapping the Invisible Landscape*; Sack, *Homo Geographicus*; Pellow, *Landlords and Lodgers*.
13. "Racial terror lynchings" is Bryan Stevenson's term meant to recognize the full scope and impact of American history of lynchings on Black communities. For more, see the Equal Justice Initiative: www.eji.org. On gentrification, see Lipsitz, *How Racism Takes Place*.
14. hooks, "Homeplace: A Site of Resistance." Following her wishes to focus on her message rather than her name, I do not capitalize bell hooks's name.

15. McKittrick, "On Plantations, Prisons, and a Black Sense of Place."
16. Hartman, *Scenes of Subjection*, 67.
17. Slocum, *Black Towns, Black Futures*, 9.
18. Giancarlo, "Spatializing Black Culture"; Hunter et al., "Black Placemaking."
19. Hunter et al., "Black Placemaking."
20. In U.S. society, Black people live under the white gaze, as African American writers and scholars have carefully theorized and documented. The white gaze supports white supremacist structures by determining who has the right to occupy space and who does not, thereby maintaining control over spatial and social dynamics. Explaining how the white gaze serves to limit the cultural and social expression of Black people, George Yancy powerfully reflects on the embodied experience of being a Black man, moving through the world weighed down by constant vulnerability—shadowed by anxiety, tension, and dread. His body becomes the target of white gazes, criminalized by white gestures, barred by white gated communities, marginalized within white curricula, and rendered unfamiliar through the supposed innocence of whiteness. To be Black in an anti-Black white world, Yancy suggests, is to have one's very existence interrogated and one's perspective continually doubted.
21. Yancy, "Foreword," vii, viii. See Morrison, "Toni Morrison on Writing"; Paris and Alim, "What Are We Seeking to Sustain?"; Yancy, *Black Bodies, White Gazes*; Blackwell, "Why People of Color Need Spaces without White People."
22. Campt, "Black Visuality and the Practice of Refusal," 25.
23. Ford, "Close-up."
24. Huizinga, *Homo Ludens*, 7.
25. Caillois, *Man, Play, and Games*.
26. Douglas, *Purity and Danger*, 64.
27. Braunstein, Fulton, and Wood, "The Role of Bridging Cultural Practices."
28. Turner, *The Anthropology of Performance*; Bauman, *Verbal Art as Performance*, 11.
29. Bauman, *Verbal Art as Performance*, 9.
30. Myerhoff, "Telling One's Story," 31.
31. Yancy, "White Embodied Gazing," 244. See also Anderson, *Black in White Space*.
32. Warren and Coles, "Trading Spaces," 3.
33. Moten, *In the Break*, 742; Warren and Coles, "Trading Spaces," 391.
34. Sharpe, *In the Wake*.
35. Sharpe, *In the Wake*, 46.
36. Hobart and Kneese, "Radical Care," 2.
37. Hobart and Kneese, "Radical Care," 2–3, my emphasis.

38. Christina Sharpe also talks about the relationship between care and death, which has additional meaning in a study of Black elderly men who are sharing their final years together: "What does it look like, entail, and mean to attend to, care for, comfort, and defend, those already dead, those dying, and those living lives consigned to the possibility of always-imminent death?" Sharpe, *In the Wake*, 38.
39. African American anthropologist and writer Zora Neal Hurston theorized and explored "the obvious fact that Negroes love and hate and fight and play and strive and travel and have a thousand and one interests in life like other humans." Hurston, "Art and Such."
40. Ain-Davis and Craven Del Hierro, *Feminist Ethnography*.
41. Shuman, *Other People's Stories*.

### 2. Denver's History of Racism

1. Five Points gets its name from the five-point intersection at Washington Street, 27th Street, 26th Avenue, and Welton Street. This was too much to fit on the sign marking this busy streetcar stop, so it was shortened to Five Points in 1881. Five Points was among the first neighborhoods to develop outside the original congressionally mandated boundaries awarded to Denver in 1864.
2. Denver residents commonly refer to this vibrant district as the RiNo. However, RiNo is not the official name of the neighborhood; instead, it is the moniker of a nonprofit arts organization that has become synonymous with the area.
3. Hudson Lindenberger, "Take a Brewery Tour through RiNo," *5280*, September 13, 2016, https://www.5280.com/take-a-brewery-tour-through-rino/.
4. Goodstein, *Park Hill Promise*.
5. Goodstein, *Curtis Park, Five Points, and Beyond*.
6. Mauck, *Five Points Neighborhood of Denver*.
7. Goodstein, *Curtis Park, Five Points, and Beyond*; Simmons and Simmons, *Five Points Neighborhood*.
8. Goodstein, *Curtis Park, Five Points, and Beyond*.
9. Simmons and Simmons, *Five Points Neighborhood*.
10. Singer and actor Paul Robeson performed and stayed at the Rossonian. The Harlem Globetrotters also stayed there, although there is no evidence that they performed there. The Rossonian often had more white than Black patrons at its peak in the 1940s.
11. Elena Enbrown, "All That Jazz," *Enbrown* (blog), February 14, 2011, https://enbrown.wordpress.com/2011/02/14/all-that-jazz.
12. Goodstein, *Curtis Park, Five Points, and Beyond*.

13. Elise Schmelzer, "The KKK Ruled Denver a Century Ago. Here's How the Hate Group's Legacy Is Still Being Felt in 2021," *Denver Post*, June 6, 2021, https://www.denverpost.com/2021/06/06/denver-kkk-history/.
14. Goodstein, *In the Shadow of the Klan*.
15. Stephens and Larson, *African Americans of Denver*.
16. Mauck, *Five Points Neighborhood of Denver*.
17. Goldberg, *Hooded Empire*, 13.
18. Lay, *The Invisible Empire in the West*, 50.
19. Schmelzer, "The KKK Ruled Denver a Century Ago."
20. Goldberg, "Denver: Queen City of the Chicago Realm," 49.
21. For example, in 1923 Stapleton gave permission for the not-so-secret local Klan order to use the city auditorium for a lecture despite protests from citizens, especially Jews, Blacks, and Catholics. Soon thereafter, the public learned that Stapleton's newly appointed safety manager was a Klansman who had accepted the position with the understanding that he would be appointed city attorney within ninety days. Goldberg, *Hooded Empire*.
22. Julie Turkuaz, "Family History Haunts G.O.P. Candidate for Governor in Colorado," *New York Times*, July 24, 2018, https://www.nytimes.com/2018/07/24/us/colorado-governor-stapleton.html.
23. Wasinger, "From Five Points to Struggle Hill."
24. Goldberg, "Denver: Queen City of the Chicago Realm," 43.
25. "Negro Home Bombed by Autoists," *Rocky Mountain News*, July 8, 1921, Western History and Genealogy Department, Denver Public Library.
26. This was a common story throughout northern and western states, as described in James Loewen's *Sundown Towns*.
27. Newsum, "Cold War Colorado."
28. Mead & Hunt, "Nuestras Historias," accessed May 18, 2025, https://meadhunt.com/preserving-significant-latino-sites/.
29. Redlining robbed Black families of generational wealth and is a major reason the typical white family today has almost eight times the wealth of a typical Black family. Michelle Singletary, "Being Black Lowers the Value of My Home: The Legacy of Redlining," *Washington Post*, October 23, 2020, https://www.washingtonpost.com/business/2020/10/23/redlining-black-wealth/.
30. George Brown later became a Colorado politician and served as the nation's first Black lieutenant-governor.
31. George Brown, "Denver Negros Find Prejudices Haven't Vanished," *Denver Post*, September 24, 1951.
32. Noel and Leonard, *Denver: Mining Camp to Metropolis*, 235.
33. Noel and Leonard, *Denver: Mining Camp to Metropolis*.

34. Living in Northeast and North Park Hill was particularly problematic because homes lay directly in the flight path for Denver's Stapleton Airfield. Postwar economic growth increased traffic in and out of the airport.
35. R-0 (residential) zoning in old Park Hill maintained only single-family homes in order to preserve the area's social stability and property values at a time of racial change. The Park Hill Action Committee used zoning to keep this an area of detached homes occupied by nuclear families. Members monitored their blocks for violations of the R-0 zoning restrictions. Homeownership was also carefully connected to whiteness. Writes Cole, "In Park Hill, R-0 zoning was used to keep neighborhood property values high and its residential character intact at a time when the once all-white area was becoming racially integrated. Even though the neighborhood was, in many ways, racially tolerant, zoning enforcement targeted African-American and Hispanic residents of Park Hill." Cole, "R-0," vi–vii.
36. Noel and Leonard, *Denver: Mining Camp to Metropolis*, 374.
37. The *Denver Blade* was an African American newspaper that offered news and perspectives from Colorado's Black communities—voices that were ignored by mainstream press. John M. Wallace, "Greater Five Points: The Things I Remember," *Denver Blade*, September 1961, quoted in Cherland, "No Prejudice Here," 26.
38. Park Hill was 97 percent white in 1960 and 3 percent Black, with only one Black family owning a home there. By 1966, 60.2 percent of the residents of Park Hill were Black. By the end of the 1960s, the figure had shifted again, to nearly 50 percent white and 50 percent Black, but the income level was maintained at "affluent and middle-class." Goodstein, *Park Hill Promise*.
39. Cole, "R-0."
40. Charles Roos, "Racial Bias Subtle but Real," *Denver Post*, October 17, 1963.
41. Noel and Leonard, *Denver: Mining Camp to Metropolis*.
42. Historian Albert M. Camarillo writes that as people of color moved into western cities, "the combination of federal laws, blockbusting real estate practices, and fear led to the wholesale departure of whites from many formerly segregated communities." Camarillo, "Blacks, Latinos, and the New Racial Frontier," 49.
43. "Park Hill Neighborhood History," Denver Public Library Special Collections and Archives.
44. Goodstein, *Park Hill Promise*.
45. During the first half of the twentieth century, racially restrictive covenants prevented people of color from establishing residency in certain neighborhoods. The federal government began to act against these actions in 1917, and in 1948 the U.S. Supreme Court held that inserting racially restrictive

covenants into deed instruments was not enforceable. However, this kind of covenant remained common, including across Denver's neighborhoods and subdivisions—such as Bonnie Brae, Burns Brentwood, Clayton, Crestmoor, Park Hill, and Regis Heights, among others. It was not until 1968, when the Fair Housing Act passed, that housing discrimination became prohibited by law. History Colorado, accessed May 18, 2025, https://www.historycolorado.org/story/do-you-know-place/2019/12/18/denvers-neighborhood-history-polo-club-place. See Thompson, "Art Branscombe," 38.

46. *Ghettoization* refers to the process in which marginalized communities or neighborhoods experience concentrated poverty, limited resources, and social isolation.
47. Longino, "The Park Hill Action Committee," 83.
48. Goodstein, *Park Hill Promise*.
49. Noel and Leonard, *Denver: Mining Camp to Metropolis*.
50. Cherland, "No Prejudice Here."
51. Denver's first zoning code dates to 1925, when, under Mayor Stapleton, the city was divided into residential, commercial, and industrial areas. The ordinance was supposed to promote "health, safety, morals, or general welfare." The predominantly white areas of town were zoned for single-family housing, while areas occupied by minorities were more likely to be zoned for multifamily housing. The political influence of the Ku Klux Klan prevented minorities from moving geographically. The 1955 Denver zoning code further exacerbated the city's racial and social divisions. Residential zoning was divided into these categories: R-0, the most restrictive, prohibited the renting out of any parts of the property; R-1, single family; R-2 allowed duplexes and townhomes; and R-3 and R-4 allowed multifamily housing. The code defined "family" as a group of people related by "blood, marriage, and adoption" and defined R-0 zoning as areas where "children and their parents would thrive" and where nontraditional households were excluded. See Gosia Kung, "Zoning Codes—Tools for Segregation or Creating Complete Neighborhoods?" *Denver Urbanism* (blog), February 18, 2014. https://denverurbanism.com/2019/02/zoning-codes-segregation-or-complete-neighborhoods.html.
52. Cole, "R-0."
53. Goodstein, *Park Hill Promise*.
54. PHAC defined "integrated" as any block with at least one Black family and expected the overall Black population to be no higher than the overall Black population of Denver, 7 to 8 percent.
55. The Northeast Park Hill Civic Association is a citizen's organization that focused mostly on the Northeast's nitty-gritty issues, such as paving neigh-

borhood alleys and maintaining regular and reliable trash pickup. Park Hill Action Committee and Northeast Park Hill NEPHCA, "Facts on Housing for Negroes," July–August 1965, 1–2, box 1, folder 7, PHAC-GPHC Records, University of Denver.

56. Goodstein, *Park Hill Promise*.
57. Park Hill Action Committee and Northeast Park Hill Action Committee, 1965.
58. From its emergence in the early twentieth century, Park Hill was considered Denver's most refined area. The original Park Hill saw itself as the ultimate suburb, "located above the confines of 19th century." See Goodstein, *Park Hill Promise*, 7.
59. Cole, "R-0," 87.
60. "Park Hill Neighborhood History." A population analysis illustrates Park Hill's racial divide during that era. Northeast Park Hill's population grew from 688 residents in 1950 to 9,312 in 1960. The Census Bureau counted 440 nonwhites among them during that same time period. By 1970 Northeast Park Hill's population of 9,659 consisted of 1,068 white and 8,591 Black residents. Similarly, in North Park Hill between 23rd Avenue and Martin Luther King Boulevard, there were 4,614 white and 9,176 Black residents. South (white) Park Hill, by contrast, had 10,587 white and 708 Black residents. See Goodstein, *Park Hill Promise*.
61. "Greater Park Hill: Denver, Colorado," Great Places in America: Neighborhoods. American Planning Association, accessed May 18, 2025, https://www.planning.org/greatplaces/neighborhoods/2008/greaterparkhill.htm.
62. "Greater Park Hill: Denver, Colorado."
63. Modan's book *Turf Wars*, exploring the politics of place, delves into the processes by which community members construct and challenge perceptions and visions of their neighborhoods, navigating the intersections of race, class, and space.
64. "Yard Sign Mania," *Park Hill News*, November 2024, p. 7.
65. Park Hill Neighbors for Equity in Education, accessed May 18, 2025, https://phnee.org/about/.

### 3. Charles Hall

1. Richard Melzer, "Many Fought for Their Dreams," *Valencia County News Bulletin*, 2019, https://news-bulletin.com/many-fought-for-their-dreams/.

### 4. Northeast Park Hill

1. Campt, "Black Visuality and the Practice of Refusal."
2. Sara Fleming, "The Battle over the Future of Park Hill Is about More Than a Golf Course," *SOS Denver* (blog), December 2019, https://sosdenverdotnet

.files.wordpress.com/2019/12/the-battle-over-the-future-of-park-hill-is-about-more-than-a-golf-course.pdf. The City of Denver divides "Greater Park Hill" into three administrative neighborhoods (retaining a single zip code): South, North, and Northeast. In this chapter, I explore how these geographic labels carry significant ideological weight, a factor contingent on which Park Hill neighborhood you live in. Although I use these geographic distinctions for the three neighborhoods to aid readers in identifying the particular Park Hill neighborhood under discussion, I do so reluctantly, since the geographic labels can be racially marginalizing.

3. Grieser, *The Black Side of the River*, 19.
4. "Park Hill Neighborhood History," accessed May 18, 2025, https://history.denverlibrary.org/neighborhood-history-guide/park-hill-neighborhood-history.
5. For a full accounting of the rise and fall of Dahlia Shopping Center, see Goodstein, *Park Hill Promise*, 472–80.
6. Prior to Mike Johnston's election as Denver mayor in 2013, he served in the Colorado Senate from 2009 to 2017. Throughout his term, and for some time after, Johnston located his office on the corner of 33rd and Holly.
7. Amanda M. Faison, "Neighborhood Buzz: Madison Street," *5280*, October 22, 2010, https://www.5280.com/neighborhood/.
8. Kuvo Jazz, "Greater Park Hill Homes Tour and Street Fair," accessed May 18, 2025, https://www.kuvo.org/greater-park-hill-homes-tour-and-street-fair/.
9. "Park Hill Garden Walk," Greater Park Hill Community, accessed May 18, 2025, https://parkhillgardenwalk.org/.
10. "Park Hill 4th of July Parade," Greater Park Hill Community, accessed May 18, 2025, https://parkhillparade.com/.
11. Tilove, *Along Martin Luther King*, 5–6.
12. "rough around the edges": dipdipderp, "Living in Park Hill area—Harold Lambert Court?" *Reddit*, accessed May 18, 2025, https://www.reddit.com/r/sheffield/comments/lv4yyx/living_in_park_hill_area_harold_lambert_court/; "advising potential residents": sydewayzsoundz, "Help! Need an honest opinion of Northeast Park Hill," *Reddit*, https://www.reddit.com/r/Denver/comments/2kj79a/help_need_an_honest_opinion_of_northeast_park_hill/.
13. PBS News Hour, "Inclusive Wellness Center Is an Oasis for a Neighborhood Left Behind," March 21, 2017, https://www.pbs.org/newshour/show/inclusive-wellness-center-oasis-neighborhood-left-behind.
14. The "Summer of Violence" refers to a period lasting four months during 1993 characterized by a surge in youth violence, numerous fatalities, and

the imposition of life sentences on dozens of teenagers. Micah Smith, "30 Years Later: Revisiting Denver's Deadly 'Summer of Violence,'" *Denver 7*, August 14, 2023, https://www.denver7.com/news/local-news/30-years-later-revisiting-denvers-deadly-summer-of-violence.

15. Migoya, "Denver's Pot Businesses Mostly in Low-Income, Minority Neighborhoods," *Denver Post*, January 23, 2017, https://www.denverpost.com/2016/01/02/denvers-pot-businesses-mostly-in-low-income-minority-neighborhoods/.

16. Montbello is a neighborhood, like Park Hill, located in Denver's northeast corner. Over the years, the community also transitioned from predominantly white to majority Black and then shifted again. As of 2023, Montbello is majority Latino. See "Montbello Neighborhood History," Denver Public Library Special Collections and Archives, accessed May 18, 2025, https://history.denverlibrary.org/neighborhood-history-guide/montbello-neighborhood-history.

17. McKittrick, *Demonic Grounds*.

18. Campt, "Black Visuality and the Practice of Refusal."

19. A moral geography maps a moral framework onto a spatial context (e.g., "We must whisper whenever coming to church"). Modan shows how creating a moral geography is "all about showing that you fit in and how you fit in." Modan, *Turf Wars*, 90. See also Hill, "The Voices of Don Gabriel."

20. This review has since been removed.

21. Chapman and Brunsma in *Beer and Racism* suggest that the craft industry culture is exclusively white, while Paulsen and Tuller, *Crafting Place*, contend that craft beer plays a seminal role in the process of gentrification, operating both as a catalyst for gentrification and a signpost to consumers that gentrification is taking place. See Anderson, "The White Space," 21.

22. Blunt, "Collective Memory and Productive Nostalgia."

23. Smitherman, *Black Talk*, 169.

24. Urban Land Conservancy, "In Memory of Geri Grimes," *Urban Updates*, June 2022.

25. Summers, *Black in Place*, 32.

### 5. Robert Taylor

1. Asante and Hall, *Rooming in the Master's House*.

### 6. A Black Social and Cultural Nexus

1. Mondschein, *The Summer of 1967—Northeast Park Hill*, 3–4.
2. Goodstein, *Park Hill Promise*, 491.

3. Light and Young, "Toponymy as Commodity," 442.
4. Winter, "Sites of Memory," 312.
5. Alim, *You Know My Steez*.
6. Johnstone, *Stories, Community, and Place*, 121.
7. Zeisel, "A Sense of Place."
8. Pickering and Keightley, "The Modalities of Nostalgia."
9. Alim, *You Know My Steez*; Alim and Smitherman, *Articulate while Black*.
10. Anderson, "The White Space."
11. Blackwell, "Why People of Color Need Spaces without White People."
12. Alim, *You Know My Steez*, 97.
13. Drawing on his own fieldwork in the Bay Area and Ice Cube's film *Barbershop*, Alim discusses how the Black barbershop serves as "'the Black man's country club,' a safe place to fraternize, build and maintain genuine relationships, and express yourself freely, without fear of being censored or censured by external forces." Alim, *You Know My Steez*, 82.
14. Fred Moten and Saidiya Hartman, "To Refuse That Which Has Been Refused to You." *Chimurenga*, October 19, 2018, https://chimurengachronic.co.za/to-refuse-that-which-has-been-refused-to-you-2/.

*7. Herman Carr*

1. Haskins, *Glory Road*, 21.
2. Haskins, *Glory Road*, 24.
3. Haskins, *Glory Road*, 18.
4. Black journalist Ida B. Wells wrote that many accusations of rape stemmed from consensual interracial relationships that had been discovered by white women's disapproving relatives. See Viñas-Nelson, "Interracial Marriage in 'Post-Racial' America."
5. Perkins, *Home Is a Dirty Street*, 26.
6. Franklin, "Invisibility Syndrome and Racial Identity Development," 772.
7. Combs, "Black (and Brown) Bodies Out of Place."
8. Tom Goldman, "Hall of Fame Coach Haskins Dies," National Public Radio, September 8, 2008, https://www.npr.org/templates/story/story.php?storyId=94394564.

*8. Talking Shit inside the Card Room*

1. Folklorists: Abrahams, *Talking Black*; Kochman, *Black and White*; Laudun, "'Talking Shit' in Rayne." Sociolinguists: Smitherman, *Talkin and Testifyin*. Sociologists: Guzman, "Talking Shit, Egos, and Tough Skin."
2. Gates, *The Signifying Monkey*.

3. Abrahams, *Talking Black*; Kochman, *Black and White*.
4. Guzman, "Talking Shit, Egos, and Tough Skin."
5. Abrahams, *Talking Black*, 40.
6. Kochman, *Black and White*.
7. More information on my transcription practices can be found in the front matter: Notes on Transcription.
8. Kochman, *Black and White*; Labov, "Rules for Ritual Insults;" Smitherman, *Talkin and Testifyin*.
9. Brown describes these off-color clever responses as "what white folks call verbal skills." Brown, *Die Nigger Die!*, 29.
10. Indirect communication is common within African American speech styles. Morgan delineates two distinct forms of indirectness: "pointed" and "baited," which hinge on the manner of address used. Morgan, *Language, Discourse and Power* and Morgan, *Speech Communities*. See Mitchell-Kernan, "Signifying and Marking." In "pointed" indirectness, a speaker aims to convey a message to a mock recipient that is actually intended for someone else and is implicitly understood as such. On the other hand, baited indirectness lacks a predetermined target. As Morgan explains, "The speaker may not have anyone in particular in mind and, in fact, lures potential targets into positions that challenge their social face." Morgan, *Language, Discourse and Power*, 50. In this scenario, it's the response behavior of the listener, not the calculated targeting by the speaker, that performatively determines the target addressee. Morgan notes that this audience-centric approach aligns with local-knowledge and cultural language ideologies, which dictate that an utterance is directed toward whoever perceives it as true. See also Morgan, *Speech Communities*, 135–39.
11. Guzman, "Talking Shit, Egos, and Tough Skin." Mr. Taylor's assertion is corroborated by Guzman's comprehensive review of the history of the dozens. Guzman traces its origins from Dollard's seminal work on the "dialectic of insult." See Dollard, "The Dozen." Scholars across disciplines have investigated this verbal exchange, characterized by playful insults devoid of malice or intent to incite violence. While initially observed among Black youth in the South, subsequent analyses have explored its prevalence and its various psychosocial functions: releasing aggression, socializing speakers into cultural norms of masculinity and sexuality, and honing verbal skills for status enhancement. Labov emphasizes that the absurdity of the insults is crucial for maintaining the playful nature of the exchange, while Kochman highlights the reciprocation of insults as a factor in sustaining playfulness and increasing tolerance for racial provocations. See Labov, "Rules for Ritual Insults" and Kochman, *Black and White*. Kelley, Guzman points out, criticizes

attempts to impose misinterpreted meanings onto the dozens, arguing that it primarily serves the simple, emotional purpose of eliciting laughter. See Kelley, *Yo' Mama's Disfunktional!*
12. Bateson, "A Theory of Play and Fantasy."
13. Bateson, "A Theory of Play and Fantasy."
14. Limón, "Carne, Carnales, and the Carnivalesque."
15. Anderson, *Code of the Street*.
16. Bateson, "A Theory of Play and Fantasy," 40.
17. Abrahams, *Talking Black*, 37.
18. Simmel, "The Sociology of Sociability."
19. Bauman, "Performance," 262.
20. Csikszentmihalyi, *Flow*.
21. Mr. Hall's musical coda feels like the backdrop of an emotionally charged, highly competitive football game where either team could have won. The men may not have even known this popular sports song's historically Black roots as one of the earliest jazz tunes ever to evolve into a standard. "Tiger Rag" became so popular that in 1931 Harry De Costa wrote the lyrics that the Mills Brothers recorded in 1934. See Gracyk, "'Tiger Rag.'"
22. If Mr. Taylor had been without a ready line to respond to Mr. Buford, he would have been considered "out of face." See Goffman, *Interaction Ritual*.
23. Fine and Corte, "Group Pleasures."
24. Podilchak, "The Social Organization of Fun," 688.
25. Price, "Why Having Fun Is the Secret to a Healthier Life."
26. The Black Joy movement represents a profound response to systemic oppression, rooted in resistance, resilience, and the reclamation of Black humanity. As Britany Packnett notes, "Joy is resistance," suggesting that happiness can serve as a powerful act of defiance against a world that seeks to undermine it ("I'm an Activist, and Joy Is My Resistance," *Self*, August 21, 2017, https://www.self.com/story/charlottesville-joy-is-resistance). Kim Pham further elaborates, asserting that conscious expressions of joy are crucial in countering the pervasive effects of racism and oppression, enabling communities to thrive despite systemic barriers ("Celebrating Black Joy as an Alternative Form of Resistance and Reclaiming of Humanity," Voice of OC, February 1, 2021, https://voiceofoc.org/2021/02/celebrating-black-joy-as-an-alternative-form-of-resistance-and-reclaiming-of-humanity/). Finally, Staynova ("An Ethnography of Joy") highlights how the "ethnography of joy" captures these expressions within communities, illustrating how communal celebrations act as forms of resistance that affirm identity and foster belonging.
27. We can think of this form of communication as related to the *cypher*—the "quintessential space in which people create hip-hop." See Hill and Petchauer,

*Schooling Hip-Hop*. The cypher embodies hip-hop's roots as a form of individual and communal expression. Individual artists take turns performing and supporting one another in a friendly, communal competition that includes any enthusiastic spectators who might cheer and applaud. See Kuttner and White-Hammond, "(Re)building the Cypher." The cypher provides an opportunity for each artist to shine and to boast of his own skill individually while in the context of a collective. The cypher, while treated as a competition, also relies on collaboration. Poet Abiodum Oyowele describes the cypher as a "circumference [of] protection" where "everyone is free and they want to be tight like that, together like that." Fitzgerald, *Freestyle*. See also Alim, *Roc the Mic Right*.

28. Daniels, "The Significance of Blues for American History," 15.
29. Schafer, "Irony from the Underground," 45.
30. Floyd, *The Power of Black Music*.
31. Bialostok and Watson, "Older Black Men Playing Dominoes."

## 10. The Business of Intimacy

1. Forstee, "A New Framing for an Old Sociology of Intimacy."
2. Sennett, *The Fall of Public Man*, 5.
3. Linde, *Working the Past*.
4. Wright, *Black Boy*, 172.
5. Linde, *Working the Past*.
6. Hanif Abdurraqib, "A World of Black Intimacy at the Card Table," *New York Times Magazine*, February 24, 2021, 2, https://www.nytimes.com/2021/02/24/magazine/a-world-of-black-intimacy-at-the-card-table.html.
7. Pearson, Child, and Carmon, "Rituals in Dating Relationships."
8. Mauss, *The Gift*.
9. Richards-Greaves, "'Say Hallelujah Somebody' and 'I Will Call upon the Lord.'"
10. Smitherman, *Talkin and Testifyin*.
11. Kochman, "Force Fields in Black and White Communication."
12. Daniel and Smitherman, "How I Got Over."
13. Jefferson, Sacks, and Schegloff, "Notes on Laughter in the Pursuit of Intimacy."
14. Cameron and Kulick, *Language and Sexuality*, 115.
15. Coates, "Talk in a Play Frame."
16. Smitherman, *Talkin and Testifyin*.
17. Durkheim, *The Elementary Forms of Religious Life*.
18. Limón, "Carne, Carnales, and the Carnivalesque."

19. Jefferson, Sacks, and Schegloff, "Notes on Laughter in the Pursuit of Intimacy."
20. Coates, "Talk in a Play Frame."

*11. D-Ray Edwards*

1. Weil, *The Need for Roots*.

*12. Endings*

1. Ezekiel Emanuel, "Why I Hope to Die at 75," *The Atlantic*, October 2014, https://www.theatlantic.com/magazine/archive/2014/10/why-i-hope-to-die-at-75/379329.
2. Hill, *The Deacons for Defense*, 70.
3. Nyawalo, "From 'Badman' to 'Gangsta,'" 461.
4. Kopano, "Rap Music as an Extension of the Black Rhetorical Tradition," 204; Carter, *Keepin' It Real*.
5. Anderson, "The White Space."
6. Hobart and Kneese, "Radical Care," 3.

# Bibliography

*Archival Materials*

Park Hill Action Committee and Northeast Park Hill. NEPHCA, University of Denver.

Western History and Genealogy Department, Denver Public Library.

*Published Work*

Abrahams, Roger. *Talking Black*. Rowley MA: Newbury, 1976.

Ain-Davis, Dana, and Krista Craven Del Hierro. *Feminist Ethnography: Thinking through Methodologies, Challenges, and Possibilities*. Lanham MD: Roman and Littlefield, 2016.

Alexander, Bryant. "Racializing Identity: Performance, Pedagogy, and Regret." *Cultural Studies ↔ Critical Methodologies* 4, no. 1 (2004): 12–27.

Alim, Samy. *Roc the Mic Right: The Language of Hip Hop Culture*. New York: Routledge, 2006.

———. *You Know My Steez: An Ethnographic and Sociolinguistic Study of Styleshifting in a Black American Speech Community*. Durham: Duke University Press, 2004.

Alim, Samy, and Geneva Smitherman. *Articulate while Black: Barack Obama, Language, and Race in the U.S.* Oxford: Oxford University Press, 2012.

Anderson, Elijah. *Black in White Space*. Chicago: University of Chicago Press, 2021.

———. *Code of the Street: Decency, Violence, and the Moral Life of the Inner City*. New York: Norton, 1999.

———. "The White Space." *Sociology of Race and Ethnicity* 1, no. 1 (2015): 10–21.

Asante, Molefi, and Ronald Hall. *Rooming in the Master's House: Power and Privilege in the Rise of Black Conservatism*. Boulder: Paradigm, 2011.

Bateson, Gregory. "A Theory of Play and Fantasy." In *Steps to an Ecology of Mind*, edited by Gregory Bateson, 177–93. London: Paladin, 1955.

Bauman, Richard. "Performance." In *International Encyclopedia of Communication* 3, 262–66. New York: Oxford University Press, 1989.

———. *Verbal Art as Performance*. Long Grove IL: Waveland Press, 1984.

Bialostok, Steve, and Marcus Watson. "Older Black Men Playing Dominoes: Talking Shit and Creating Black Place." *Transforming Anthropology* 30, no. 6 (2022): 34–47.

Blackwell, Kelsey. "Why People of Color Need Spaces without White People." *The Arrow*, August 9, 2018.

Blunt, Alison. "Collective Memory and Productive Nostalgia: Anglo-Indian Homemaking at McCluskiegani." *Environment and Planning D: Society and Space* 21, no. 6 (2003): 717–38.

Bourdieu, Pierre. *The Logic of Practice*. Stanford: Stanford University Press, 1990.

———. "Social Space and Symbolic Power." *Social Theory* 7, no. 1 (1989): 14–25.

Braunstein, Ruth, Brad Fulton, and Richard Wood. "The Role of Bridging Cultural Practices in Racially and Socioeconomically Diverse Civic Organizations." *American Sociological Review* 79, no. 4 (2014): 705–25.

Brown, R. H. *Die Nigger Die! A Political Autobiography of Jamil Abdullah al Amin*. New York: Dial Press, 1969.

Bucholtz, Mary. "The Politics of Transcription." *Journal of Pragmatics* 32, no. 10 (2000): 1439–65.

Caillois, Roger. *Man, Play, and Games*. Champaign: University of Illinois Press, 1958.

Camarillo, Albert M. "Blacks, Chicanos, and the New Racial Frontier in American Cities of Color: California's Emerging Minority-Majority Cities." In *African American Urban History since World War II*, edited by Kenneth L. Kusmer and Joe W. Trotter, 19–38. Chicago: University of Chicago Press, 2009.

Cameron, Deborah, and Don Kulick. *Language and Sexuality*. Cambridge: Cambridge University Press, 2003.

Campt, Tina. "Black Visuality and the Practice of Refusal." *Women & Performance: A Journal of Feminist Theory* 29, no. 1 (2019): 79–87.

———. "The Visual Frequency of Black Life: Love, Labor, and the Practice of Refusal." *Social Text* 140, no. 3 (2019): 25–46.

Carter, Prudence L. *Keepin' It Real: School Success Beyond Black and White*. New York: Oxford University Press, 2007.

Chapman, Nathaniel, and David Brunsma. *Beer and Racism: How Beer Became White, Why It Matters, and the Movements to Change It*. Bristol: Bristol University Press, 2020.

Cherland, Summer. "No Prejudice Here: Racism, Resistance, and the Struggle for Equality in Denver, 1947–1994." PhD diss., University of Nevada, Las Vegas, 2014.

Coates, Jennifer. "Talk in a Play Frame: More on Laughter and Intimacy." *Journal of Pragmatics* 39, no. 1 (2007): 29–49.

Cole, Erin. "R-0: Race, Sexuality and Single-Family Zoning in Denver's Park Hill and Capitol Hill Neighborhoods, 1956–1989." PhD diss., University of New Mexico, 2014.

Combs, Barbara. "Black (and Brown) Bodies Out of Place: Towards a Theoretical Understanding of Systematic Voter Suppression in the United States." *Critical Sociology* 42, nos. 4–5 (2016): 535–49.

Csikszentmihalyi, Mihaly. *Flow: The Psychology of Optimal Experience*. New York: HarperPerennial, 1990.

Daniel, Jack, and Geneva Smitherman. "How I Got Over: Communication Dynamics in the Black Community." In *Cultural Communication and Intercultural Contact*, edited by Donal Carbaugh, 27–40. New York: Routledge, 1990.

Daniels, Douglas Henry. "The Significance of Blues for American History." *Journal of Negro History* 70, nos. 1–2 (1985): 14–23.

Dollard, John. "The Dozens: Dialectic of Insult." *American Imago* 1, no. 1 (1939): 3–25.

Douglas, Mary. *Purity and Danger: An Analysis of Concepts of Pollution and Taboo*. London: Routledge, 1966.

Durkheim, Emile. *The Elementary Forms of Religious Life*. New York: Free Press, 1995.

Farrington, Charles. "Language Variation and the Great Migration: Regionality and African American Language." PhD diss., University of Oregon, 2019.

Fine, Gary, and Ugo Corte. "Group Pleasures: Collaborative Commitments, Shared Narrative, and the Sociology of Fun." *Sociological Theory* 35, no. 1 (2017): 64–86.

Fitzgerald, Kevin, dir. *Freestyle: The Art of Rhyme*. The Center for Hip-Hop Education/Organic Films. DVD. Palm Pictures, 2004.

Floyd, Samuel A., Jr. *The Power of Black Music. Interpreting Its History from Africa to the United States*. New York: Oxford University Press, 1995.

Ford, J. E. "Close-up: Fugitivity and the Filmic Imagination." *Black Camera* 7, no. 1 (2015): 110–14.

Forstee, Clare. "A New Framing for an Old Sociology of Intimacy." *Sociology Compass* (2017). https://compass.onlinelibrary.wiley.com/doi/abs/10.1111/soc4.12467.

Franklin, Anderson J. "Invisibility Syndrome and Racial Identity Development in Psychotherapy and Counseling African American Men." *Counseling Psychologist* 27 no. (1999): 761–93.

Gates, Henry Louis. *The Signifying Monkey*. New York: Oxford University Press, 1989.

Giancarlo, Alexandra. "Spatializing Black Culture through the Placemaking Tradition of the Rural Louisiana Creole Boucherie." *Geographical Review* 111, no. 1 (2021): 1–19.

Goffman, Erving. *Interaction Ritual*. New York: Doubleday, 1967.

Goldberg, Robert. "Denver: Queen City of the Chicago Realm." In Lay, *The Invisible Empire in the West*, 39–66.

———. *Hooded Empire: The Ku Klux Klan in Colorado*. Champaign: University of Illinois Press, 1981.

Goodstein, Phil. *Curtis Park, Five Points, and Beyond: The Heart of Historic East Denver*. Denver: New Social, 2014.

———. *In the Shadow of the Klan: When the KKK Ruled Denver 1920–1926*. Denver: New Social, 2006.

———. *Park Hill Promise: The Question for an Idyllic Denver Neighborhood*. Denver: New Social Publications, 2012.

Gracyk, Tim. "'Tiger Rag'—The Original Dixieland Jazz Band (1918)." 2002. https://www.loc.gov/static/programs/national-recording-preservation-board/documents/TigerRag.pdf.

Grieser, Jessica. *The Black Side of the River: Race, Language, and Belonging in Washington, D.C.* Washington DC: Georgetown University Press, 2022.

Guzman, Joseph. "Talking Shit, Egos, and Tough Skin: Humor among Elite Black Men." *Journal of Contemporary Ethnography* 49, no. 5 (2020): 613–37.

Hartman, Saidiya. *Scenes of Subjection: Terror, Slavery, and Self-Making in Nineteenth-Century America*. New York: W. W. Norton, 1997.

Haskins, Don. *Glory Road*. New York: Hachette, 2005.

Hill, Jane. "The Voices of Don Gabriel: Responsibility and Self in a Modern Mexicano Narrative." In *The Dialogic Emergence of Culture*, edited by Dennis Tedlock and Bruce Mannheim, 97–147. Urbana: University of Illinois Press, 1995.

Hill, Lance. *The Deacons for Defense: Armed Resistance and the Civil Rights Movement*. Chapel Hill: University of North Carolina Press, 2004.

Hill, Marc, and Emery Petchauer. *Schooling Hip-Hop: Expanding Hip-Hop Based Education Across the Curriculum*. New York: Teacher College Press, 2013.

Hobart, Hiʻilei Julia Kawehipuaakahaopulani, and Tamara Kneese. "Radical Care: Survival Strategies for Uncertain Times." *Social Text* 38, no. 1 (2020): 1–16.

hooks, bell. "Homeplace: A Site of Resistance." In *Yearning: Race, Gender, and Cultural Politics*, edited by bell hooks, 383–90. Boston: South End Press. 1990.

Huizinga, Johan. *Homo Ludens: A Study of the Play-Element in Culture*. Kettering OH: Angelico Press, 1955.

Hunter, Marcus Anthony, Mary Pattillo, Zandria F. Robinson, and Keeanga-Yamahtta Taylor. "Black Placemaking: Celebration, Play, and Poetry Theory." *Culture & Society* 33, nos. 7–8 (2016): 31–56.

Hurston, Zora Neale. "Art and Such." In *Reading Black, Reading Feminist: A Critical Anthology*, edited by Henry Louis Gates Jr., 21–26. New York: Meridian Books, 1990.

Jefferson, Gail, Harvey Sacks, and Emmanuel Schegloff. "Notes on Laughter in the Pursuit of Intimacy." In *Talk and Social Organization*, edited by G. Button and J. R. E. Lee, 152–205. Bristol: Multilingual Matters, 1987.

Johnstone, Barbara. *Stories, Community, and Place: Narratives from Middle America*. Bloomington: Indiana University Press, 1990.

Jones, Taylor. "Variation in African American English: The Great Migration and Regional Differentiation." PhD diss., University of Pennsylvania, 2020.

Kelley, Robin D. G. *Yo' Mama's Disfunktional! Fighting the Culture Wars in Urban America*. Boston: Beacon Press, 1997.

Kirkland, David. "Black Masculine Language." In *The Oxford Handbook of African American Language*, edited by Sonja Lanehart, 834–49. Oxford: Oxford University Press, 2015.

Kochman, Thomas. *Black and White: Styles in Conflict*. Chicago: University of Chicago Press, 1981.

———. "Force Fields in Black and White Communication." In *Cultural Communication and Intercultural Contact*, edited by Donal Carbaugh, 193–218. Mahwah NJ: Lawrence Erlbaum, 1990.

Kopano, Baruti. "Rap Music as an Extension of the Black Rhetorical Tradition: 'Keepin' It Real.'" *Western Journal of Black Studies* 26, no. 4 (2002): 204–14.

Kuttner, Paul, and Mariama White-Hammond. "(Re)building the Cypher: Fulfilling the Promise of Hip Hop for Liberation." In *The Organic Globalizer Hip Hop: Political Development and Movement* Culture, edited by Christopher Malone and George Martinez, 43–58. New York: Bloomsbury, 2015.

Labov, William. "Rules for Ritual Insults." In *Sociolinguistics*, edited by Nikolas Coupland and Adam Jaworski, 472–86. London: Palgrave, 1997.

Laudun, John. "'Talking Shit' in Rayne." *Journal of American Folklore* 125, no. 497 (2012): 304–26.

Lay, Shawn, ed. *The Invisible Empire in the West: Toward a New Historical Appraisal of the Ku Klux Klan of the 1920s*. Chicago: University of Illinois Press, 2003.

Light, Duncan, and Craig Young. "Toponymy as Commodity: Exploring the Economic Dimensions of Urban Place Names." *International Journal of Urban and Regional Research* 39, no. 3 (2014): 435–50.

Limón, José. "Carne, Carnales, and the Carnivalesque: Bakhitinian Batos, Disorders, and Narrative Discourse." *American Ethnologist* 16, no. 3 (1989): 471–86.

Linde, Charlotte. *Working the Past: Narrative and Institutional Memory*. New York: Oxford University Press, 2009.

Lipsitz, George. *How Racism Takes Place*. Philadelphia: Temple University Press, 2011.

Loewen, James. *Sundown Towns: A Hidden Dimension of American Racism*. New York: Touchstone, 2006.

Longino, Charles. "The Park Hill Action Committee: A Study of the Legitimation Process of Community Involvement." Master's thesis, University of Colorado Boulder, 1962.

Low, Setha. *Spatializing Culture: The Ethnography of Space and Place*. New York: Routledge, 2017.

———. "Towards an Anthropological Theory of Space and Place." *Semiotica* 2009, no. 175 (2009): 21–37.

Mauck, Laura. *Five Points Neighborhood of Denver*. Mt. Pleasant SC: Arcadia, 2001.

Mauss, Marcel. *The Gift: The Form and Reason for Exchange in Archaic Societies*. Abingdon UK: Routledge Classics, 2002.

McKittrick, Katherine. *Demonic Grounds*. Minneapolis: University of Minnesota Press, 2006.

———. "On Plantations, Prisons, and a Black Sense of Place." *Social and Cultural Geography* 12, no. 8 (2011): 947–62.

Mitchell-Kernan, Claudia. "Signifying and Marking: Two Afro-American Speech Acts." In *Directions in Sociolinguistics: The Ethnography of Communication*, edited by John Gumperz and Dell Hymes, 161–79. New York: Holt, Rinehart and Winston, 1972.

Modan, Gabriella. *Turf Wars: Discourse, Diversity, and the Politics of Place*. Malden MA: Wiley-Blackwell, 2007.

Mondschein, Jules. *The Summer of 1967—Northeast Park Hill*. Denver: Commission on Community Relations, 1967.

Morgan, Marcyliena H. *Language, Discourse and Power in African American Culture*. Cambridge: Cambridge University Press, 2002.

———. *Speech Communities*. Cambridge: Cambridge University Press, 2014.

Morrison, Toni. "Toni Morrison on Writing without the 'White Gaze.'" PBS, *American Masters*. https://www.pbs.org/wnet/americanmasters/toni-morrison-on-writing-without-the-white-gaze/14874/.

Moten, Fred. *In the Break: The Aesthetics of the Black Radical Tradition*. Minneapolis: University of Minnesota Press, 2003.

Myerhoff, Barbara. *Numbering Our Days*. New York: Simon and Schuster, 1980.

———. "Telling One's Story." In *Stories as Equipment for Living: Last Talks and Tales by Barbara Myerhoff*, edited by Marc Kaminsky and Mark Weiss, 28–59. Ann Arbor: University of Michigan Press, 2007.

Nasir, Na'ilah Suad, and Maxine McKinney de Royston. "Power, Identity, and Mathematical Practices Outside and Inside School." *Journal for Research in Mathematics Education* 44, no. 1 (2013): 264–87.

Newsum, Dani Renee. "Cold War Colorado: Civil Rights Liberals and the Movement for Legislative Equality, 1945–1959." Master's thesis, University of Colorado Boulder, 2012.

Noel, Thomas, and Stephen Leonard. *Denver: Mining Camp to Metropolis*. Boulder: University Press of Colorado, 1990.

Nyawalo, Mich. "From 'Badman' to 'Gangsta': Double Consciousness and Authenticity, from African American Folklore to Hip Hop." *Popular Music and Society* 36, no. 4 (2013): 460–75.

Ochs, Elinor. "Transcription as Theory." In *Developmental Pragmatics*, edited by Elinor Ochs and Bambi Schieffelin, 43–72. New York: Academic Press.

Paris, Django, and H. Samy Alim. "What Are We Seeking to Sustain through Culturally Sustaining Pedagogy? A Loving Critique Forward." *Harvard Educational Review* 8, no. 1 (2014): 85–100.

Paulsen, Krista, and Haley Tuller. *Crafting Place: Craft Beer and Authenticity in Jacksonville, Florida*. Morgantown: West Virginia University Press, 2017.

Pearson, Judy C., Jeffrey T. Child, and Anna F. Carmon. "Rituals in Dating Relationships: The Development and Validation of a Measure." *Communication Quarterly* 59, no. 3 (2011): 359–79.

Pellow, Deborah. *Landlords and Lodgers: Socio-Spatial Organization in an Accra Community*. Chicago: University of Chicago Press, 2002.

Perkins, Useni. *Home Is a Dirty Street*. Chicago: Third World Press, 1975.

Pickering, Michael, and Emily Keightley. "The Modalities of Nostalgia." *Current Sociology* 54 (2006): 919–41.

Podilchak, Walter. "The Social Organization of Fun." *Leisure and Society* 8, no. 2 (1985): 685–92.

Price, Catherine. "Why Having Fun Is the Secret to a Healthier Life." TED2022, April 2022. https://www.ted.com/talks/catherine_price_why_having_fun_is_the_secret_to_a_healthier_life/.

Prince, Sabiyha. *African Americans and Gentrification in Washington, D.C.: Race, Class and Social Justice in the Nation's Capital*. New York: Routledge, 2014.

Richards-Greaves, Gillian. "'Say Hallelujah Somebody' and 'I Will Call upon the Lord': An Examination of Call-and-Response in the Black Church." *Western Journal of Black Studies* 40, no. 3 (2016): 192–204.

Rickford, John, and Russel Rickford. *Spoken Soul: The Story of Black English*. New York: Wiley, 2000.

Ryden, Kent. *Mapping the Invisible Landscape: Folklore, Writing, and the Sense of Place*. Iowa City: University of Iowa Press, 1993.

Sack, Robert. *Homo Geographicus*. Baltimore: Johns Hopkins University Press, 1997.

Schafer, W. J. "Irony from the Underground: Satiric Elements in Invisible Man." In *Twentieth Century Interpretations of Invisible Man*, edited by J. M. Reilly, 39–47. Englewood Cliffs NJ: Prentice Hall, 1970.

Sennett, Richard. *The Fall of Public Man*. Cambridge: Cambridge University Press, 1977.

Sharpe, Christina. *In the Wake: On Blackness and Being*. Durham: Duke University Press, 2016.

Shuman, Amy. *Other People's Stories: Entitlement, Claims and the Critique of Empathy*. Champaign: University of Illinois Press, 2010.

Simmel, Georg. "The Sociology of Sociability." *American Journal of Sociology* 55, no. 3 (1949): 254–61.

Simmons, Laurie, and Thomas Simmons. *Five Points Neighborhood: Denver Neighborhood History Project, 1993–94*. Denver: Front Range Research Associates, 1995.

Slocum, Karla. *Black Towns, Black Futures: The Enduring Allure of a Black Place in the American West*. Chapel Hill: University of North Carolina Press, 2019.

Smitherman, Geneva. "Black Language and the Education of Black Children." *Black Scholar* 23, no. 1 (1997): 28–35.

———. *Black Talk: Words and Phrases from the Hood to the Amen Corner*. New York: Mariner Books, 2000.

———. *Talkin and Testifyin*. Detroit: Wayne State University, 1986.

Spears, Arthur. "African-American Language Use: Ideology and So-Called Obscenity." In *African American English*, edited by Salikoko Mufwene, Guy Bailey, John Baugh, and John R. Rickford, 226–50. New York: Routledge, 1998.

Staynova, Yana. "An Ethnography of Joy: Entrepreneurship among Latinx Communities in East Los Angeles." *American Anthropologist* 126, no. 3 (2024): 635–46.

Stephens, Ronald, and La Wanna Larson. *African Americans of Denver*. Mount Pleasant SC: Arcadia Publishing, 2008.

Summers, Brandi. *Black in Place: The Spatial Aesthetics of Race in a Post-Chocolate City*. Chapel Hill: University of North Carolina Press, 2019.

Thompson, Cooper. "Art Branscombe." In *White Men Challenging Racism: 35 Personal Stories*, edited by Cooper Thompson, Emmett Schaefer, and Harry Brod, 37–44. Durham NC: Duke University Press, 2009.

Tilove, Jonathan. *Along Martin Luther King: Travels on Black America's Main Street*. New York: Random House, 2003.

Turner, Victor. *The Anthropology of Performance*. New York: PAJ, 1987.
Viñas-Nelson, Jessica. "Interracial Marriage in 'Post-Racial' America." *Origins: Current Events in Historical Perspective*. History Departments of The Ohio State University and Miami University (July 2017). https://origins.osu.edu/article/interracial-marriage-post-racial-america.
Warren, Chezare, and Justin A. Coles. "Trading Spaces: Antiblackness and Reflections on Black Education Futures." *Equity and Excellence in Education* 53, no. 3 (2020): 382–98.
Wasinger, Holly. "From Five Points to Struggle Hill: The Race Line and Segregation in Denver." *Colorado Heritage* (2005): 28–39.
Weil, Simone. *The Need for Roots*. London: Penguin Classics, 1943.
Winter, Jay. "Sites of Memory." In *Memory: Histories, Theories, and Debates*, edited by Susannah Radstone and Bill Schwarz, 32–324. New York: Fordham University Press, 2010.
Wright, Richard. *Black Boy*. New York: Harper and Brothers, 1945.
Yancy, George. *Black Bodies, White Gazes: The Continuing Significance of Race in America*, 2nd ed. Lanham MD: Roman and Littlefield, 2017.
———. "Foreword." In *The Logic of Racial Practice: Explorations in the Habituation of Racism*, edited by Brock Bahler, vii–xiii. Lanham MD: Roman and Littlefield, 2021.
———. "White Embodied Gazing, the Black Body as Disgust, and the Aesthetics of Un-Suturing." In *Body Aesthetics*, edited by Sherri Irvin, 244–62. Oxford: Oxford University Press, 2016.
Zeisel, John. "A Sense of Place." *New Scientist* 189, no. 2541 (2006): 50–55.

# Index

*Page numbers in italics indicate illustrations.*

Abdurraqib, Hanif, 155
acoustic intensity, 102, 120, 122
adjacency pairs, 120
Ain-Davis, Dana, 19
Alim, Samy, 90, 92, 201n13
All Fives, 6–7. *See also* dominoes playing
Anderson, Ed, 182
Anderson, Elijah, 67, 92, 122
anthropology, 4, 19, 184, 191n3
Army, racism in, 108–9, 140–42
Aurora CO, 65, 92

baited indirectness, 202n10
banking discrimination, 30, 33
banter. *See* talking shit
barbershops, Black, 12–13, 47, *94*, 94–95, 201n13
Bauman, Richard, 17
belonging, 15–17, 61–67, 99–100, 102–3, 175, 203n26
Benny Hooper's, 26, 90–91
Billups, Chauncey, 3
*Black Boy* (Wright), 153
Black Joy movement, 203n26
Bloods, 55, 58, 88, 144
the blues, 134
Blunt, Alison, 67

Bob, 89
Bourdieu, Pierre, 13
Brad, 12
Branscome, Art, 33
Brown, George, 30, 195n30
Brown, James, 63
Brown, R. H., 202n9
*Brown v. Board of Education*, 185
Buford, Mr., 137–47; about, 14–15, 18, 23, *118*, 137, *138*, 144–47; in the Army, 140–42, 143; childhood of, 137–40; death of, 163, *165*, 165–67, 181; dominoes playing and, 1, 51, 99; intimacy and, 150–53, 154–60, 162, 163–65, 167; nostalgia and, 90; talking shit and, 14, 119, 120, 125, 127, 128–31, 133; as a young adult, 142–44
Bush, George W. and Laura, 111
businesses and cultural hubs, Black, 53–58, *54*, *56*, *57*, 60, 66–67

call and response, 158–59, 162
Camarillo, Albert M., 196n42
Cameron, Deborah, 161
Campt, Tina, 16, 63
Candlish, William, 28
Capitol Hill, 25

card room of Hiawatha Davis Recreation Center: about, 5, 6, 8–9, 84, 85, 88; age and health and, 183–84; author and, 2, 3–4, 5, 9–11, 13–15; demise of, 187–89; displacement and, 51; intimacy in, 154–65, 167–68; placemaking and, 16, 93, 135; play-frames and rituals and, 16–17; sign for, 5, *188*, 189; talking shit and, 8. *See also* dominoes playing
caregiving, 18–19, 156, 167–68, 194n38
Carmon, Anna F., 157
Carr, Herman, 105–15; about, 23, 105, *106*, *118*, *126*; author and, 1, 14; as a child, 107–8; death of, 113–15, 181; dominoes playing of, 112–14, 183; Don Haskins and, 106–7, 111–12; in the military, 108–9; nostalgia and, 90–91; placemaking and, 93–94; Robert Taylor and, 112–13, 114, 115; as a working adult, 109–11
Carr, Shelton Delano, 111
"The Changing Character of the Park Hill Neighborhood" meeting, 33–34
Chapman, Walter R., 29
Child, Jeffrey T., 157
Civil Rights Act of 1964, 185
Coates, Jennifer, 161, 162
cocaine, 55, 87. *See also* drugs
Cole, Erin, 196n35
collective memories, 153–54
Colorado Fair Housing Act of 1959, 24, 32, 36
Colored Men's Department, 91
Commission on Community Relations, 32, 86–87
construction cranes, 23
conversational dueting, 161
cool pose, 122

Core Programs of Denver Parks and Recreation, 183
cotton picking, 43, 73–75, 138
COVID-19 pandemic, 167, 182, 184
Craven Del Hierro, Krista, 19
creativity, 184
Crips, 55, 88, 144
croker sack story, 73, 74–75
Csikszentmihalyi, Mihaly, 128
Cummings, Bobby: about, 47, 53, 63, 179–80, 183; death of, 179–80; dominoes playing and, 3–5, 10, 97–100, 179–80
Cynthia, 63–67, 71
cypher, 203–4n27

Dahlia Campus for Health and Well-Being, 53–54
Dahlia Square Shopping Center, 53, 87, 169–70
Daniels, Douglas Henry, 134
daps, 6, 13, 192n5
Dave, 91–92, 97–98
Davis, Hiawatha, Jr., 83
Deacons for Defense and Justice, 186
Deep South district of Denver, 25
Deluxe Recreation Parlor and Ex-Serviceman's Club, 26
Denver CO, 23–39; background and overview of, 23–24; Five Points as a Black community in, 24–27, 194n1; housing in, 30–37, 53, 61, 196n35, 196n45, 197n51; KKK in, 27–29, 195n21; population in, 25, 27, 29–30, 52, 196n38, 198n60; redlining in, 29–30, 195n29. *See also specific neighborhoods of*
*Denver Blade*, 32, 196n37
Denver Doers Club, 27
Denver Interracial Committee, 28

Denver Parks and Recreations: background and overview and, 6, 10; dominoes tournament and, 99; gentrification and, 100; personnel and, 97–98, 100, 171, 172, 175; programs of, 132, 182–83. *See also specific recreation centers*
Denver Post, 23, 28, 30, 32, 36
Denver Star, 28
Denver Statesman, 28
Denver Times, 27–28
Denver Water Board, 30
desegregation, 33, 37, 38
displacement, 15, 51, 58, 65, 69–70, 71, 92–93
dominoes playing: background and overview of, 1, 3–5, 192nn6–7; scoring of, 6–8, 13; shit talk and, 128; slamming and, 3, 7–8, 102; tile shuffling and, 13–14; tournaments for, 3, 10, 97–100, 179–82, 192n6. *See also under specific people*
Donald, 92–93
Douglas, Mary, 17
D-Ray, 169–78; about, 23, *118*, 169–71, *170*; athletics and, 169, 171, 172–73; childhood and education of, 172; dominoes playing and, 173–75, 181; intimacy and, 154–60, 162, 163–65, 166–67; Levert and, 175–77; music and, 133, 134; talking shit and, 1, 14, 119–20, 131, 173, 174–77; as a witness to history, 178
drugs, 55, 60, 64, 87–88
Durkheim, Emile, 161

Edwards, Donald "D-Ray." *See* D-Ray
Enbrown, Elena, 26
exercise room at Hiawatha Davis Recreation Center, 51, 84, 100

Ex-Serviceman's Club, 26

"The Facts of Negro Housing" flyer, 36
Fair Housing Act of 1959, Colorado, 24, 32
Fair Housing Act of 1968, U.S., 197n45
Five Points: background and overview of, 24, *31*, 194n1; birth of, 24–27; decline of, 29–30, 32, 110; KKK and, 27–29; nostalgia for, 90–91, 92
5280, 24
food, 11, 38, 188, 189
Franklin, Anderson J., 110
Freddie, 122–24, 169
fun, 124–25, 156. *See also* joy

gangs, street, 55, 68–69, 87–88, 89, 144
Gates, Henry Louis, 117
gentrification: of Five Points, 24; Hiawatha Davis Recreation Center and, 51, 61–62, 100–101, 102; of North and Northeast Park Hill, 51–52, 60, 61, 66–72, 186; placemaking and, 86, 90, 92, 102, 200n21
George: about, 7, 18, 80–81, *126*, 166, 181, 188; dominoes playing and, 95–96, 112, 125–27, 128–30
ghettoization, 33–34, 197n46
"gift"-giving, 158
Gish, Ward, 28–29
Glen, 115, 133, 173
Glenarm Recreation Center, 91, 169, 172
*Glory Road* (Haskins), 106–7
Goodstein, Phil, 25, 88
Greater Park Hill Community (GPHC), 37–38
*Greater Park Hill News*, 37
Grimes, Geraldine "Geri," 67–71
grocery stores, 11, 53, 54–55, 188, 189

Grover: about, 118; author and, 2–3, 4–5, 9; D-Ray and, 169, 173, 174; talking shit and, 8, 119, 121, 122–24, 134; white gaze and, 101

Hall, Charles, 41–49; about, 23, 41–42, 183–84; author and, 4, 9, 14, 18–19; croker sack story and, 73, 74–75; discovery of Denver by, 44–46; dominoes playing and, 1, 8, 47–48, 181, 182, 187–89; education of, 43–44; intimacy and, 150–52, 159, 163; music and, 134; placemaking and, 93, 95; post-COVID pandemic and, 48–49; in Roswell, 42–44; talking shit and, 119, 120, 125–31, 133; as a young adult, 46–47
Hancock, Michael, 63, 85–86
Harlem Globetrotters, 43, 194n10
Hartman, Saidiya, 15
Haskins, Don, 106–7, 111–12
Haynes, Happy, 88
Hiawatha Davis Jr. Recreation Center: background and overview of, 2, 5; beginnings of, 88–89; changes at, 99–101, 102, 171; description of, 83–86, 84–85, 93; gentrification and, 51, 61–62, 100–101, 102; nostalgia and, 64, 86; placemaking and, 89–92, 95–100, 102–3, 186; post-COVID, 182–83; weight room at, 51, 84, 100. *See also* card room of Hiawatha Davis Recreation Center; Skyland Recreation Center
hip-hop, 186, 203n27
Hobart, Hiʻilei, 19
Hollins, Harry, 172
the Holly, 53–55, 62. *See also* Holly Square; Park Hill Shopping Center

Holly Area Redevelopment Project (HARP), 67
Holly Square, 53, 54, 54–57, 62, 67–69, 87, 169–70. *See also* Park Hill Shopping Center
Holly Street, 60, 83, 87, 169–70
Holmes, Clarence, 28
*Home Is a Dirty Street* (Perkins), 110
homeplaces, 15
*Homo Ludens* (Huizinga), 121
hood, 24, 67
hooks, bell, 15, 192n14
Hooper, Benny, 26–27, 90–91
House of Hair, 12–13
housing, 30–37, 53, 61, 196n35, 196n45, 197n51
Huizinga, Johan, 121
Hurston, Zora Neale, 19, 194n39

income, household, 52–53
indirect shit talk, 120–21, 202n10
insider-outsider status of author, 13–15
integration, 29, 36–37, 141, 185, 197n54
interracial relationships, 29, 108, 201n4
intimacy, 149–68; background and overview of, 149; in the card room, 154–65, 167–68; of goodbye, 163–67; shared racism experiences and, 149–54; talking shit and, 155–59, 161

Jared, 62
jazz, 26, 132–33, 134, 204n27
Jefferson, Gail, 161
Jerry, 98–99
*Jerry Springer*, 154
Jim Crow practices, 30, 108, 185–86
Johnson, Lyndon, 34, 86
Johnston, Mike, 59, 199n6

Johnstone, Barbara, 90
Jonesboro AL, 184–86
joy, 131–32, 203n26. *See also* fun

"keeping things real," 186
Keith, 87–88, 175
King, Martin Luther, Jr., 34
Kneese, Tamara, 19
Kochman, Thomas, 158–59, 202n11
Ku Klux Klan, 27–29, 186, 195n21, 197n51
Kulick, Don, 161

laughter, 41–42, 118, 132, 161, 162, 203n11
Levert, 175–77
Light, Duncan, 90
Linda, 38, 84–85, 100, 182
Lonnie, 122, 183
loudness, 102, 120, 122
lynchings, 15, 153, 154, 192n13

Mandela, Nelson, 83
Marcus, 12–13
marijuana, 60
Martin Luther King Boulevard, 30, 60
masculinity, 117–18, 126–27, 129, 156–57, 165, 177
Mauss, Marcel, 158
McKittrick, Katherine, 15
memories, 60–61, 64–66, 71, 90–91, 133–34, 153–54, 170
mental health services, 53–54
methodology, research, 9–11, 20
microbreweries, 12, 66–67, 200n21
Montbello, 62, 200n16
Mook, 91, 181–82
moral geography, 66, 200n19
Morgan, Marcyliena H., 202n10
Moten, Fred, 18, 100

music, 26, 132–35, 186, 203n21, 203n27
Myerhoff, Barbara, 184

NAACP, 28, 43
names, 4, 89–90, 171, 191n3
Nancy P. Anschutz Center, 56–57
Napoleon, 91, 123–24, 150–53
neighborhood improvement associations, 29
*News Hour*, 60
Newton, J. Q., 31–32
Nikon, Gregory, 123
Northeast Park Hill: about, 23, 24, 31, 89, 198n60; housing and real estate in, 31, 34–37, 196n34, 197n55; racism and, 38–39. *See also* Park Hill; placemaking, Black
Northeast Park Hill Civic Association, 36, 197n55
Northeast Park Hill Coalition, 37
North Park Hill, 32, 33, 52–53, 60, 66, 196n34, 198n60. *See also* Park Hill
nostalgia, 60–61, 64–66, 71, 90–91, 133–34, 153–54, 170
*Number Our Days* (Myerhoff), 184

off-color remarks, 120, 202n9
outsider status of author, 13–15
Owetta, 32–33
Oyowele, Abiodum, 204n27

Packnett, Britany, 203n26
Park Hill: about, 24, *31*, 53, 58–63, 66, 196n38, 198n58, 199n2; housing and real estate and, 30–33, 196n35; "integration" of, 33–39, 197n51, 197n54, 198n60; North Park Hill, 32, 33, 52–53, 60, 66, 196n34, 198n60. *See also* Northeast Park Hill; South Park Hill; *specific places within*

INDEX 221

Park Hill Action Committee (PHAC), 33–37, 196n35, 197n54
Park Hill Neighbors for Equity in Education, 38–39
Park Hill Pirates, 63–64
Park Hill Shopping Center, 53, 54, 54, 66, 67. *See also* Holly Square
Paul, 51, 98–99, 162, 169, 173, 187–88
Pearson, Judy C., 157
performance, 17, 127, 155–57, 161, 162
Perkins, Useni, 110
Perseverance mural, 83, *85*
PHAC (Park Hill Action Committee), 33–37, 196n35, 197n54
Pham, Kim, 203n26
pinochle, 2–3, 95
Pirates, Park Hill, 63–64
placemaking, Black, 51–72; background and overview of, 14–17, 51–53, 192n12; barbershops and, 94–95; businesses and cultural hubs and, 53–58, 54, 56, 57, 60, 66–67; conclusions on, 184, 187; Cynthia's story and, 63–67, 71; demographic changes and, 100–102; Geri Grimes' story and, 67–71; Hiawatha Davis Recreation Center and, 89–92, 95–100, 102–3, 186; music and, 133; nostalgia and, 90–91; Roderick's story and, 58–63, 71
place names, 89–90, 171, 194n2
play-frames, 16–17, 119, 120, 124, 162
playing the dozens, 121, 202n11
pointed indirectness, 202n10
population: in Denver, 25, 27, 29–30, 52, 196n38, 198n60; in Roswell, 42–43
poverty levels, 53
Price, Catherine, 132
Prince, Sabiyha, 52

productivity, 184

racism: in the Army, 108–9, 140–42; in Denver, 24–25, 27–30, 32–37; in Roswell, 42–44; shared experience and, 149–54; surviving, 184–89
radical care, 19
railroads, 25
Ray, 134
redlining, 29–30, 195n29
refusal, acts of, 16, 63, 71, 186
research methodology, 9–11, 20
resegregation, 35–36
resistance: gentrification and, 186; joy and, 203n26; placemaking and, 15–16, 63, 71; talking shit and, 132, 135
Richard, 55–58
RiNo (River North Arts District), 24, 194n2
rituals, cultural, 13, 16–17, 121, 155–57, 158, 161, 192n8
Robeson, Paul, 194n10
*Rocky Mountain News*, 29
Roderick, 58–63, 71
Ronnie, 8–9
Roos, Charles, 32
Rosco, 33
Rossonian Hotel and Nightclub, 26, 194n10
Roswell NM, 42–43
R-O zoning, 31, 35, 196n35, 197n51

Sacks, Harvey, 161
Safeway, 54, 188, 189
Samuel, 2
Schafer, W. J., 134
Schegloff, Emmanuel, 161
schools, 35–36, 37, 38–39, 43–44, 185
scoring dominoes, 6–8, 13

segregation, racial, 25, 28–29, 30, 36, 38–39, 107
Sennett, Richard, 149
sexual intimacies, 126–27
Sharpe, Christina, 18, 194n38
Shawn, 181
shit talking. *See* talking shit
Shuman, Amy, 19–20
signifying, 117
Silver Sneakers, 2, 84, 100
Simmel, Georg, 124
Skyland Park, 53, 63, 64
Skyland Recreation Center: beginnings of, 86–88; change to Hiawatha Davis Recreation Center, 88–89, 90, 171; memories of, 3, 64, 69, 86, 90, 101–2, 171. *See also* Hiawatha Davis Jr. Recreation Center
slamming dominoes, 3, 7–8, 102
Smitherman, Geneva, 67
sociability through conversation, 119, 124
South Park Hill: about, 36, 38, 52–53, 198n60; resident perspectives on, 62–63, 66; Roderick and, 58–60. *See also* Park Hill
space and place. *See* placemaking, Black
Stapleton, Benjamin, 26, 27–28, 195n21, 197n51
Stapleton Airport, 30, 196n34
Starbucks incident, 149–50, 151
Staynova, Yana, 203n26
stereotypes, 79
*The Summer of 1967*, 86–87
Summer of Violence, 60, 199n14
Summers, Brandi, 71

talking shit, 117–36; as "a whole lot of nothing," 1, 124–27; background and overview of, 8–9, 117, 192n8; current events and, 135; fun and joy and, 131–32; Herman Carr and, 112–13; intimacy and, 155–59, 161; as a jazz band, 133–34; play and, 16–17, 128–31; rhetorical features of, 117–21; by "youngsters," 122–24
Taylor, Robert Truman, 73–81; about, 23, *74*, 80–81, *114*, *118*, *126*, 187–89; on Blacks, 79, 81, 184; as a child and young adult, 73–77, 79; dominoes playing and, 1, 4, 7–8, 18, 94–96, 181, 187–89; Herman Carr and, 112–13, 114, 115; intimacy and, 150–52, 160; music and, 132, 133; in North Park Hill, 77–78; talking shit and, 14, 17, 120–21, 125–27, 128–31, 133
telling other people's stories, 19–20
Temple Emanuel, 25
33rd Avenue, 53, 54, *56*, *57*, 170
*Tiger Rag*, 129, 203n21
tile shuffling, 13–14
Till, Emmett, 108
Tilove, Jonathan, 60
tournaments, domino, 3, 10, 97–100, 179–82, 192n6
Trapper: about, 12, 48, 92, *185*; death of, 186; domino playing and, 8, 133, 180; intimacy and, 114, 161, 166, 183; racism and, 184–86; talking shit and, 120–21
Troy, 187–88
Turner, Victor, 17

Union Station, 23
Urban Land Conservancy (ULC), 55, 67

Wallace, John M., 32
Walter, 179
War on Poverty, 86

Webb, Wellington, 88, 93
weight room at Hiawatha Davis Recreation Center, 51, 84, 100
Wells, Ida B., 101n4
Welton Street, 24, 26, 110
Western State College, 44
white flight, 33, 86, 196n42
white gaze, 16, 101, 193n20
Will, 122–23
Wilson, Nemiah, 109–10
Winter, Jay, 90
"A World of Black Intimacy at the Card Table" (Abdurraqib), 155
Wright, Richard, 153

Yancy, George, 193n20
Yarborough, Buford. *See* Buford, Mr.
YMCA, 26, 91
Young, Craig, 90

Zeisel, John, 91
zoning, 31, 35, 196n35, 197n51

In the Anthropology of Contemporary North America series:

*America's Digital Army: Games at Work and War*
Robertson Allen

*Governing Affect: Neoliberalism and Disaster Reconstruction*
Roberto E. Barrios

*Playing to the End: Elder Black Men, Placemaking, and Dominoes in Denver*
Steve Bialostok

*Public Land and Democracy in America: Understanding Conflict over Grand Staircase-Escalante National Monument*
Julie Brugger

*Come Now, Let Us Argue It Out: Counter-Conduct and LGBTQ Evangelical Activism*
Jon Burrow-Branine

*White Gold: Stories of Breast Milk Sharing*
Susan Falls

*Mexicans in Alaska: An Ethnography of Mobility, Place, and Transnational Life*
Sara V. Komarnisky

*Prison Town: Making the Carceral State in Elmira, New York*
Andrea R. Morrell

*Holding On: African American Women Surviving HIV/AIDS*
Alyson O'Daniel

*Rebuilding Shattered Worlds: Creating Community by Voicing the Past*
Andrea L. Smith and Anna Eisenstein

*Songs of Profit, Songs of Loss: Private Equity, Wealth, and Inequality*
Daniel Scott Souleles

*Back to America: Identity, Political Culture, and the Tea Party Movement*
William H. Westermeyer

*Religious, Feminist, Activist: Cosmologies of Interconnection*
Laurel Zwissler

To order or obtain more information on these or other University of Nebraska Press titles, visit nebraskapress.unl.edu.

www.ingramcontent.com/pod-product-compliance
Lightning Source LLC
Chambersburg PA
CBHW030620230426
43661CB00053B/2076